CANTI B

MONUMENTS OF RENAISSANCE MUSIC

EDWARD E. LOWINSKY
GENERAL EDITOR

BONNIE J. BLACKBURN
ASSISTANT EDITOR

VOLUME II: CANTI B

OTTAVIANO PETRUCCI

CANTI B

NUMERO CINQUANTA

VENICE, 1502

EDITED BY

HELEN HEWITT

WITH AN INTRODUCTION BY
EDWARD E. LOWINSKY

TEXTS EDITED AND ANNOTATED BY
MORTON W. BRIGGS
TRANSLATED BY NORMAN B. SPECTOR

CHICAGO AND LONDON
THE UNIVERSITY OF CHICAGO PRESS

Illustration on title page from Silvestro Ganassi
Regola Rubertina (Venice, 1542)

Library of Congress Catalog Card Number: 67-18076
THE UNIVERSITY OF CHICAGO PRESS, CHICAGO & LONDON
The University of Toronto Press, Toronto 5, Canada
© *1967 by The University of Chicago*
All rights reserved
Published 1967
Printed in the United States of America
Designed by John B. Goetz

INTRODUCTION

THE EDITION of French chansons of the late fifteenth century raises a number of problems, none of which can be regarded as settled: are all voices to be sung? If not, what criteria should be used to distinguish vocal from instrumental parts? How should one underlay the text of French chansons? Does the absence of texts in Petrucci's chanson publications, also encountered in some manuscript chansonniers of the time, such as Rome, Biblioteca Casanatense, MS 2856, or the almost entirely textless Verona, Biblioteca Capitolare, MS DCCLVII, point to instrumental performance?[1] Or is it simply a reflection of the paradoxical situation that no secular music was more popular among Italian connoisseurs at the end of the fifteenth century than the French chanson, even though Italian musicians—and presumably printers—were deficient in the knowledge and practice of the French tongue?

The first problem is whether to adhere strictly to Petrucci's text and give no more than the first few words of the chansons as he printed them. Such a procedure would be in accordance with the professed aim of this series to offer the great monuments of Renaissance music in a form as close to their original versions as possible. While this should always be the chief aim of a scholarly edition, it need not be the exclusive aim. Wherever important additions can be made without detriment to the main goal—a decisive qualification—there is no good reason why they should not be made. Professor Hewitt's mastery of the sources has made it possible for her to trace the complete texts

of about half of Petrucci's repertory in *Canti B*, as she had done before in her exemplary edition of the *Odhecaton*. To add these texts in no way detracts from her attempt to reproduce Petrucci's edition faithfully, inasmuch as his text incipits are retained in the footnotes to the music of this edition (see p. 8). Morton W. Briggs, Professor of Romance Languages at Wesleyan University, has established a critical reading of these texts and provided careful annotations.

Adding these texts confronts us with the thorny problem of how to adapt the French words to the music, rich in melismas and contrapuntal complexities and written down in manuscripts careless as to placement of the text. Fifteenth-century chansonniers do not clarify the relation between specific notes and syllables; they differ even in the manner in which the various voice-parts are provided with text.[2] In this situation, well-established scholarly practice has been to place the words as they appear in the manuscripts, or nearly so.[3]

---

[1] See the thorough discussion of this problem by Helen Hewitt in her edition of the *Odhecaton* (Cambridge, Mass., 1942), chap. 4, "The Significance of the Literary Texts" (pp. 31 ff.).

[2] See the excellent discussion of Knud Jeppesen in *Der Kopenhagener Chansonnier* (Copenhagen and Leipzig, 1927), pp. lxv ff.

[3] This practice has been followed, to cite a few examples, by J. F. R. Stainer and C. Stainer in their edition of chansons from Oxford, Bodleian Library, Canonici misc. 213, *Dufay and His Contemporaries* (London, 1898) (p. 18: "In fitting the words to the music we have endeavoured, as far as possible, to observe the exact position of the words in the manuscript"); by Jeppesen, *Der Kopenhagener Chansonnier*; by Y. Rokseth, E. Droz, and G. Thibault, *Trois chansonniers français du XVe siècle* (Paris, 1927); by Willibald Gurlitt in his edition of sixteen chansons by Gilles Binchois (*Das Chorwerk*, XXII, 1933) (p. 3: "For the rest, the text underlay follows, as closely as possible, the original source"); by J. Marix, *Les Musiciens de la cour de Bourgogne au XVe siècle* (Paris, 1937) (p. xxi: "...we have followed the manuscript as faithfully as possible..."); by Charles van den Borren, *Pièces polyphoniques profanes de provenance liégeoise (XVe siècle)* (Brussels, 1950) (p. [7]: "We have not tried to achieve

To deviate from a traditional practice so well founded requires strong reasons. For one thing, strict adherence to the text underlay in the original sources is impossible. The original treatment of text can best be shown in facsimiles.[4] For another, the far-reaching differences in various manuscripts demonstrate that the written sources of the time do not reflect so much the intent of the composer as the nonchalance of the copyist. Moreover, they reveal the prevailing attitude of Renaissance musicians who regarded notation as a system for putting down, not the maximum, but the minimum required for a musical performance. Any attempt to write down more than that was resented by the singers as an insult to their intelligence.[5] If we consider that the greatest musicians—indeed, most composers—of the age earned their livelihood as singers, we realize that the singers of the Renaissance constituted an elite of the most gifted and best educated musicians of all times.

In such a situation, to hold rigidly to the text underlay of the original means to pay too much respect to the whims of a particular copyist and to neglect the search for the composer's intent. And in the almost total absence of autographs, who is to undertake the search for the composer's meaning and intent if not the scholar who devotes his life to the study of this music? The notion that a good edition should serve the ends of study and of performance is by now an accepted standard for scholarly editions.

As in the case of *musica ficta*, Editor and General Editor in this series have joined efforts to establish the closest consonance possible between text and music, always keeping in mind the variety of performances feasible at any given period. If certain parts, in particular the contratenor, were meant to be played by instruments, if others were intended to be sung, the melodic behavior of the various parts should be found to be very different. The instrumental parts will be at times unvocal, replete with fast instrumental figures and awkward skips, at times devoid of melodic logic and continuity and in a rhythmic shape not conducive to accommodation of the text.[6] If, on the other hand, all parts were meant to be sung, a greater assimilation of the various parts to each other will be discovered, an assimilation that may take the form of rhythmic equality in homophonic settings, of melodic equality in contrapuntal settings in which each part is independent, or of thematic likeness, as in compositions making use of imitation.[7] If the composer strove for close union between words and tones, text underlay is ordinarily not too difficult a task. But if, as is often the case in fifteenth-century music, both sacred and secular, the composer's preoccupation with musical design results in a rather loose connection between text and music, if the music clothes the text as do the rich folds of drapery the human body in fifteenth-century painting and sculpture, then the editor needs all the ingenuity and experience he can gather to fit the two together. Once he tries his hand at text underlay he will note with surprise what improvements are possible and how often, even in a very melismatic part, a closer relationship between word and tone can be achieved. Among the worst faults of text underlay found in modern editions of chansonniers

an adaptation of the text to the notes with regard to practical use. The original manuscripts being, most of the time, rather imprecise in this regard, it seemed to us more in conformance with the postulates of science to keep to this imprecision, all the time observing that it is impossible, in a reduction in modern notation, to arrive at a faithful reproduction in the smallest details of these 'à peu près'"); by Wolfgang Rehm, a student of Gurlitt's, in his edition of *Die Chansons von Gilles Binchois* (Mainz, 1957) (p. 14*: "The text underlay followed, as far as feasible, the sources"); by Howard M. Brown, *Theatrical Chansons of the Fifteenth and Early Sixteenth Centuries* (Cambridge, Mass., 1963) (p. x: "Text underlay follows the sources as closely as possible, but some adjustments have been necessary").

[4] Such facsimiles are available in numbers adequate for study of the problem. Not only are most editions generally provided with them—whole manuscripts have been published in facsimile editions. See, for example, the *Facsimile Reproduction of the Manuscripts Sevilla 5-I-43 and Paris n. a. fr. 4379 (Pt. I)*, with an introduction by Dragan Plamenac, *Publications of Mediaeval Musical Manuscripts*, No. 8 (Brooklyn: Institute of Mediaeval Music, 1962), or the edition of *Codex Escorial Chansonnier, Biblioteca del Monasterio El Escorial, Signatur: Ms. V. III. 24*, ed. Wolfgang Rehm, *Documenta Musicologica, Zweite Reihe: Handschriften-Faksimiles 2* (Kassel, 1958).

[5] See Tinctoris' contemptuous remarks on the notation of accidentals, which any competent musician knows how to use without such help (cf. the Foreword to the first volume of the present series, *Musica nova*, ed. H. Colin Slim [Chicago, 1964], p. viii). This was also the opinion of Eugénie Droz and Geneviève Thibault, who in their edition of *Trois chansonniers français* (p. 107) wrote: "It would have almost wounded the pride of a trained singer or a skilful minstrel to believe them ignorant of the rules of correct declamation, or of the rules of counterpoint [*musica ficta*]."

[6] See nos. 12, 13, 16, 19, where two parts sing the text in canon or in canonic imitation while the others play an instrumental accompaniment. In other chansons, one voice alone sings to the accompaniment of instruments (nos. 14, 24, 51).

[7] These types rarely appear in their pure forms during the period under discussion. Mixtures of homophony and imitation are found in nos. 15, 23, 27, 33; mixtures of free and imitative counterpoint occur in nos. 22, 45, 46; prevailingly imitative technique is displayed in nos. 9, 17, 34, 39. No. 28 shows a chanson with an instrumental prelude.

are the interruption of one word by a pause[8] and the holding of one syllable over repeated notes.[9] The practice of spreading a number of syllables more or less evenly over long melismas obstructs the understanding of the words; it can often be successfully replaced by pulling the sentence together at the beginning of the melodic phrase and placing the melismas at the end of the textual phrase. Accentuation can be improved in many cases,[10] although it will hardly ever be perfect, at least not before the second half of the sixteenth century.

Although the scribes of Masses and motets were often the same as those of chansons—this is particularly true in mixed anthologies—modern editors of Latin church music have proceeded with more freedom in the matter of text underlay than is generally shown by editors of chanson manuscripts. This is the more surprising since the principle of a good and natural accentuation would seem to be more vital in music sung in the vernacular than in that sung in Latin.

Stoquerus' rules of text underlay for the "older" composers, of Josquin's generation, apply also to the chanson.[11] In the older style it is legitimate to divide a chain of semiminims and to place one syllable under each group of two.[12] In contrast to the rules valid for the "modern" composers of Willaert's generation, here it is permitted to place a syllable below the note following a run. But exceptions occur. For instance, the rule that the short note following a dotted note should share the syllable with the preceding note is cheerfully ignored in popular songs with fast and

natural declamation.[13] Stoquerus' sanction, in exceptional cases, to apply more than one syllable to a ligature aids in solving a knotty problem in Josquin's *Baisés moy*[14] and in avoiding a barbarism in Brumel's *Ave, Ancilla Trinitatis*.[15]

Sometimes unusual problems call for unusual solutions. In De Vigne's chanson with double text, French and Italian (no. 32), the famous Italian text *Fortuna d'un gran tempo* can be applied easily to tenor and contratenor. The French text *Franc coeur, qu'as tu a soupirer* fits the soprano, but halfway through we run out of text. The discovery that at mid-point the soprano takes up the *Fortuna* melody suggests placing the *Fortuna* text where its melody appears. The four lines of the French text go well with the preceding portion of the part; two lines of the Italian poem fit beautifully the rest of the soprano part. The effect is astonishing and humorous, reminiscent of a favorite genre of Renaissance music, the quodlibet. If the combination of a French and an Italian text in one and the same voice part is unusual, it is no more so than the combination of two melodies in one part. It appears a perfect symbol of the symbiosis of French and Italian music, so characteristic of the Italian Renaissance, comparable also to the use of French chansons as *cantus firmi* in Mass compositions or in motets of the time, and no more astonishing than the macaronic verse in the Italian literature of the period. Moreover, it may be regarded as the revival of a habit well known from the medieval motet in which not only French texts appeared in motetus and triplum of a work based on an excerpt from Gregorian Chant, but in which even Latin and French appeared occasionally mixed in the same part.

Another unusual problem occurs in the anonymous chanson *Mon père m'a mariée* (no. 17). The composition allows easy text underlay in all voices; the words can be fitted in syllabic style save for the melismatic phrase endings. Here is a chanson whose vocal character seems incontestable. Strangely, at the very end (mm. 50 ff.), a two-note motif surrounded by rests occurs in all four voices and seems to thwart any attempt at intelligent text underlay. "My father married me off," says the chanson, "when I was no more than a child. He gave me to an old man of nearly sixty. And I, who am no more than fifteen, shall I thus

---

[8] Of course, in previous periods the interruption of one word by pauses was a part of the physiognomy of the vocal style. One has only to open Nino Pirrotta's great series of *The Music of Fourteenth-Century Italy* (American Institute of Musicology, 1954——) to find innumerable examples of such interruptions in the secular music of the *Trecento*, many of them set in a manner that allows no other interpretation.

[9] Yet, even the editors of this volume must plead guilty to committing this fault once, in an exceptional case: in Compère's *Lourdault* (no. 5), the first phrase ends on a five-note slide with the first note repeating the preceding tone. In this particular situation we preferred good accentuation to observance of an otherwise well-nigh inviolable rule. Nor should it be forgotten that the notation of the time offered no possibility to the composer to tie the two notes together, if this were what the composer wanted.

[10] For one example, see the Foreword to Vol. I of this series, pp. xiv–xvii, and the commentary on p. xix.

[11] See Edward E. Lowinsky, "A Treatise on Text Underlay by a German Disciple of Francisco de Salinas," *Festschrift Heinrich Besseler* (Leipzig, 1961), pp. 231–51; 236–41.

[12] See, for example, no. 27, mm. 26 (S), 27 (A, B), etc.

[13] See no. 17, mm. 5, 6 (S), etc., or again no. 27 (*passim*).

[14] No. 34; see mm. 31–32 (T and B).

[15] No. 39, mm. 31–32 (S).

pass my time? You, who are here present, I pray you, be my judges." "Je vous en prie, jugez-en." Now if one simply repeats the text, including the two-note motif, the chanson will end in the following manner: "Je vous en prie, jugez-en, je vous, je vous, je vous en prie, jugez-en."

Not only is it possible to provide the questionable passage with text, the ensuing reading echoes the sobbing of the unhappy girl in a most expressive manner. In a chanson so well adapted to the text, in which both the melancholy of the girl and her youthfulness are expressed so naturally, the latter in the rhythm of her chatter, the former in the minor mode, such an interpretation must be allowed as a definite possibility.

In the editions of the present series we shall not hesitate to make use of repetitions of text phrases, or parts thereof. The printing of such repetitions in italics will mark them as editorial additions.[16] Such repetitions are now assumed to have been part and parcel of the performance practice of the time, and there is no reason to suppose that they were confined to music of the religious sphere.

The use of italics for editorial additions of text will be limited to editions of manuscripts and prints offering the full text. In the present volume italics will not be used, since, with the exception of *Virgo celesti* (no. 2), Petrucci did not provide his edition with texts. Moreover, Professor Briggs has taken the texts from different sources, and at times, from modern editions of monophonic chansonniers.

The application of rules and principles of text underlay, like the use of the principles of *musica ficta*, does not necessarily lead to identical results. Indeed, editors will soon discover that the same principles can result in different solutions, some better than others. But assuredly, they will lead to more singable versions of the great chanson literature of the Renaissance than the principle of following the original text distribution. Inclusion of facsimiles and the printing of text repeti-

tions in italics will help in providing some idea of the text as it appears in the original sources.

The addition of translations of the French verses is in harmony with our view of the texts as an integral part of the musical work of art. The idea of offering translations of the poetic texts was originally suggested to me by the late Noah Greenberg, whose untimely death at the height of his powers has deprived America of her most inspired interpreter of Renaissance music. He felt keenly the need to know the meaning of the texts if the music was to be sung with understanding. Not only is poetry in any foreign tongue hard to grasp; old French poses particular problems of spelling, syntax, and vocabulary.

I am indebted to Dr. Mary-Jo Fink, Professor of Romance Languages at the University of Louisville, for advice and help in my initial struggles with this problem, and I am grateful to Professor Norman B. Spector of the University of Chicago for the gallantry with which he undertook the trying and delicate task of rendering the texts into English. His patience and willingness to experiment, as we tried out various versions in prose and in rhyme, were exemplary.

The lack of inhibition in much of this poetry may astonish the reader. Indeed, the question may well be raised whether it is in good taste to translate some of these verses that border on the obscene. But should we assume that only Frenchmen, or editors, are mature enough to read such verse? It is the purpose of the MONUMENTS OF RENAISSANCE MUSIC to open the world, the whole world, of Renaissance music to the scholar and performing musician. Without a proper understanding of the texts the social milieu of the Renaissance composer cannot be adequately understood, the meaning of the music cannot be justly appreciated, the chansons cannot be performed in the right vein and spirit. Moreover, these chansons are a vital part of the contemporary scene. Rabelais' wit, fun, and foolery, and some of his ribald irreverent themes, derive in good part from the chansons that he knew so well and quoted so abundantly. Indeed, the time is at hand not only for musicians and musicologists, for students of literature and theater, but for the historian of culture as well to study the music of the Renaissance and its texts as an indispensable aspect of the tone, temper, and imagination of the age.[17]

---

[16] Here we should like to suggest an improvement over the method used in our example in Vol. I, *La plus bruiant, celle qui toutes passe*. There we printed all duplications of text phrases in italics, even where the "repetition" marked, in fact, a passage in which the original had text and where the first appearance of the text actually constituted the editorial addition. We suggest marking in italics not only the real repetitions but also anticipations of a text phrase so that the modern edition will point with greater accuracy to the text distribution of the original.

[17] A vivid picture of the all-pervading part of music in the daily life, work, and play of the Renaissance man is given in

In the struggle with the question of prose versus rhymed translations, the power of rhyme and rhythm to mitigate the risqué, and even occasional crudeness, was a revelation. This is why in the end we chose poetic translations, even though the difficulties of meeting rhyme and meter are enormous and perfection remains a goal continually slipping from one's grasp.

The repertory of Petrucci's *Canti B* offers a variety of problems in *musica ficta*, which we shall discuss in the order of their difficulty. We shall proceed from the notational to the musical, from the simple to the involved, from the intriguing to the enigmatic.

The flat before the f″ in the soprano, whether as key signature (no. 19) or as accidental (no. 28, mm. 45 and 54; no. 44, m. 63), leaves the tone unchanged, indicating only that the note lies outside the Guidonian hand that extends to e″. *Canti B* provides the rare instance of an F-flat in the bass. Pierre de la Rue's *Tous les regretz* (no. 22) for four voices has no key signature in soprano, alto, and tenor. But the bass has the sub-bass clef and a flat for the F below the G which is the lowest tone of the Guidonian system. Since *musica ficta* was defined as lying *extra* (or *praeter*) *manum Guidonis*,[18] and since e″ and G were the highest and lowest tones, respectively, of the Guidonian system, f″ as well as F were provided by some literal-minded scribes with a flat—paradoxically, but not without some logic.[19]

That *musica ficta* was a problem not only for the modern editor but also for the old musicians is evident from the variety of accidentals and key signatures found in various sources. Petrucci gives no key signature for the four voices of *Vray Dieu, qui m'y confortera* (no. 4), but MS Brussels 11239 offers ♮; ♭; ♮; ♭.

André Pirro's *Histoire de la musique de la fin du XIVe siècle à la fin du XVIe* (Paris, 1940), particularly in chap. 1, "La musique et la société mondaine. La musique et l'église," and chap. 4, "La musique et le théâtre. La musique instrumentale. La musique italienne," and in Howard M. Brown's *Music in the French Secular Theater, 1400–1550* (Cambridge, Mass., 1963). See also Edward E. Lowinsky, "Music in the Culture of the Renaissance," *Journal of the History of Ideas*, XV (1954), 509–53 (now also available in the Harper Torchbook, *Renaissance Essays from the Journal of the History of Ideas*, ed. P. O. Kristeller and P. Wiener [New York, 1967]).

[18] See Edward E. Lowinsky, "Renaissance Writings on Music Theory," *Renaissance News*, XVIII (1965), 361–62.

[19] Pietro Aron demanded the notation of a flat before f″ in his *De Institutione harmonica* (1516), Book II, chap. 4 (see Edward E. Lowinsky, "The Function of Conflicting Signatures in Early Polyphonic Music," *Musical Quarterly*, XXXI [1945], 227–60; 255).

Comparison shows that Petrucci's version allows more freedom. Alto and bass often need a B-flat which can be provided by application of the ordinary rules of *musica ficta*, but in several passages where the B ascends to C (e.g., alto, mm. 42, 47, or bass, mm. 42, 44, 45), or for the formation of the triad of E minor (m. 43), or for melodic progressions from E to the lower fourth B and back (superius, mm. 43–44), the B-natural is required. Of course, with a key signature of one flat for alto and bass, the B-natural could also be provided by *musica ficta* rules, but Petrucci's key signature seems less ambiguous.

A beautiful example of the composer's ability to thwart the editor's desire to eliminate diminished fifth chords is shown in Jean Braconnier's *Amours me trocte par la pance* (no. 33), m. 82. Here the diminished fifth occurs on the accented beat in slow motion with the leading tone in the bass—that is, in the most exposed position. Nevertheless, it is precisely what the composer wanted, and he has seen to it that no *musica ficta*-happy singer can counter his intention. The bass moves from A to E; the preceding chord is A minor. To try to edit out the diminished fifth would land the singer in a situation worse than the one he would hope to escape. And if we look at the text, "le courtault est mort," we see at once that the composer wished the plaintive sound of the displeasing dissonance to illustrate his text.

Another example of a similar dilemma occurs in the opening measures of Obrecht's *J'ay pris amours* (no. 3) where the descent of the soprano from B-natural to E prevents the bass (m. 3) from singing the B-flat required by the rules of *musica ficta*. But Obrecht is skilful enough to conceal the awkward bass line in an attractive harmonic progression in four parts.

On the other hand, no. 41 offers a counter-example of what a piece would sound like without the *musica ficta* implied by the composer. The anonymous author of *Mon père m'a donné mari* is not a particularly gifted composer, but without the added accidentals the work would neither sound pleasing nor would it achieve the intended melancholic expression of the "ill-wed," the *malmaridade*.

Musica ficta offers a valuable clue to the puzzling question of authenticity in the case of the double version of Josquin's *Baisés moy* for four (no. 34) and for six parts (no. 37). Not only is the six-part version awkward and full of clumsy dissonances, it obscures the charming *musica ficta* design of Josquin's invention

— one of the happiest finds of this great harmonic discoverer: the opening phrase leads from D major to G major to C major, expressing felicitously the lover's desire in the guise of the striving from secondary dominant through dominant to tonic. It is a mark of Josquin's genius that this harmonic progression, accompanied by graceful melody and rhythm, is wrapped up in a double canon. But it took the system of *musica ficta* to enable the singer then, and the editor today, to execute the harmonic design so carefully planned by Josquin. The six-part version, adding a third pair of canon voices, renders the execution of the *musica ficta* design impossible. Where we need C-sharp in the soprano, the third canon introduces C in the bass, and the same occurs with F-sharp, and finally in measure 6 the bass introduces B-flat, forcing the soprano to flatten the B just before the leading tone needed for the cadence on C. As a result, the transparency of Josquin's four-part texture becomes a heavy six-part setting, the gracefulness of the syncopated seventh changes to the clumsiness of the full ninth chord rooted on the tonic, the ingenious modulatory design turns into a monotonous and harsh-sounding insistence on a harmonic circumscription of C, in which a flattened seventh, incongruously, appears just before the leading tone and the affirmation of the tonic. The addition of the third canon betrays, in its most unfavorable light, a facet of fifteenth-century musical mentality: the intellectual ambition to triumph over difficulty is allowed to ruin an artistic conceit; pedantry wins over elegance. And nothing illustrates the permissiveness of the age in the face of a work of art more blatantly than the publication of the graceful original together with the bungled version in one and the same print, and during the composer's lifetime, at that. The only compensation lies in Petrucci's adding Josquin's name to the original and withholding it from the arrangement.

A similar situation obtains in Lannoy's *Cela sans plus* (no. 16), which Petrucci prints with a bass part added by Johannes Martini, as Professor Hewitt established on the basis of comparison with nine other sources, eight of which transmit the work for three parts. Only one manuscript (Rome, Biblioteca Casanatense, MS 2856) offers a reading in four parts, attributing the bass to Martini and specifying its character as *si placet*, that is, an optional addition. If Gombosi regarded the chanson as "decidedly the thinnest composition I have ever encountered" (see note 40 of the Commentaries), he did so from the vantage point of Obrecht's full-bodied style and his four-part arrangement of Lannoy's tenor (see no. 13). The fact that no fewer than eight contemporary sources transmit Lannoy's work in its original three-part setting is proof that the aesthetic ideal that animated its composer, simplicity and transparency paired with melodic grace and rhythmic elegance, was fully appreciated at its time. Arrangements such as Obrecht's work or the addition of a bass part as essayed by Johannes Martini are characteristic of the lack of respect in which "the original"—any original—was held at that time, and of the change in taste. Martini not only disturbs the serenity and lightness of Lannoy's texture but also his tonal and harmonic relationships by providing the bass with the key signature of one flat. This demands various adjustments in the three upper parts by means of *musica ficta* that were far from Lannoy's mind. They are the cause of the ambiguities and complications in the modal picture, whose original design the reader can easily reconstruct by adjusting *musica ficta* for the three upper parts without reference to Martini's bass.

A number of compositions in *Canti B* illustrate the significance of *musica ficta* as an artistic principle capable of transforming the harmonic character of a work and of giving it a new tonal dimension. It is surely no accident that we find this imaginative play with *musica ficta* in the works of the finest composers of the time, in chansons by Josquin, Compère, La Rue, and Brumel.

Unfortunately, we lack the full text of Compère's *Et dunt revenis vous* (no. 29). It must have been a very humorous poem, to judge from the character of rhythm and melody, from the fast note repetitions indicating a parlando style of recitation, the gay upbeats, the echoing back and forth of short call motives between lower and upper duos, the stretto imitation of busy little motives in stepwise motion, the hocket phrases near the end. The piece stresses the major sound of Mixolydian, but in the last third of the composition (mm. 40–45 and 55 to the end) B-flat and E-flat invade the G major sound to indulge in a coy flirtation with G minor for the sake of contrast and surprise. The alto (in mm. 40 and 54) anchors the F so well that a raising of the soprano's F to F-sharp, in keeping with the rest of the piece, is impossible. To avoid tritone progressions the tenor (m. 41) has no choice but to flatten the B. The soprano, however, having a held-out note on A and a cadential F-sharp in the alto just preceding it, can go on to B-natural (m. 42) without ill effect. The next phrase repeats B-flat and draws E-flat in its train; that it is correctly construed appears from the varied repeat at the end where the need for B-flat, and hence for E-flat, is underlined by the repetition of the soprano motif (mm. 55 and 57) that allows no other interpretation.

In Pierre de la Rue's *Ce n'est pas jeu* (no. 7) the play with *musica ficta* takes on symbolic and expressive meaning. Professor Hewitt has stressed the "advanced compositional character" of this work. This goes well with the advanced tonal design apparent in its unusual exposition. The structure of the exposition is best understood if one omits the soprano. A sequence of imitations at two-measure intervals then stretches from alto to tenor and bass with complete regularity. Irregular, and therefore hinting at some special design, are the pitch levels at which the imitations enter. Instead of, say, tonic, tonic, tonic (very frequent), or tonic, dominant, tonic, dominant (no. 29), the subject enters on tonic, subdominant, subdominant of the subdominant.

In this design the soprano was either added as an afterthought—it presents the four last measures of the subject a fifth higher than the alto—or, more likely, it entered two measures earlier with the beginning of the theme, but was shortened so as to create a two-part entry and to offset the excess of symmetry and regularity which such a beginning would have caused. At any rate, the entry of the soprano lying a fifth above the alto fitted the tonal scheme of the work precisely.

The question raised by such a scheme is whether the motif, and in particular its ending (*ut re mi fa mi*), should be solmizated alike in all voices. This would lead to the use of E-flat in the alto and A-flat in the tenor and bass. By changing the second half of the motif in the bass and intoning it a tone higher, the D-flat is avoided, which facilitates the tonal coherence of the exposition.

The unusual imitation scheme proceeding in the cycle of lower fifths seems to be intended to produce this order of transpositions. As a further hint of this intention, the composer arranged the imitations with such complete regularity that they lead the performer to use identical solmization.

Pierre de la Rue's work was not the first published composition to use such a design. *Canti B*'s predecessor, the *Odhecaton*, contained Josquin's three-part *Fortuna d'un gran tempo*,[20] which has been shown to contain a similar, yet bolder, modulatory scheme designed to depict symbolically Fortune's fickleness. This interpretation was later corroborated by the extraordinary *Fortuna* composition of Matthaeus Greiter, published in Basel in 1553, in which every chromatic tone was unmistakably indicated and the net of modulations extended from F major to F-flat major, involving even B-double flat.[21]

To add to the surprising relationship of Pierre de la Rue's chanson with Josquin's *Fortuna*, a careful reading of the text, and particularly its beginning,

> *Ce n'est pas jeu*
> *d'estre sy fortunée*

reveals that the lady considers her melancholy plight a trick in Fortune's old game. This interpretation is strengthened by the return of the exposition at the end to another text in which the unhappy maiden accuses her *grant destinée*. Thus we may include Pierre de la Rue's chanson among the works written around 1500 in which *musica ficta* is used to create a sound symbol of the Goddess Fortuna.

But the most astonishing piece in regard to *musica ficta* is certainly Brumel's *Noé, noé, noé* (no. 25). It is worthwhile to study this work to arrive, if possible, at greater certainty concerning the composer's intention. It has a key signature of one flat in all voices and would normally be considered as written in transposed Dorian. From the beginning a great number of E-flats are needed and, as Professor Hewitt's collations show, are in fact written out in various sources.

The work falls into three clearly defined sections: measures 1–20 are set in a prevailingly homophonic style; at measure 21 a six-tone motif goes through all voices in stretto, beginning on the first, second, third, and fourth beats of the measure. The motif, originally in minor, recurs in major and is transposed from F to B-flat, requiring E-flat; a clear-cut homophonic cadence (mm. 30–33) concludes this section. The final section begins in measure 33 with the motif of a falling third:

[20] *Odhecaton*, no. 74. See Edward E. Lowinsky, "The Goddess Fortuna in Music, with a Special Study of Josquin's *Fortuna dun gran tempo*," *Musical Quarterly*, XXIX (1943), 45–77.

[21] Edward E. Lowinsky, "Matthaeus Greiter's *Fortuna*: An Experiment in Chromaticism and in Musical Iconography," *Musical Quarterly*, XLII (1956), 500–519, and XLIII (1957), 68–85.

This motif appears in each voice four times in ascending sequence. From measure 39 on, the motif of the falling third is extended to the motif of the descending triad. Again it appears in all voices, but this time in descending sequence. Both motives are clear-cut and persistent; they are framed by pauses; their rhythmic and melodic shape remains identical save for those minor changes effected by sequential treatment. If the motif of the falling third occurs sixteen times, that of the descending triad appears no less than twenty-one times.

What needs to be recognized first is the extraordinary character of this construction: whereas sequences in themselves are nothing unusual in the style of this period, such rhythmic, metric, and motivic regularity, such constant repetition and sequence involving motives of such melodic and rhythmic simplicity are unusual. Obviously, the composer wanted to arouse attention. By the time the sequence arrives at B-flat as the initial note, the motif of the triad is so well established that to bend it into a motif of a diminished triad would run counter not only to the rule prohibiting the use of imperfect intervals, but also to the carefully built up expectation. Expectation deceived can be used as an artistic device of a high order if what follows is of a higher imaginative value. But here it would be expectation disappointed. Moreover, several sources demand the E-flat, so that in their versions the fourth appearance of the descending triad would have to be changed from a reading of A-flat, F, D-flat, to A-F-D. This, however, would not only involve a diminished triad in alto and bass (mm. 44–46), but also a direct leap of a tritone in soprano and tenor (mm. 44–45), albeit separated by a rest. But the insistence on the triad motif and the joining of the four parts in stretto imitation result in a structure so tightly fitted together that only a chromatic interpretation can explain the singularity of the design. And only a chromatic interpretation results in a flawless reading and logical harmonic and thematic construction.

There is some difficulty about how to construe the ending. If Brumel had intended to go to F-flat and A-double flat, he could have done so by moving his transposition further to G-flat and C-flat and on to C-flat and F-flat. This he did not do. To leap suddenly to F-flat and A-double flat in measures 51–52 would therefore seem ill-advised. Nor is an ending on G-flat major likely. Only one to two measures before such an ending the harmonic progression centers on F

minor. The C-flat in measures 54–55 would have to be introduced suddenly without adequate preparation and justification. The resulting harmonic progression is unconvincing in a context so carefully established to develop a logical modulatory scheme.

It seems that the best exit from the chromatic labyrinth can be gained in measures 52–53, where B-flat minor would turn to F major and lead, through a repeat and reaffirmation of F major, to a cadence on G minor. The section from measure 39 to the end would then be construed in the fashion shown on the opposite page.

We have concentrated on the positive evidence for the chromatic interpretation of Brumel's provocative work. There is also evidence of a negative kind. I refer to examples in which entrance into a chromatic modulation would be followed by loss of tonal continuity and where an exit could not be found. For instance, in *Avant, avant* (no. 38) it would be possible to err into chromatic constructions at measure 15 by matching the original B-flat in the bass with B-flat in the tenor and E-flat in the soprano, which would bring A-flat, D-flat, G-flat, etc., in its train. But not only could we gain no exit from such an involvement, the ensuing modulation is wild and arbitrary rather than carefully arranged by leading into the circle of fifths through stepwise escalation. It simply does not work. Neither does a later passage at measure 30 where one might wish to continue a B-flat in the alto with an ensuing E-flat, A-flat, etc., in alto, soprano, and other parts.

Passages like these prove two points: (1) it takes superior ability on the part of the composer to so set his contrapuntal parts that they mesh perfectly in the achievement of a chromatic modulation; and (2) it is impossible for a modern editor to impose such constructions at will and have them result in superior readings if they are not designed by a most circumspect and able craftsman in the first place.

It is one thing to propose and logically establish so extraordinary a chromatic modulation; it is another to account for it, particularly when it appears as early as 1502. But Brumel's bold venture is not an isolated phenomenon. It fits very well with similar experiments of the time, above all with Josquin's *Fortuna d'un gran tempo* from the *Odhecaton* and with Pierre de la Rue's *Ce n'est pas jeu* of the present volume. It goes only one step in the circle of fifths beyond Josquin's work, which involves B-flat, E-flat, A-flat, and D-flat. Of course,

Josquin's Absalon motet, too, goes to G-flat,[22] but we do not know when it was composed and thus the question of influence cannot be decided with documentary certainty, although his unmatched harmonic genius would point to Josquin's priority. Brumel's work also fits into the general stylistic relationship observed between Brumel and Josquin.[23] Finally, it is of interest that Alfonso d'Este I, Duke of Ferrara, invited Brumel to become his chapelmaster. Ferrara, throughout the sixteenth century, was a musical center of progressive tendencies, and the Duke, who issued his invitation in 1505, may well have been familiar with the work published in Venice in 1502.

It is unfortunate that we do not have the original text of Brumel's *Noé, noé, noé*. A number of texts of the period begin with *Noé*, but none that we have come across would fit Brumel's piece. Without the text we lack the chief clue to, and confirmation of, the chromatic interpretation. For no chromatic experiments are known in vocal music of the age in which there is not a convincing connection between the text and the use of chromaticism or modulatory transposition. Even in a more conventional work such as De Orto's *D'ung aultre amer* (no. 24), with its astonishing canons, the appearance of B-flat, E-flat, and A-flat in the same measure seems provoked by the word "change" in the text (m. 30), which, in the terminology of the time, would naturally be associated in the composer's mind with the idea of mutation.[24] Thus we can only hope that a source may yet be discovered that transmits Brumel's extraordinary composition with its original text.

Small as *Canti B* appears, compared with the *Odhecaton* and *Canti C* which are respectively double and triple its size, its chanson collection contains an amazing diversity of styles, moods, and temperaments.

The crystalline beauty and elegance of Josquin's *Comment peult avoir joye* (no. 19), with its bright sound of Ionian, contrasts with the somber sound of Pierre de la Rue's songs of unhappy love, with their low bass tessitura descending to D and C (nos. 7 and 22), written in modal counterpoint rendered more expressive through use of rugged dissonance (in no. 28,

mm. 21–23, the dissonance of three fourths piled on top of each other combined with syncopation marks the words "I die"). The virtuoso technique of Ninot le Petit, Compère, Vaqueras, and Lourdault, alias Jean Braconnier, the masters of the "modern," freely composed chanson, with its airy texture, light homophony, and voice pairing, its tripping rhythms, its cultivation of the upbeat, its fast parlando, and its Gallic wit and drive co-exists with the modest skill of anonymous composers responsible, say, for the simple homespun *cantus-firmus* arrangement of *Una moza falle yo* (no. 26), a piece without imagination or individuality, the most ordinary sort of *Gebrauchsmusik*. Works of a thoroughly unified contrapuntal texture, such as chansons by Raulin (no. 6) or Ghiselin (no. 42), alternate with works of the most varied textures. Compère's *Et dunt revenis vous* (no. 29), for example, is a study in contrasts: fugal imitation is followed by homophony, slow motion by fast, rolling melody by speech-like tone repetitions, low by high voices, downbeat by upbeat phrases, normal rhythm by hocket-like syncopations, major by minor. Chansons observing the old modes are followed by others foreshadowing modern major, such as Agricola's *Je vous emprie* (no. 46) and others already mentioned (no. 19) or yet to be discussed (no. 27). Compositions of the old masterful contrapuntists Busnois or De Orto alternate with works in which popular inspiration survives, such as the magnificent *Réveillez-vous, Piccars* (no. 9).

This song of war appears to be a survival of a sort of popular polyphony that must have been widespread at the time. It deserves a closer look. A battle song of enduring appeal, as Professor Hewitt has shown, it combines simplicity of melody, straightforward meter, rousing rhythm, and careless counterpoint with parallel fifths (mm. 9 and 38) and a series of extraordinarily strong and at times crude dissonances (mm. 7:4, 11:4, 14:4, 18:1, 18:4, 30:2, 32:4, 38:2, 41:4, 42:2, 45:4, 46:1, 47:3, 49:4, 50:1, 50:4). A number of these are what we have called, in another context,[25] "tonal dissonances," that is, frictions not sanctioned by the laws of modal counterpoint nor subject to its rules of preparation and resolution, but explicable in terms of an increasing sense of tonality and a growing intensity of cadential direction (see, for example, the

[22] See Edward E. Lowinsky, *Secret Chromatic Art in the Netherlands Motet* (New York, 1946), pp. 24–25.

[23] See G. Reese, *Music in the Renaissance* (New York, 1954), pp. 240, 260 ff.

[24] See Edward E. Lowinsky, "The Goddess Fortuna in Music," p. 67.

[25] Edward E. Lowinsky, *Tonality and Atonality in Sixteenth-Century Music* (2d rev. printing; Berkeley and Los Angeles, 1962), pp. 12–13, 20–24.

beautiful dominant seventh chord, m. 18:4, even though it appears weakened by the anticipation of the note of resolution). This goes well with the strong feeling for tonal-harmonic relationships manifest in the net of modulations spreading from D Dorian through A minor (mm. 5 and 10) to F major (m. 16), tending for a moment even toward B-flat major (mm. 20–21), going back to F (m. 24), from there to C major (m. 29), and again back to F (m. 39), and then, in a final circling motion, returning toward A minor (m. 47) and D minor.

Traits such as these can be found in Italian popular polyphony of the time, published by Petrucci in his great collections of frottole.[26] *Réveillez-vous* is, on a higher level of contrapuntal craftsmanship, a Flemish counterpart of these Italian works; it allows us to savor that sturdier brand of Flemish polyphony used for popular occasions of which a great part must have disappeared.[27] Characteristically, music of this kind— and no. 10 is another example of it—comes down anonymously. Nor should it be assumed that it was ever completely isolated from the more refined and sophisticated polyphony of the great masters; its appearance in their company alone is sufficient to disprove such a notion.[28] I should suppose that these "anonymi" were smaller masters from provincial centers who were engaged in meeting the immense demand for music on all levels of social life in the old Netherlands.

The man who was most receptive to this less polished style of popular polyphony was Jacob Obrecht; the dissonances that one can find in his *Cela sans plus* (no. 13), for instance, are reminiscent of the dissonance treatment in *Réveillez-vous*. Yet, Obrecht's great line of melody and rhythmic and metric variety set his work far apart from the simpler, rough-hewn style of our Anonymous.

The variations in the level of craftsmanship in *Canti B* are enormous. Both Josquin's *Comment peult avoir joye* (no. 19) and Bulkyn's *Or sus* (no. 36) are based on canon. Bulkyn's chanson, with its lame pace

and uninspired melody, its ineffective cadences, not to speak of the parallel fifths between the canon voices (mm. 10 and 19, and their repeats in mm. 29 and 38), is an immense contrast to the animation and ease with which canon parts and counterpoints roll along in Josquin's composition. What offers a challenge to a great master is a burden for the unskilled composer.

The variations in the outlook of the composer are no less large. There is a wide gulf between the performer-oriented art of De Orto's canonic tour de force and the audience-oriented art of the Ninot, Compère, Lourdault generation. Indeed, De Orto's fantastic artifice in his *D'ung aultre amer* (no. 24), brilliantly resolved by Professor Hewitt, does not add, but detracts from the audible part of the music. Certainly the parallel octaves at the end, the unprecedented skip of a seventh in two parts in parallel fifths (mm. 29–30), and most of all, the non-integrated harmonic whole of the piece, are part of the payment exacted for the intricate design. The intellectual part of the composition cannot be heard or appreciated by anyone save the performer. This is *l'art pour l'art* with a vengeance.

It is astonishing how completely this aspect of the art has vanished in the music of the younger generation of chanson composers. A piece such as Ninot's *Et la la la* (no. 27) is a hit tune of the first order. Its major sound, racy rhythms and regular accents, homophonic simplicity, "tonal" dissonances (mm. 17:4, 22:1), parlando style and vernacular speech character remove it resolutely both from the courtly air of the Burgundian chanson and the intellectual posture of the Flemish canonic chanson. It took a genius such as Josquin to prove that there need be no conflict between these two seemingly irreconcilable worlds. A piece such as *Baisés moy* (no. 34), consisting of a double canon, is at once a fantastic feat of technical skill and a perfect specimen of the modern chanson with its air of irony and good-humored laughter, its lighthearted melodies and light-footed rhythms, and its enchanting lifelike chatter.

But Josquin is too complex an artist and thinker not to have left some creations whose enigmatic character is hard to penetrate. Professor Hewitt, with her peculiar knack for cracking even the most baffling canonic mysteries, has solved the canonic instruction of Josquin's *L'homme armé* with which Petrucci opens his *Canti B*. The question remains why Josquin should have used it at all, for the piece itself is not only

---

[26] *Ibid.*, chap. 1.

[27] For reference to an unpublished manuscript of carols with Flemish and Latin texts written in a primitive contrapuntal style, see Lowinsky, "Music in the Culture of the Renaissance," p. 518.

[28] Howard M. Brown, in his *Music in the French Secular Theater* (p. 134 and p. 273), has shown that *Réveillez-vous* is built on a monophonic popular chanson, some lines of which were sung in a French farce.

peculiarly unattractive, but also quite un-Josquinian. Where else in Josquin's *oeuvre* would one find such ungraceful melody, such unrelenting homophony, such plodding and monotonous rhythm?

Is it possible that these puzzling traits have their origin in a symbolic intention? The instructions begin with the word "Canon" framed by two dots. Now in Josquin's time "canon," in French usage, also signified "cannon." The two peculiar dots may possibly have been symbols for cannon balls—a symbolism perhaps not too far-fetched in a chanson on

> *l'homme armé, l'homme armé*
> *l'homme armé doibt on douter.*

Could it be that Josquin's *L'homme armé* embodied a symbol of the man who, under the burden of armor, cannot move forward except in slow and heavy steps? Could the unrelenting homophony be intended to symbolize the soldiers' marching step? Such an interpretation is out of tune neither with Josquin's often demonstrated delight in symbolism nor with the abnormal character of the piece itself, nor indeed with Josquin's times—so full of war and strife and upheaval. But in Josquin's work, unlike De Orto's, the symbolism becomes an audible part of the musical work; it transcends the narrow boundaries of intellectual artifice accessible only to the artificer and his guild brothers.[29]

Petrucci's editor, starting *Canti B* with the symbol of the man of arms created by Josquin, follows it with Compère's prayer to the Blessed Virgin Mary who, in her pity for mankind, looks down with mercy upon her servants. The *cantus firmus* with its ascending hexachord scale was perhaps suggested by the association with the hymn tune *Ut queant laxis*, from which Guido of Arezzo derived the six solmization syllables of the hexachord[30]; it may represent symbolically the ascent of the prayer to the "heavenly virgin." It may also be a symbol of Mary, the *scala regni caelestis*:[31] Again, this symbolism is audible not only in the *cantus firmus* itself, but in the anticipatory imitation of the alto in the very beginning of the piece, which points clearly to the "heavenly scale" of the Virgin Mary.

Nothing illustrates more poignantly the sturdy innocence of the Renaissance musician than the co-existence in one volume of songs of love—going through the whole gamut of love's desire, delight, deceit, and distress—with songs of war and musical prayers to the Blessed Virgin Mary (nos. 2 and 39), a co-existence gradually abandoned in the chansonniers of the more self-conscious, reform-minded sixteenth century, but characteristic of the chansonniers of the fifteenth century, in which heaven and earth are still close to each other and the turn from an earthly love to the adoration of the heavenly Virgin is easy and natural.

I cannot close this Introduction without thanking Mrs. Tiffany Blake of Chicago for the generous gift that made it possible to provide the present volume with an extraordinary number of illustrations which will aid the scholar as well as delight the eye.

EDWARD E. LOWINSKY

CHICAGO, ILLINOIS

[29] The artillery-loving Alfonso I, Duke of Ferrara (1476–1534), accompanied his device *Loco et tempore*, also *à lieu et temps*, with a cannon ball. Although documented for the time of the battle of Ravenna (1512), it is possible that the device is considerably earlier than that (see Jacopo Gelli, *Divise, motti, e imprese di famiglie e personaggi Italiani* [2d rev. ed.; Milan, 1928], nos. 1103 and 1104). The possibility that Josquin, who wrote his *Missa Hercules Dux Ferrariae* for the Duke's father, should have composed his *L'homme armé* as a musical device for the young Alfonso, before he became duke, is an intriguing thought.

[30] See Ludwig Finscher, *Loyset Compère (c. 1450–1518), Life and Works* (American Institute of Musicology, 1964), p. 125.

[31] In the *Te Matrem Dei laudamus* Mary is hailed as the *scala regni caelestis*. This image found further dissemination in the Neo-Latin and Italian poetry of the time. Battista Marchese Paolaccino, Bishop of Reggio, incorporated it into a Latin elegy. Leonardo Giustiniani (1388–1446) rendered the elegy in the form of an Italian canzonetta in honor of the Virgin, which began with these words:

> *Maria Vergine bella*
> *Scala: che ascendi, e guidi a l'alto cielo*

(see Gio. Maria Crescimbeni, *De' Comentari intorno all'istoria della volgar poesia*, Vol. II, Part II, Lib. V [Venice, 1730], pp. 246–47).

PREFACE

IN THE preface to the modern edition of *Odhecaton A* by the Mediaeval Academy of America in 1942, gratitude was expressed to a large number of persons who assisted in the preparation of that edition. To a degree they also helped with this edition of *Canti B*. It was the suggestion of Professor Heinrich Besseler that as I gathered information on the *Odhecaton* I should deal similarly with *Canti B* and *C*. A great deal of research on *Canti B*, therefore, had already been completed before the *Odhecaton* appeared.

During the academic year 1943–44 I had the privilege of working at Yale University as a Sterling Fellow. I am most grateful to that institution for the award that gave me a full year in which to put my notes in order and write a commentary on *Canti B*. The late Professor Schrade kindly read each chapter as it was completed and made many valuable observations.

The award of a John Simon Guggenheim Memorial Fellowship for 1947–48 gave me a year in Paris, where I tried to take advantage of the extensive resources of the Bibliothèque Nationale. The French musicologists were most helpful to me. Mme la Comtesse de Chambure permitted me to study photostats of the Nivelle de la Chaussée Chansonnier. M. Marc Pincherle arranged for me to talk on *Canti B* before the French Société de Musicologie, and Mme Nanie Bridgman trained a group of singers and instrumentalists who performed most delightfully several works from the anthology. M. Vladimir Fédorov was also helpful to me in countless ways.

On my return to the United States and to college teaching, my bulky manuscript was consigned to a shelf, where it remained until 1963, when Professor Edward E. Lowinsky, General Editor of the MONUMENTS OF RENAISSANCE MUSIC, invited me to publish Petrucci's trilogy of chansonniers in his new series.

As the use of microfilm has increased enormously since 1942, my library now contains a filmed copy of virtually every manuscript I once traveled to Germany, Switzerland, Italy, France, or Belgium to consult. I should like to acknowledge the help of several colleagues in assembling this film collection: Professors Howard M. Brown, Edward E. Lowinsky, Gwynn McPeek, Martin Picker, Dragan Plamenac, and Gustave Reese, all of whom have shown great generosity in allowing me to have copies of films in their own libraries. I should also like to thank a pupil of mine, Arthur Wolff, who helped me by ordering certain films from European libraries or from the Archives in Kassel.

I wish to thank the Mediaeval Academy of America for graciously permitting me to continue the edition of the Petrucci anthologies in the University of Chicago series. Both Professor Willi Apel and the late Otto Gombosi read my manuscript in its first draft. Professor Howard M. Brown of the University of Chicago read my first revision and made many interesting and valuable suggestions. Professor Lowinsky spent countless hours in condensing, improving, arranging, and rearranging the material in search of the best possible presentation. He has also made the final decision in matters of *musica ficta* and text underlay. I can never thank him adequately for all he has done for me.

H. H.

NORTH TEXAS STATE UNIVERSITY
DENTON, TEXAS

CONTENTS

ILLUSTRATIONS

THE EDITIONS
OF 1502 AND 1503

THE PRESENT volume contains an edition of the second of the three anthologies of secular part-music published by Ottaviano dei Petrucci in Venice between 1501 and 1504. The first of these, the *Harmonice Musices Odhecaton: A*, not only inaugurated this series but also marked the inception of Petrucci's distinguished career as a music publisher. The second and third volumes of the series were given somewhat simpler titles in Petrucci's native tongue: *Canti B numero Cinquanta* (the "B Songs, Fifty in Number") and *Canti C numero Cento Cinquanta* (the "C Songs, One Hundred Fifty in Number"). Although the *Odhecaton* has received the widespread attention proportionate to its importance in the history of music printing, there exists no comparable literature dealing with *Canti B* or *Canti C*.

When Anton Schmid published his work on Petrucci in 1845,[1] no copies of *Canti B* or *Canti C* were known to have survived. That Petrucci had actually published them, however, was known from their citation by Conrad Gesner in his *Pandectae* of 1548.[2] It was not until 1855 that one copy each of the *Odhecaton* and *Canti B* were unearthed at the Liceo Musicale in Bologna. They were discovered by one of the professors of the Liceo, Gaetano Gaspari, who became its first librarian when this position was created the following year. According to Claudio

Sartori,[3] the bookshelves were in a chaotic state, so that Gaspari's first task was to set things in order. Nearly everything there had once been a part of Padre Martini's personal library.

Gaspari's discovery of the two Petrucci anthologies was made known in an article by Angelo Catelani,[4] who was both a friend of Gaspari and librarian of the Estense Library in Modena. Catelani described both volumes in detail and reproduced the title page and colophon of *Canti B*.[5]

The colophon of *Canti B* reads:

Impressum Venetiis per Octavianum Petrutiu(m) Forosemp(ro)nie(n)sem die 5 Februarii Salutis anno 1501. Cum privilegio invictissimi Dominii Venetiaru(m) q(uod) nullus possit cantum Figuratum Imprimere sub pena in ipso privilegio contenta. (See Plates I and II.)

(Printed in Venice by Ottaviano Petrucci, a native of Fossombrone, the fifth day of February in the year of Salvation 1501. With the privilege of the most invincible Dominion of the Venetians, that no one else may print Figured Music under the penalty contained in said privilege.)

Between this imprint and Petrucci's emblem occurs the register of the signatures:

Registrum A B C D E F G. Omnes q(ua)terni.

When a large sheet of paper is folded in eighths, a

---

[1] *Ottaviano dei Petrucci da Fossombrone, der erste Erfinder des Musiknotendruckes mit beweglichen Metalltypen, und seine Nachfolger im sechzehnten Jahrhunderte* (Vienna, 1845).

[2] *Pandectarum sive Partitionum universalium Conradi Gesneri . . .*, Book I, p. 82, "Cantus quinquaginta signati B."

[3] *Die Musik in Geschichte und Gegenwart*, IV (1955), s.v. "Gaetano Gaspari," cols. 1412–14.

[4] "Bibliografia di due stampe ignote di Ottaviano Petrucci," *Gazzetta musicale di Milano*, XIV (1856). Published separately: Milan, 1856; reprinted by the Bolletino Bibliografico, Milan, 1932.

[5] See Claudio Sartori, *Bibliografia delle opere musicali stampate da Ottaviano Petrucci* (Florence: Leo S. Olschki, 1948), p. 44.

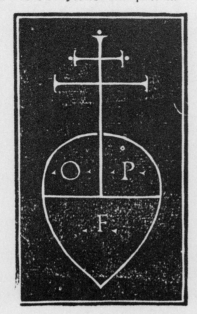

Imp:eſſum Venetiis per Octauianum Petrutii Foroſempnié
ſem die ς Februarii Salutis anno 1501 Cū3 priuilegio inuictiſſi
mi Domini Venetiarūcp nullus poſſit cantum Figuratum Im
p:imere ſub pena in ipſo priuilegio contenta.

Regiſtrum A B C D E F G. Omnes quaterni.

PLATE I.   *Canti B*, edition of 1502, Colophon.

booklet or "gathering" of four smaller sheets results. Since all the gatherings of *Canti B* were of the same size, Petrucci could express this fact very concisely by writing "omnes quaterni," that is, "All [the gatherings are] in fours." To ensure that the gatherings would be assembled in the correct order for binding, Petrucci placed the letter A in the lower right-hand corner of the first sheet of the first gathering—the remaining sheets being marked A ii, A iii, and A iiii—letter B similarly on the first sheet of the second gathering, and so on. Letters (or numbers) so used are called signatures. Petrucci tells us that seven letters of the alphabet were needed: A–G. *Canti B*, then, fills twenty-eight (7×4) folios or one hundred and twelve (4×28) pages.

The date given in the colophon, February 5, 1501, requires explanation, for it seems to be earlier than the date of dedication of the *Odhecaton: A*, May 15, 1501. Catelani tried to explain away this discrepancy by suggesting that the *B* volume had actually not been issued until some months after the printing took place. Fétis offered a more plausible interpretation: that the

Venetian year at that time began on Easter.[6] But it was Carlo Castellani who produced the correct solution in 1888 when he pointed out that the Venetian year then began on March first.[7] Thus, dates falling within the months of January or February have to be adjusted to conform with the Gregorian calendar, and Petrucci's "February 5, 1501" should read "February 5, 1502" according to our reckoning today. *Canti B*, then, did follow (not precede) the *Odhecaton: A*, and the three volumes were indeed issued in the order A, B, C.

In 1879 an acquisition was made by the Library of the Conservatoire National de Musique et de Déclamation, Paris: one copy each of the *Odhecaton*, *Canti B*, and *Canti C*. From available published accounts, the history

[6] François Fétis, "Note sur la découverte récente des plus anciens monuments de la typographie musicale, et, par occasion, sur les compositeurs belges du XVme siècle," *Bulletins de l'Académie Royale des Sciences, des Lettres et des Beaux-Arts de Belgique*, 2d ser., XI (1861), 272.

[7] *I Privilegi di stampa e la proprietà letteraria in Venezia* (2d ed.; Venice, 1889). For information on the Venetian calendar, see pp. 17, 23, 40, 64. See also Gustave Reese, "The First Printed Collection of Part-Music (the Odhecaton)," *Musical Quarterly*, XX (1934), 48; or Sartori, *Bibliografia*, p. 39.

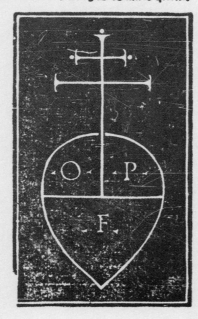

PLATE II.   *Canti B*, edition of 1503, Colophon.

of this acquisition is not quite complete. Jean-Baptiste Weckerlin, at that time librarian of the Conservatory, commented that "in this year, 1879, we were able to intercept on their way to Bordeaux some rare volumes coming out of Spain. One was the *Harmonice Musices Odhecaton*, printed at Venice in 1502 and 1503 by Petrucci, to whom we generally attribute the invention of movable type for music, a complete and unique copy...."[8] In calling this item "complete," Weckerlin meant that it included all three volumes of the series: A, B, and C. In terming it "unique," he was quite justified, for today it is still as true as it is remarkable that no other library in the world possesses copies of all three volumes of Petrucci's first series.[9]

That same year the purchase was announced by Weckerlin in a "Note on the *Odhecaton* of Petrucci and the *Liber Missarum* of Carpentras" (another rare volume bought at the same time). In reference to the obscure history of the former, Weckerlin mused: "Oh, well! mysterious Spain concealed a complete copy of this treasure, in the remotest part of some convent library, no doubt; as yet we do not know."[10] A briefer announcement appeared in *Le Ménestrel*; several of the composers were named, with a remark (intended to stress their eminence) to the effect that "they were the Rossinis and the Aubers of that time."[11] That French musicologists may be justly proud of their good fortune in having obtained these three anthologies is even more true today than it was when Weckerlin could write: "The appearance of a complete copy of this most rare volume, printed by Petrucci, was bound, of course, to make a sensation in the world of musicologists; consequently, letters of congratulation

[8] Bibliothèque du Conservatoire National de Musique et de Déclamation: *Catalogue bibliographique*, ed. Jean-Baptiste Weckerlin (Paris, 1885), pp. 372–400. Also published separately as *Petrucci: Harmonice musices odhecaton, avec notice* (Paris, 1885); see p. xxviii.

[9] The adjusted dates of the Paris volumes are: May 25, 1504 (*Odhecaton*); August 4, 1503 (*Canti B*); February 10, 1504 (*Canti C*).

[10] "Note sur l'*Odhecaton* de Petrucci et le *Liber Missarum* de Carpentras," *Revue et gazette musicale de Paris*, XLVI (1879), 380.

[11] *Le Ménestrel*, XLV (1878–79), 414.

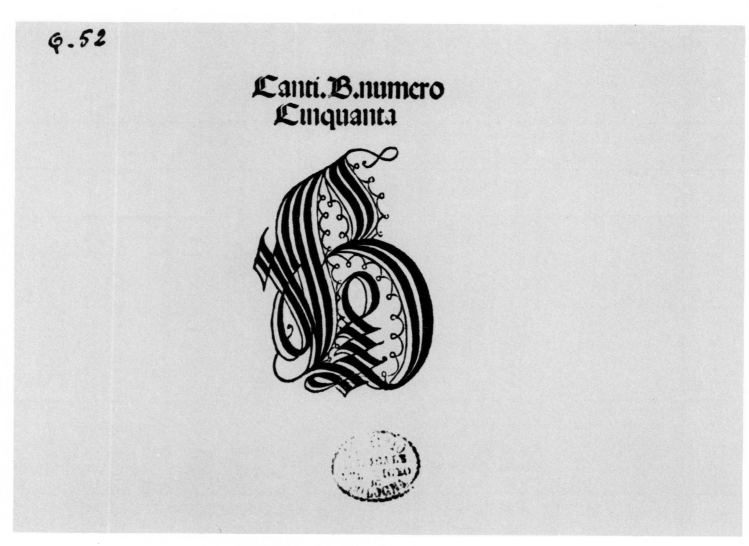

PLATE III. *Canti B*, edition of 1502, Title Page.

from Belgium, Italy, Germany, England, and so on, arrived for us at the time of purchase of this little treasure, unique thus far."[12]

In the Bibliothèque Nationale there is still preserved a copy of the *Catalogue d'une petite collection de livres rares et précieux d'ouvrages sur la musique en vente aux prix marqués: Chez Charles Lefebre, libraire* (Bordeaux, 1879). In this dealer's catalogue (p. 15) there is the following entry, whose inconsistencies in the use of italics, capital letters, and so on, are retained here:

Petrucci (Octavius), *Harmonice* musices Odhecaton (A). *Impressum Venetiis,* 1504. *Canti B.* numero cinquanta, *Impressum Venetiis,* 1503. *Canti* (c) N° cento cinquanta. *Impressum* Venetiis per Octavinum Petrutium. Forosem, 1504–1503. —Ensemble un fort vol. in-4° oblong gothique rel. 1000 fr.

These entries can be no other than the volumes purchased by the Conservatoire, but where Lefebre obtained them seems never to have been determined.

Since all three anthologies were of the same format and, in fact, were bound together under one cover,

Weckerlin could describe them as one: "a little volume in-4° oblong, sixteen centimeters high and a little more than twenty-two and a half centimeters wide [6.3 × 8.86 in.]."[13] Haberl added further details: "The paper is excellent, firm, smooth, as if calendered, and after almost four hundred years has a parchment-like tone. The printer's ink is a brilliant and deep black, and nevertheless does not shine through to the other side; the leaves are elegantly rounded at the corners—in a word: 'this first musical print competes with the most beautiful modern printed music, even surpasses it in individual parts.'"[14] Nearly a hundred years later Claudio Sartori wrote similarly that "in the elegance of the type and in the clarity of the impression the *Odhecaton* has remained the unexcelled model in the history of music printing."[15]

[13] *Ibid.*
[14] Franz Xavier Haberl, "Drucke von Ottaviano Petrucci auf der Bibliothek des Liceo filarmonico in Bologna: Ein bibliographischer Beitrag zu Anton Schmid's *Ottaviano dei Petrucci* (Wien, 1845)," *Monatshefte für Musikgeschichte,* V (1873), 55.
[15] *Die Musik in Geschichte und Gegenwart,* X (1962), *s.v.* "Petrucci," col. 1139.

[12] Weckerlin, *Catalogue,* p. 372.

4

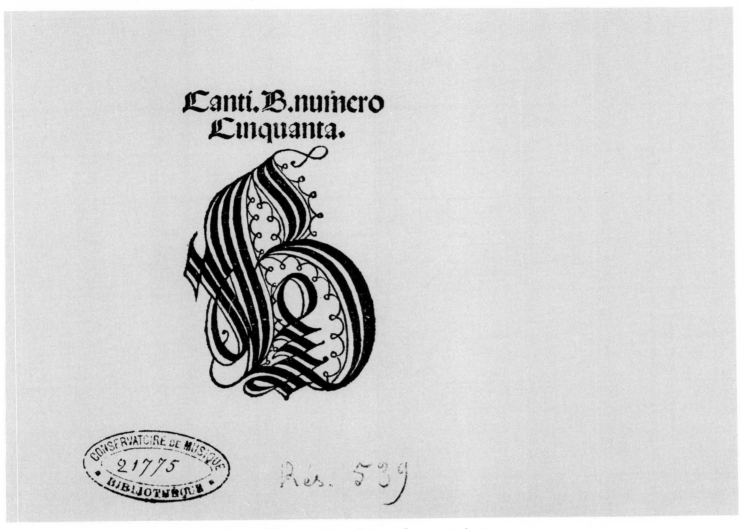

PLATE IV. *Canti B*, edition of 1503, Title Page.

The date appearing in the colophon of the Paris copy of *Canti B* is August 4, 1503 (see Plate II). Since this date does not fall within the period during which the Venetian and Gregorian calendars differ, it needs no correction. Thus, two different issues of *Canti B* are known, and only two: that of February 5, 1502, and that of August 4, 1503.

Neither the Bologna nor the Paris copy of *Canti B* shows a dedication or other accessory material. The title page reads simply: *Canti . B . numero Cinquanta*; and below these words is a very large and decorative capital *B*, measured by Weckerlin as "more than eight centimeters [3.15 in.] in height" (see Plates III and IV). On the verso of the first folio appears an index of the volume. This comprises two lists: first, a list of the four-part works (those *A quatro*, but including the few compositions for five or six parts); second, a list of those *A tre*. On folio 2 recto appears the music of Josquin's *L'omme armé*, and the remaining compositions follow—the last, Compère's *Le grant désir*, falling on folio 55 verso. Opposite this work, on the recto of an unnumbered folio, stands the colophon and, beneath it, Petrucci's device, familiar through its use in all his publications (see Plates I and II).

Although its title would lead us to believe that *Canti B* contains fifty (*cinquanta*) compositions, the actual count is fifty-one. Indexes of the contents of the Bologna copy have been published by Catelani,[16] Haberl,[17] Eitner,[18] Vernarecci,[19] Torchi,[20] and Sartori[21]; of the Paris copy, by Weckerlin[22] and Sartori.[23] The most reliable indexes are found in Sartori's *Bibliografia*.[24]

[16] Catelani, "Bibliografia," pp. 6–7.
[17] Haberl, "Drucke von Petrucci," pp. 55–56.
[18] The various incipits are scattered throughout Robert Eitner's *Bibliographie der Musik-Sammelwerke des XVI. and XVII. Jahrhunderts* (Berlin, 1877).
[19] Augusto Vernarecci, *Ottaviano de' Petrucci da Fossombrone, inventore dei tipi mobili metallici fusi della musica nel secolo xv* (2d ed.; Bologna, 1882), pp. 238–40.
[20] Luigi Torchi, "I Monumenti dell'antica musica francese a Bologna," *Rivista musicale italiana*, XIII (1906), 578–80.
[21] Sartori, *Bibliografia*, pp. 42–43.
[22] Weckerlin, *Catalogue*, pp. 381 ff.
[23] Sartori, *Bibliografia*, pp. 65–66.
[24] Sartori, *ibid.*, pp. 35–37 (*Odhecaton A*), 65–66 (*Canti B*), 70–73 (*Canti C*).

5

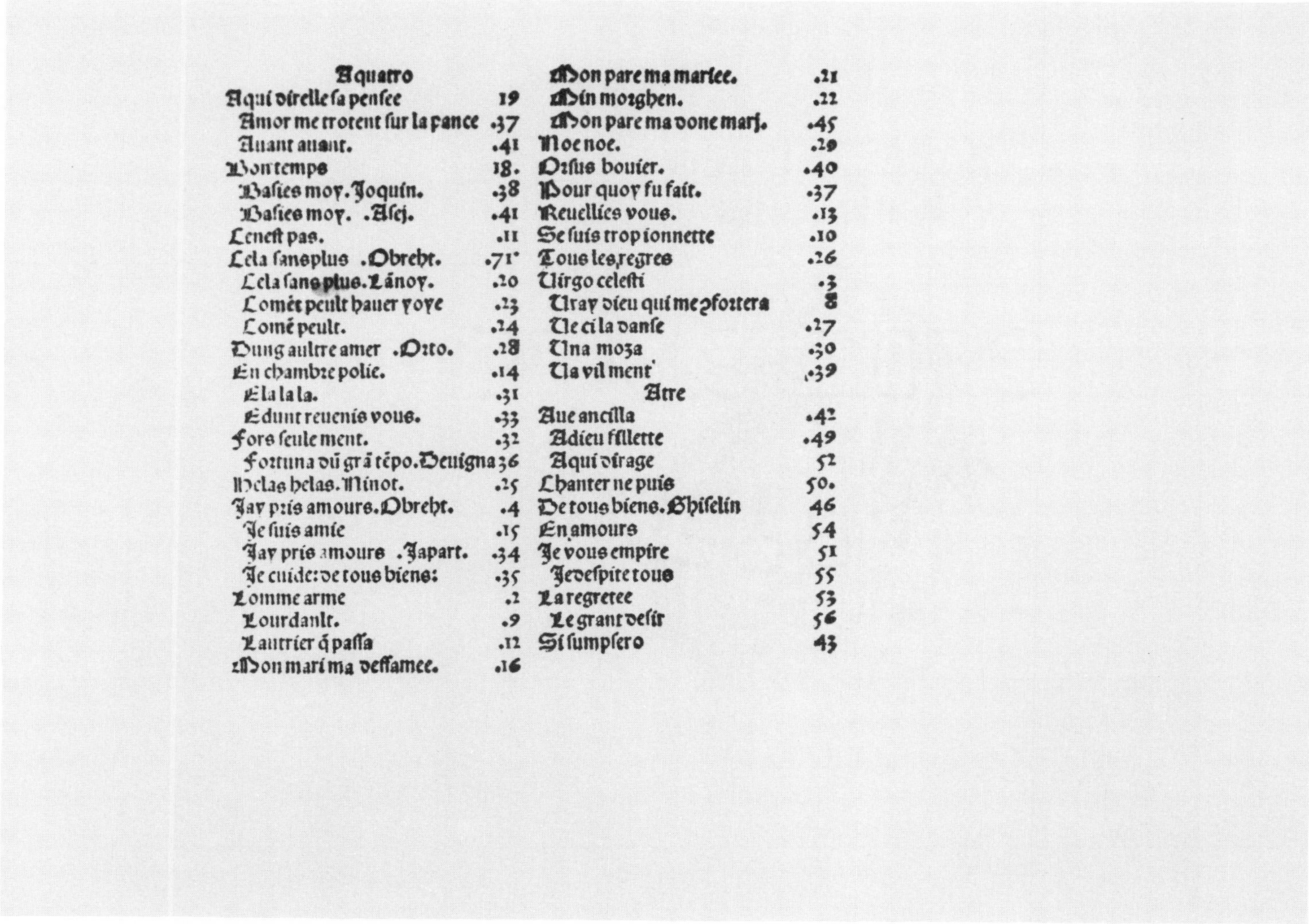

PLATE V. *Canti B*, edition of 1502, Table of Contents.

Sartori states that the volume printed in 1503 "is a reprint of the first edition of *Canti B* of February 5, 1502."[25] If he means only that both collections contain the same pieces of music, he is right. He points out that the type was reset for the index and other lettered parts of the volume: "The index of this reprint differs from [that of] the first edition. In it we find, in fact, that the numbering of the pages is marked partly in arabic numbers, partly in roman numerals."[26]

A comparison of the indexes of the two books (see Plates V and VI) shows minor differences in spelling as well as in style of numeration; there seems no doubt that the type was reset. The index gives the names of seven composers (of eight compositions): Obreht (nos. 3 and 13), Lannoy (no. 16), Ninot (no. 21), Orto (no. 24), Japart (no. 30), Josquin (no. 34), and Ghiselin (no. 42). Six of the seven names confirm composers' names given with the music in the body of the volume. The seventh, in the index alone, tells us the composer of no. 16, "La(n)noy," by which is meant Colinet de

[25] *Ibid.*, p. 65.
[26] *Ibid.*

Lannoy. The two editions of *Canti B* agree in this respect; no new names were added in the edition of 1503, no names were withdrawn.

A careful comparison, page by page, of the Paris and Bologna copies shows that the type was also reset for the music of the later printing. (It might be said that the second "edition" was not necessarily an improvement upon the first, as would be assumed today. It is merely different.) A few examples will suffice to show the kinds of variation that make this a certainty:

1. The stem of a minim or semiminim (or the stems of a group of these notes) will extend downward in one edition, upward in the other; a stem may be straight in one copy, crooked or (in one or two instances only) broken in the other.

2. A few notes may appear at the end of a staff in one copy, at the beginning of the next in the other.

3. The metric signature may be in the fourth space in one copy, in the third space in the other; or, in the third space in one copy, on the second line in the other.

4. Two notes, such as *brevis*, *longa*, may be written in ligature in one copy, as individual notes in the other; or, more frequently, two semibreves may appear as separate

6

A quatre

Aqui direlle sa pensee 19
Amours me trotet sur la pance 37
Auant auant 4i
Bon temps xviii
Baßies moy. Josquin. 38
Baßies moy. Ascl. 4i
Ce nest pas xi
Ce la sans plus. Obreht xvii
Cela sans plus. Lauoy 20
Comet peult hauer voye 23
Comet peult. 24
Dung aultre amer. Orto 28
En chambre polie xiiii
Ela la la. xxxi
Edunt reuenis vous xxxiii
Fors seule ment. 32
Fortuna dun gra tepo Deuigna 36
Delas helas. Minot 25
Jay pris amours. Obreht iiii
Je suis amie xv
Jay pris amours. Japart xxxiiii
Je cuide: de tous biens 35
Lomme arme 2
Lourdault. 9
Lautrier q passa xii
Mon mari ma deffamee xvi

Mon pere ma marsee xxi
M En morghen 22
Mon pere ma done mari xxxv
Moe noe 29
Orsus bouier. xxxx
Pour quoy fu fiat. xxxxvii
Reuellies vous 13
Se suis trop ionnette. x
Tous les regres 26
Virgo celesti 3
Vray dieu qui me pfortera 8
Ue cil la danse. 17
Una moza 30
Ua vil ment 39

Atre

Aue, ancilla xxxxii
Adieu fillette xxxxviiii
A qui dirage 52
Chanter ne puis 50
De tous biens. Ghi elln xxxxvi
En amours liiii
Je vous emprie 5i
Je despite tous lv
La regrettee liii
Le grant desir lvi
Si sumpsero xxxxiii

PLATE VI. *Canti B*, edition of 1503, Table of Contents.

notes in one copy, in a *ligatura cum opposita proprietate* in the other.

5. An individual semibreve rest may depend from the fourth line in one copy, from the third line in the other.
6. A *corona* may be placed higher in one copy than in the other.
7. The dot following a note may fall in a certain space in one copy, in the space above or below it in the other.
8. A leger line may be very short in one copy, many times as long in the other.
9. Five individual pages in the Bologna copy contain only five staves, whereas the Paris copy shows six staves uniformly throughout.

Although a difference of one kind or another may be found on every page, these discrepancies are not noticeable in the transcriptions, for they are not of a kind to alter the values of either notes or rests. They do, however, prove that *Canti B* received not a second printing but a second edition.

In a few places the second edition of 1503 seems to be correcting errors detected in the first edition:

1. Folio 41 was incorrectly numbered "35" in the first edition, but corrected to "41" in the second edition.

2. The elaborate capital "A" needed to start the incipit *Auant auant* (no. 38) was lacking in the first edition, but is present in the second.

3. In no. 11 (f. 15) the last word of the incipit is incomplete, reading merely "fori" in the first edition, but corrected to "forier" in the second edition.

4. In no. 50 (f. 54') a minim rest placed above the fifth line in the first edition has been brought within the staff in the second edition.

In other places, however, one may prefer the first edition. Sartori has already reported a number of pages that are incorrectly numbered in the second edition, although correctly numbered in the first.

1. The second word of the incipit of no. 29 shows the modern spelling "dont" in the first edition, but the variant "dunt" in the second edition.

2. In no. 47 (m. 57:4) the F in the contra is incorrectly a semiminim in the second edition, though correctly a minim in the first edition.

Other than this small error in no. 47, only one other difference is noted in the readings. In no. 28 the *superius*, m. 15:3–4, reads b′ dotted quarter, c″ eighth in the Bologna copy, but is changed to a′ half note in

7

Bologna copy; edition of 1502

Paris copy; edition of 1503

the Paris copy. Since the manuscript sources agree in showing the a′, it is probable that the change in reading was intended as a correction; if so, the b′ in the tenor should also have been changed to a′ (see above).

Sartori says that Petrucci's "printing process was effected in three stages: the lines were printed first, then the notes, and finally the words of the text, the decorated initials, the numbers of the index, and the page numbers."[27] This would seem to be true, for many empty staves may be seen in the volumes, and occasionally a letter will overlap the stem of a note. Heads of notes fall on line or space with the greatest accuracy, yet, contrary to the custom today, the double bar at the ends of the voice parts always extends a little above and below the staff.

The transcriptions were made from photostats of the Paris copy of the edition of 1503. The titles, in both the commentaries and the music, are taken from the edited texts, and Petrucci's original text incipits are indicated in a footnote to the music. Where no text sources could be found, the text incipits are preserved in their original spellings, except for the addition of punctuation and accents. When no continuation of the text beyond the incipit could be found, the section on text is ordinarily omitted.

The notes on the literary texts for the present edition of *Canti B* follow in the main the pattern set by Miss Isabel Pope in her work on the literary texts of the *Odhecaton*. When the text appears in various sources, the clearest and most complete version has been chosen. Capitalization and syllabification are in conformance with present French usage; accentuation and punctuation generally follow modern practice. All words abbreviated in the manuscripts appear in com-

plete form; consonantal *i* and *u* are written *j* and *v*. With such poems as the *rondeau*, the *virelai*, and the *romance*, only the first few words of the refrain are given once it has been stated. Any other corrections or changes are explained in the notes.

Apart from such minor modernizations the basic texts remain unchanged. No attempt has been made, for example, to correct slight variations in spelling. The confusion between *s* and *z* in endings, between singular and plural forms, and the like, stand as evidence of a language still in the disorder of formation. The text and music constitute a unit which a corrected text could not maintain, and the original text lends a degree of liveliness and spontaneity which a modernized version must surely lose.

Of the elements of the printing—words and music—the music is the more carefully done and the more accurate. It is for his skill in the printing of music with movable type that Petrucci is celebrated. In 1929 an example of his art—from *Canti B*—was used by Kinsky to illustrate early music printing, together with the comment: "His prints—true masterpieces of typography—are of a perfection later never attained again."[28]

As for the music itself, *Canti B* is forward-looking, whereas the *Odhecaton* is retrospective. Most of the settings are arrangements of strophic chansons, either with or without refrains. These settings allowed the composer the greatest freedom in treating the wide variety of verse forms. A few of the popular songs are still extant today in monophonic manuscripts, which also preserve the words. A few of the pieces, such as Hayne's setting of a *rondeau layé*, *La Regretée*

[27] Sartori, "Petrucci," col. 1139.

[28] *Geschichte der Musik in Bildern*, comp. Georg Kinsky (Leipzig, 1929), p. 72.

(no. 48), are examples of free composition, although their texts are one of the courtly *formes fixes*—strict forms whose popularity was now waning after three centuries of steady use. Compère and Brumel have contributed motets; both are fine works and their texts are at hand. A number of the pieces seem not to have been written to be sung and may represent early attempts to write instrumental music.

The Petrucci volume itself shows only one piece with complete text: Compère's motet *Virgo celesti* (no. 2). All other texts appearing in the present volume have been found elsewhere. If the words appear in all voices in a contemporary source they are introduced into all voices in *Canti B*. If, on the other hand, a particular work is a setting of a popular tune which we have in monophonic form only, two procedures have been followed: (1) the text has been placed in all voices if the music seems to allow; (2) the text has been placed only in the parts showing the borrowed melody if the remaining parts do not adapt themselves to singing. There are many pieces whose texts could not be found at all.

The composers represented in the collection range from the well-known masters of the day, Josquin des Prez, Loyset Compère, and Antoine Brumel, to such shadowy figures as Bulkyn, De Vigne, Raulin, or Vaqueras. Possibly our inability to identify some composers today lies in the fact that they were more singers than composers, for all these men were employed in secular courts or chapels, great or small.

LIST OF SOURCES
WITH *SIGLA*

IN THIS section are reported manuscripts, early printed works, and modern publications which contain pieces from *Canti B*. The symbol "cf." before the *Canti B* number means that only part of the work is found in the source; this part may be one or more voices, or it may be merely the words of a song that the two pieces of music have in common.

The manuscripts are listed alphabetically according to the city in which they are found; the contemporary publications are listed by publisher; and the modern sources are listed alphabetically by author of article or book, or editor of complete works. A brief bibliography follows each manuscript; the book or article cited contains some information on the manuscript—brief or extended. Bibliographical details of modern editions cited in "Manuscripts" (A) and "Early Printed Books" (B) will be found in section C, "Modern Editions." The number following the publisher's name in section B is taken from *Recueils imprimés: XVIᵉ–XVIIᵉ siècles (Répertoire International des Sources Musicales)*, edited by François Lesure (Munich, 1960).

In referring to manuscript or print, use will be made of the *siglum* (established for manuscript) or short title which directly precedes the full title of the manuscript or publication in the following lists.

A. MANUSCRIPTS

AUGSBURG 142ᵃ
Augsburg, Staats- Kreis- und Stadtbibliothek, MS 142ᵃ (*olim* 18) (contains the dates 1458 and 1513).
Robert Eitner, "Ein Liedercodex aus dem Anfange des

sechzehnten Jahrhunderts," *Monatshefte für Musikgeschichte*, V (1873), 117–22; some facsimiles.
Hans Michael Schletterer, "Katalog der in der Kreis- und Stadt-Bibliothek, dem Staedtischen Archive und der Bibliothek des historischen Vereins zu Augsburg befindlichen Musikwerke," *Beilage 3 zu den Monatsheften für Musikgeschichte*, X–XI (1878–79), MS No. 18 (Codex 142ᵃ), p. 3.
Smijers, *Josquin des Prez: Wereldlijke Werken*, II, v (Ger. trans., vii).
Wolf, *Notationskunde*, I, 444–45.
Canti B 40

BASEL F. X. 1–4
Basel, Universitäts-Bibliothek, MSS F. X. 1–4 (16th c.).
Julius Richter, "Katalog der Musik-Sammlung auf der Universitäts-Bibliothek in Basel (Schweiz)," *Beilage zu den Monatsheften für Musikgeschichte*, XXIII (1891), 43–54.
Smijers, *Josquin des Prez: Wereldlijke Werken*, III, v (Ger. trans., viii).
Wolf, *Isaac: Weltliche Werke*, p. 169.
Wolf, *Notationskunde*, I, 445.
Canti B 5, 22, 28; cf. *Canti B* 1, 16

BERLIN 78. B. 17 (poetry only)
Berlin, Kupferstichkabinett, MS 78. B. 17 (Hamilton 674) (*Die Liederhandschrift des Cardinals de Rohan*) (ca. 1470).
Modern edition: Löpelmann, *Liederhandschrift des Cardinals de Rohan*.
Canti B 3, 24, 28, 30, 31 (T, B), 42; cf. *Canti B* 47

BOLOGNA Q 16
Bologna, Civico Museo Bibliografico Musicale, MS Q 16 (15th c.).
Luigi Torchi, "I Monumenti dell'antica musica francese a Bologna," *Rivista musicale italiana*, XIII (1906), 499.
Canti B 16, 47

BOLOGNA Q 17
Bologna, Civico Museo Bibliografico Musicale, MS Q 17 (*ca.* 1500).
> *Catalogo della Biblioteca del Liceo Musicale di Bologna*, comp. Gaetano Gaspari (4 vols.; Bologna, 1890–1905), III, 196.
> Jeppesen, *Kopenhagener Chansonnier*, p. lxxiii.
> Torchi, "Monumenti," pp. 499–501.
> Wolf, *Isaac: Weltliche Werke*, p. 170.
> Wolf, *Notationskunde*, I, 447.
> Wolf, *Obrecht: Motetten*, II, v (Ger. trans., vii).
>> *Canti B* 5, 16, 19; cf. *Canti B* 1

BOLOGNA Q 18
Bologna, Civico Museo Bibliografico Musicale, MS Q 18 (16th c.).
> Knud Jeppesen (ed.), with poetry ed. by Viggo Brøndal, *Die mehrstimmige italienische Laude um 1500: das 2. Laudenbuch des Ottaviano dei Petrucci (1507) in Verbindung mit einer Auswahl mehrstimmiger Lauden aus dem 1. Laudenbuch Petrucci's (1508) und aus verschiedenen gleichzeitigen Manuskripten* (Leipzig and Copenhagen, 1935), pp. lxiii–lxiv.
> Torchi, "Monumenti," pp. 502–3.
>> *Canti B* 15, 18, 25; cf. *Canti B* 19

BOLOGNA Q 19
Bologna, Civico Museo Bibliografico Musicale, MS Q 19 (Diane de Poitiers Codex) (bears the date "1518 adi. 10. d. zugno").
> Edward E. Lowinsky, "The Medici Codex: A Document of Music, Art, and Politics in the Renaissance," *Annales musicologiques*, V (1957), 61–178 (pages 98–106 deal with the manuscript Bologna Q 19).
> Torchi, "Monumenti," p. 502.
>> *Canti B* 28; cf. *Canti B* 16

BRUSSELS 228
Brussels, Bibliothèque Royale de Belgique, MS 228 (*Album de Marguerite d'Autriche*) (*ca.* 1520).
> Charles van den Borren, "Inventaire des manuscrits de musique polyphonique qui se trouvent en Belgique," *Acta musicologica*, V (1933), no. 7, pp. 120–25.
> Smijers, *Josquin des Prez: Wereldlijke Werken*, I, v (Ger. trans., ix).
> Wolf, *Notationskunde*, I, 447.
> Modern edition of the poetry: Françon, *Albums poétiques*, pp. 204–55; Gachet, *Albums et oeuvres poétiques*, pp. 71–95.
> Modern edition of the music: Picker, *Chanson Albums*.
>> *Canti B* 7, 22, 28; Cf. *Canti B* 21

BRUSSELS 11239
Brussels, Bibliothèque Royale de Belgique, MS 11239 (*Chansons de Marguerite*) (*ca.* 1500).
> Van den Borren, "Inventaire," V, no. 8, pp. 125–27.
> Wolf, *Notationskunde*, I, 447.
> Wolf, *Obrecht: Motetten*, IV, v (Ger. trans., vii).

Modern edition of the poetry: Françon, *Albums poétiques*, pp. 184–203; Gachet, *Albums et oeuvres poétiques*, pp. 61–69.
Modern edition of the music: Picker, *Chanson Albums*.
>> *Canti B* 4, 7, 22, 40

COPENHAGEN 291⁸
Copenhagen, Kongelige Bibliotek, MS Thott 291⁸ (*ca.* 1470–80).
> Geneviève Thibault and Eugénie Droz, "Le Chansonnier de la Bibliothèque Royale de Copenhague," *Revue de Musicologie*, VIII (1927), 12–35 (facsimile of f. 18'–19 opp. p. 12; modern edition of four pieces, pp. 15–35).
> Modern edition: Jeppesen, *Kopenhagener Chansonnier*.
>> Cf. *Canti B* 24

COPENHAGEN 1848
Copenhagen, Kongelige Bibliotek, MS Thott 1848 (*ca.* 1525).
> Dragan Plamenac, "A Postscript to 'The "Second" Chansonnier of the Biblioteca Riccardiana,'" *Annales musicologiques*, IV (1956), 261, n. 1.
>> *Canti B* 37, 51; cf. *Canti B* 14, 15, 16, 34, 41

CORTONA 95–96, PARIS 1817
Cortona, Biblioteca Comunale, MSS 95, 96 (Altus, Superius); Paris, Bibliothèque Nationale, Nouv. acq. fr. 1817 (Tenor).
> *I Manoscritti della Libreria del Comune e dell'Accademia Etrusca di Cortona*, comp. Girolamo Mancini (Cortona, 1884), pp. 53–54 (MSS 95, 96).
> Smijers, *Josquin des Prez: Wereldlijke Werken*, II, v (Ger. trans., vii).
> Wolf, *Isaac: Weltliche Werke*, pp. 170–71.
> Wolf, *Notationskunde*, I, 448 (MSS 95, 96), 457 (Paris 1817).
> Modern edition of the poetry after Cortona 95, 96: Renier, "Mazzetto di poesie"; after Paris 1817: Gröber, "Liederbücher von Cortona."
>> *Canti B* 5, 11, 34; cf. *Canti B* 23, 28, 32

DIJON 517
Dijon, Bibliothèque Municipale, MS 517 (*ca.* 1470–80).
> Jeppesen, *Kopenhagener Chansonnier*, pp. xxiv–xxv.
> Stéphen Morelot, "Notice sur un manuscrit de musique ancienne," *Mémoires de la Commission des Antiquités du Département de la Côte-d'Or*, IV (1856), 133–60, and musical appendix of 24 unnumbered pages. Also published separately as *De la musique au XVᵉ siècle: Notice sur un manuscrit de la Bibliothèque de Dijon* (Paris, 1856).
> Wolf, *Notationskunde*, I, 448.
> Modern edition of 26 works: Edward Barret, "The Dijon Chansonnier: Contents, Forms, Transcriptions" (M.A. Thesis, University of Louisville, 1964).
> Modern edition of folios 1–56; Droz, *Trois chansonniers français*.
>> Cf. *Canti B* 3, 24, 30

FLORENCE 107bis

Florence, Biblioteca Nazionale Centrale, MS Magl. XIX, 107bis (16th c.).

Bianca Becherini, *Catalogo dei manoscritti musicali della Biblioteca Nazionale di Firenze* (Kassel: Bärenreiter, 1959), no. 40, pp. 42–44.

Smijers, *Josquin des Prez: Motetten*, III, vi (Ger. trans., ix).

Wolf, *Notationskunde*, I, 449.

Wolf, *Obrecht: Missen*, III, ii–iii (Ger. trans., vi).

Canti B 11, 23; cf. *Canti B* 16

FLORENCE 164–167

Florence, Biblioteca Nazionale Centrale, MS Magl. XIX, 164–167 (16th c.).

Becherini, *Catalogo*, no. 67, pp. 69–71.

Smijers, *Josquin des Prez: Motetten*, I, v (Ger. trans., ix).

Wolf, *Notationskunde*, I, 450.

Wolf, *Obrecht: Wereldlijke Werken*, p. vi (Ger. trans., p. xi).

Canti B 11, 27, 28

FLORENCE 176

Florence, Biblioteca Nazionale Centrale, MS Magl. XIX, 176 (*ca.* 1500).

Becherini, *Catalogo*, no. 69, pp. 72–75.

Jeppesen, *Kopenhagener Chansonnier*, p. lxxii.

Wolf, *Notationskunde*, I, 450.

Canti B 6, 16

FLORENCE 178

Florence, Biblioteca Nazionale Centrale, MS Magl. XIX, 178 (16th c.).

Becherini, *Catalogo*, no. 70, pp. 75–77.

Jeppesen, *Kopenhagener Chansonnier*, p. lxii.

Wolf, *Isaac: Weltliche Werke*, p. 172.

Wolf, *Notationskunde*, I, 450.

Wolf, *Obrecht: Wereldlijke Werken*, p. vi (Ger. trans., p. xi).

Canti B 16, 19, 30, 46

FLORENCE 229

Florence, Biblioteca Nazionale Centrale, MS Banco Rari 229 (*olim* Magl. XIX, 59) (*ca.* 1500).

Becherini, *Catalogo*, no. 28, pp. 22–29.

Jeppesen, *Kopenhagener Chansonnier*, p. lxxii.

Wolf, *Isaac: Weltliche Werke*, pp. 171–72.

Wolf, *Notationskunde*, I, 450.

Wolf, *Obrecht: Wereldlijke Werken*, p. vi (Ger. trans., p. xi).

Canti B 16, 30, 46; cf. *Canti B* 41

FLORENCE 2439

Florence, Biblioteca del Conservatorio "L. Cherubini," MS 2439 (Fondo Basevi) (16th c.).

Léon de Burbure, "Étude sur un manuscrit du XVIe siècle, contenant des chants à quatre et à trois voix; suivie d'un *post-scriptum* sur le *Bellum Musicale*, de Cl. Sebastiani," *Mémoires couronnés et autres mémoires*

publiés par *l'Académie Royale des Sciences, des Lettres et des Beaux-Arts de Belgique*, XXXIII (1882), no. 6.

Jeppesen, *Kopenhagener Chansonnier*, p. lxxii.

Wolf, *Isaac: Weltliche Werke*, p. 171.

Wolf, *Notationskunde*, I, 450–51.

Wolf, *Obrecht: Missen*, III, iii (Ger. trans., vi).

Cf. *Canti B* 28

FLORENCE 2442

Florence, Biblioteca del Conservatorio "L. Cherubini," MS 2442 (three part-books only; Bassus wanting) (16th c.).

Pubblicazioni dell'Associazione dei Musicologi Italiani. Catalogo delle Opere Musicali . . . Serie IV, 1° vol., Città di Firenze, Biblioteca del R. Conservatorio di Musica (Parma, 1929), p. 246.

Smijers, *Josquin des Prez: Wereldlijke Werken*, II, v (Ger. trans., vii).

Wolf, *Notationskunde*, I, 451.

Canti B 22, 27, 33; cf. *Canti B* 14, 41

FLORENCE 2794

Florence, Biblioteca Riccardiana, MS 2794 (15th c.).

Bianca Becherini, "Alcuni canti dell' 'Odhecaton' e del codice fiorentino 2794," *Bulletin de l'Institut historique belge de Rome*, XXII (1942–43), 327–50.

Jeppesen, *Kopenhagener Chansonnier*, p. lxxii.

Dragan Plamenac, "The 'Second' Chansonnier of the Biblioteca Riccardiana (*Codex 2356*)," *Annales musicologiques*, II (1954), 105, n. 1.

Wolf, *Notationskunde*, I, 450.

Canti B 46

GREIFSWALD E^b 133

Greifswald, Universitäts-Bibliothek, MS E^b 133 (originally four part-books; Superius and Bassus only survive today) (16th c.).

Dragan Plamenac, "Music Libraries in Eastern Europe: A Visit in the Summer of 1961 (Pt. II)," *Music Library Association Notes*, XIX (1962), 412–13.

Wolf, *Isaac: Weltliche Werke*, p. 172.

Wolf, *Notationskunde*, I, 451.

Wolf, *Obrecht: Wereldlijke Werken*, p. vi (Ger. trans., p. xi).

Canti B 25, 40

HEILBRONN X. 2

Heilbronn, Gymnasialbibliothek, MS X. 2 (Bassus only) (16th c.).

Edwin Mayser, *Alter Musikschatz* (*Mitteilungen aus der Bibliothek des Heilbronner Gymnasiums*, II) (Heilbronn, 1893), pp. 77–78.

Wolf, *Notationskunde*, I, 451.

Wolf, *Obrecht: Motetten*, IV, v (Ger. trans., vii).

Canti B 40, 45, 47, 49, 50

LILLE 402 (poetry only)

Lille, Bibliothèque Municipale, MS 402 (16th c.).

Modern edition: Françon, *Poèmes de transition*.

Canti B 22

LONDON 20 A XVI
London, British Museum, Royal 20 A XVI (16th c.).
Augustus Hughes-Hughes, *Catalogue of Manuscript Music in the British Museum* (3 vols.; London, 1906–9), II, 127–28.
Wolf, *Notationskunde*, I, 453.
Modern edition of a few poems: Wallis, *Anonymous French Verse*; cf. also Marcel Françon, "Déclin et renaissance de la poésie" (review), *Romanic Review*, XXVI (1935), 353–57.
Canti B 46, 48

LONDON ADD. 35087
London, British Museum, MS Add. 35087 (16th c.).
Hughes-Hughes, *Catalogue of Manuscript Music*, II, 128–29.
Catalogue of Additions to the Manuscripts in the British Museum in the Years 1894–1899 (London, 1901), p. 146.
Robert Priebsch, *Deutsche Handschriften in England*, II, 289–93.
Wolf, *Notationskunde*, I, 453.
Wolf, *Obrecht: Motetten*, II, v (Ger. trans., vii).
Modern edition of the songs with Dutch texts: Wolf, *Oud-Nederlandsche Liederen*.
Cf. *Canti B* 12, 18, 19

LONDON HARLEY 5242
London, British Museum, MS Harley 5242 (16th c.).
Paule Chaillon, "Le Chansonnier de Françoise (MS Harley 5242, British Museum)," *Revue de musicologie*, XXXV (1953), 1–31.
Hughes-Hughes, *Catalogue of Manuscript Music*, II, 122–23.
Wolf, *Notationskunde*, I, 453.
Cf. *Canti B* 4

LONDON LANSDOWNE 380 (poetry only)
London, British Museum, Lansdowne 380 (16th c.).
British Museum, Department of Manuscripts: *A Catalogue of the Lansdowne Manuscripts in the British Museum. With Indexes of Persons, Places, and Matters. Printed by Command of His Majesty King George III, in Pursuance of an Address of the House of Commons of Great Britain* (London, 1819), Part II, pp. 110–11.
Canti B 3, 24, 28, 30

MODENA IV
Modena, Archivio Capitolare del Duomo, MS IV (early 16th c.).
A. Dondi, *Il Duomo di Modena* (1896).
Knud Jeppesen (ed.), *Italia sacra musica* (3 vols.; Copenhagen, 1962), II, vi.
Cf. *Canti B* 16

MORITZBURG, SAXE (poetry only)
Moritzburg (Dresden), Schlossbibliothek, MS Jean de Saxe (16th c.).

Modern edition: Françon, *Poèmes de transition*.
Canti B 22

MUNICH 322–325
Munich, Universitäts-Bibliothek, MSS 322–325, From the library of Glareanus (16th c.).
Miller, *Heinrich Glarean, Dodecachordon*, I, 29.
Wolf, *Notationskunde*, I, 455.
Wolf, *Obrecht: Motetten*, II, v (Ger. trans., vii).
Canti B 39

NEW HAVEN, MELLON
New Haven, Connecticut, Yale University, Library of the School of Music, Mellon Chansonnier (*ca.* 1480).
Manfred F. Bukofzer, "An Unknown Chansonnier of the 15th Century (the *Mellon Chansonnier*)," *Musical Quarterly*, XXVIII (1942), 14–49.
Cf. *Canti B* 1

PARIS 477 (poetry only)
Paris, Bibliothèque Nationale, Nouv. acq. fr. 477 (16th c.).
Bibliothèque Nationale: *Catalogue général des manuscrits français: Nouvelles acquisitions françaises* (4 vols.; Paris, 1899–1918), I, 73–74.
Index of this manuscript in Françon, *Poèmes de transition*, pp. 733–40.
Canti B 22

PARIS 1158 (poetry only)
Paris, Bibliothèque Nationale, Nouv. acq. fr. 1158 (16th c.).
Bibliothèque Nationale, *Catalogue général: Nouv. acq. fr.*, I, 154.
Partial index of this manuscript in Françon, *Albums poétiques*, pp. 288–89.
Canti B 22

PARIS 1597
Paris, Bibliothèque Nationale, Fonds fr. 1597 (16th c.).
Bibliothèque Impériale, Département des Manuscrits: *Catalogue des manuscrits français publié par ordre de l'Empereur: Ancien fonds* (5 vols.; Paris, 1868–92), I, 270.
Modern edition: Shipp, "Paris MS f. fr. 1597."
Canti B 5, 28, 40, 46, 48; cf. *Canti B* 12

PARIS 1717 (poetry only)
Paris, Bibliothèque Nationale, Fonds fr. 1717 (16th c.).
Bibliothèque Impériale, *Catalogue: Ancien fonds*, I, 297.
Partial index of this manuscript in Françon, *Poèmes de transition*, pp. 756–57.
Canti B 22

PARIS 1719 (poetry only)
Paris, Bibliothèque Nationale, Fonds fr. 1719 (16th c.).
Bibliothèque Impériale, *Catalogue: Ancien fonds*, I, 299.
Published in part in Schwob, *Parnasse satyrique*.
Canti B 22, 28, 45

PARIS 1722 (poetry only)
Paris, Bibliothèque Nationale, Fonds fr. 1722 ("Vers et poésies de Marguerite d'Orléans, Duchesse d'Alençon, Soeur du Roy François Premier") (16th c.).
> Bibliothèque Impériale, *Catalogue: Ancien fonds*, I, 299.
> *Canti B* 28, 48

PARIS 2245
Paris, Bibliothèque Nationale, Fonds fr. 2245 (1496).
> Bibliothèque Impériale, *Catalogue: Ancien fonds*, I, 390–91.
> Jeppesen, *Kopenhagener Chansonnier*, p. lxxi.
> Cf. *Canti B* 24

PARIS 7559 (poetry only)
Paris, Bibliothèque Nationale, Nouv. acq. fr. 7559 (*ca.* 1500).
> Bibliothèque Nationale, *Catalogue Général: Nouv. acq. fr.*, III, 169.
> Émile Picot, "Cent quarante-cinq rondeaux d'amours" (review), *Romania*, V (1876), 390–93.
> Modern edition: Bancel, *Cent quarante-cinq rondeaux.*
> Index of this manuscript in Françon, *Albums poétiques*, pp. 277–84.
> *Canti B* 22

PARIS 9346
Paris, Bibliothèque Nationale, Fonds fr. 9346 (*Le Manuscrit de Bayeux*) (a monophonic chansonnier; 16th c.).
> Gustave Reese and Theodore Karp, "Monophony in a Group of Renaissance Chansonniers," *Journal of the American Musicological Society*, V (1952), 4–15.
> Wolf, *Notationskunde*, I, 458.
> Modern edition: Gérold, *Manuscrit de Bayeux.*
> Modern edition of the poetry: Gasté, *Chansons normandes.*
> Modern edition of some of the poetry: Du Bois, *Vaux-de-Vire d'Olivier Basselin*; Wolff, *Altfranzösische Volkslieder.*
> Cf. *Canti B* 4, 14, 34, 37, 51

PARIS 12744
Paris, Bibliothèque Nationale, Fonds fr. 12744 (a monophonic chansonnier; 15th c.).
> Reese and Karp, "Monophony," pp. 4–15.
> Wolf, *Notationskunde*, I, 458.
> Modern edition: Paris-Gevaert, *Chansons.*
> Modern edition of the virelais (poetry only): Heldt, *Französische Virelais.*
> Cf. *Canti B* 4, 5, 6, 9, 12, 15, 27, 51

PARIS 15123
Paris, Bibliothèque Nationale, Fonds fr. 15123 (*Le Manuscrit Pixérécourt*) (*ca.* 1500).
> *Bibliothèque de M. G. de Pixérécourt*, ed. Charles Nodier and Paul Lacroix (Paris, 1839), no. 484, pp. 61–62.
> Bibliothèque Nationale: *Catalogue général des manuscrits*

français: Ancien supplément français (3 vols.; Paris, 1895–96), III, 319.
> Jeppesen, *Kopenhagener Chansonnier*, p. lxxi.
> Wolf, *Notationskunde*, I, 458.
> Cf. *Canti B* 24

PARIS 19182 (poetry only)
Paris, Bibliothèque Nationale, Fonds fr. 19182 (16th c.).
> Bibliothèque Nationale: *Catalogue général des manuscrits français: Ancien Saint-Germain français* (3 vols.; Paris, 1898–1900), III, 267–68.
> Index of this manuscript in Françon, *Poèmes de transition*, pp. 763–71.
> *Canti B* 22

PARIS, ROTHSCHILD 2819 (poetry only)
Paris, Bibliothèque Nationale, Henri de Rothschild Collection, MS 2819 (*Oeuvres poétiques de Jehan d'Auton*) (16th c.).
> Émile Picot (comp.), *Catalogue des livres composant la bibliothèque de feu Monsieur le baron James de Rothschild* (4 vols.; Paris, 1912), IV, 140–43.
> *Canti B* 24

PARIS, ROTHSCHILD 2973
Paris, Bibliothèque Nationale, Henri de Rothschild Collection, MS 2973 (*Le Chansonnier Cordiforme*) (15th c.).
> Picot, *Catalogue*, IV, 314–17.
> Jeppesen, *Kopenhagener Chansonnier*, p. lxxi.
> Modern edition: Kottick, "*Chansonnier Cordiforme.*"
> Cf. *Canti B* 3

REGENSBURG C 120
Regensburg, Proske-Bibliothek, Cod. C 120 (Codex Pernner; 16th c.).
> Dominicus Mettenleiter, *Aus der musikalischen Vergangenheit bayrischer Städte. I, Musikgeschichte der Stadt Regensburg* (Regensburg, 1866), p. 154.
> Smijers, *Josquin des Prez: Motetten*, IV, v (Ger. trans., vii).
> Wolf, *Isaac: Weltliche Werke*, p. 173.
> Wolf, *Notationskunde*, I, 458–59.
> Wolf, *Obrecht: Wereldlijke Werken*, p. vii (Ger. trans., p. xii).
> *Canti B* 5, 9, 15, 21, 22, 28; cf. *Canti B* 16

ROME 2856
Rome, Biblioteca Casanatense, Cod. 2856 (16th c.).
> Jeppesen, *Kopenhagener Chansonnier*, p. lxxiii.
> Wolf, *Notationskunde*, I, 459.
> Wolf, *Obrecht: Wereldlijke Werken*, p. vii (Ger. trans., p. xii).
> *Canti B* 16, 47; cf. *Canti B* 1

ROME C. G. XIII, 27
Città del Vaticano, Biblioteca Ap. Vaticana, Cappella Giulia, Cod. XIII, 27 (16th c.).
> Jeppesen, *Kopenhagener Chansonnier*, p. lxxiii.

Wolf, *Isaac: Weltliche Werke*, p. 173.

Wolf, *Notationskunde*, I, 459.

Wolf, *Obrecht: Wereldlijke Werken*, p. vii (Ger. trans., p. xii).

    Canti B 11, 16, 19, 30, 35; cf. *Canti B* 1

ROME VAT. 11953

Città del Vaticano, Biblioteca Ap. Vaticana, Codicetto Vat. lat. 11953 (Bassus part-book only) (1500–1510).

    Raffaele Casimiri, "Canzoni e mottetti dei sec. xv–xvi," *Note d'Archivio per la storia musicale*, XIV (1937), 145–60; also published separately (Rome, 1938).

    Charles van den Borren, "A proposito del codicetto Vat. lat. 11953," *Note d'Archivio per la storia musicale*, XVI (1939), 17–18.

    Canti B 4, 7, 18, 22

ST. GALL 461

St. Gall, Stiftsbibliothek, Cod. 461 (*Fridolin Sichers Liederbuch*, 1545).

    Arnold Geering, *Die Vokalmusik in der Schweiz zur Zeit der Reformation. Schweizerisches Jahrbuch für Musikwissenschaft*, VI (Aarau, 1933), *Beilage* XI, pp. 235–36; see also p. 90 and p. 188.

    Gustav Scherrer (comp.), *Verzeichniss der Handschriften der Stiftsbibliothek von St. Gallen* (Halle, 1875), p. 152.

    Wolf, *Isaac: Weltliche Werke*, p. 173.

    Wolf, *Notationskunde*, I, 462.

    Wolf, *Obrecht: Wereldlijke Werken*, p. vii (Ger. trans., p. xii).

    Modern edition: Giesbert, *Ein altes Spielbuch*.

    Canti B 28

ST. GALL 463

St. Gall, Stiftsbibliothek, Cod. 463 (*Aegidius Tschudis Liederbuch*) (Superius and Altus part-books only) (ca. 1517–20).

    Robert Eitner, "Eine Handschrift von Egidius Tschudi," *Monatshefte für Musikgeschichte*, VI (1874), 131–34.

    Ildephons Fuchs, *E. Tschudi's Leben und Schriften* (2 vols.; St. Gall, 1805), II, 175–76.

    Geering, *Vokalmusik in der Schweiz, Beilage* IX, pp. 227–32; see also pp. 91–92.

    Scherrer, *Verzeichniss*, p. 152.

    Smijers, *Josquin des Prez: Motetten*, I, v–vi (Ger. trans., ix–x).

    Wolf, *Isaac: Weltliche Werke*, pp. 173–74.

    Wolf, *Notationskunde*, I, 462–63.

    Wolf, *Obrecht: Motetten*, II, vi (Ger. trans., viii).

    Canti B 2, 40; cf. *Canti B* 16, 28, 41

ST. GALL 464

St. Gall, Stiftsbibliothek, Cod. 464 (*Aegidius Tschudi's Liederbuch*) (a duplicate of the Superius of St. Gall 463 and Bassi of five- and six-part works only) (ca. 1517–20).

    Eitner, "Eine Handschrift von Egidius Tschudi," pp. 131–34.

    Fuchs, *Tschudi's Leben*, II, 175–76.

Geering, *Vokalmusik in der Schweiz*, p. 92.

Scherrer, *Verzeichniss*, p. 152.

Smijers, *Josquin des Prez: Wereldlijke Werken*, I, v. (Ger. trans., ix).

Wolf, *Isaac: Weltliche Werke*, pp. 173–74.

Wolf, *Notationskunde*, I, 462–63.

    Canti B 2; cf. *Canti B* 16

SEGOVIA

Segovia, Catedral, Codex (without number) (15th c.).

    Higini Anglès, "Un manuscrit inconnu avec polyphonie du XVe siècle conservé à la cathédrale de Ségovie (Espagne)," *Acta Musicologica*, VIII (1936), 6–17.

    Higini Anglès, "Die spanische Liedkunst im 15. und am Anfang des 16. Jahrhunderts," *Theodor Kroyer-Festschrift* (Regensburg, 1933), pp. 67–68.

    Canti B 23, 28, 35, 39; cf. *Canti B* 41

SEVILLE 5-I-43

Seville, Biblioteca Colombina, Cod. 5-I-43 (15th c.).

    Higini Anglès, "El 'Chansonnier Français' de la Colombina de Sevilla," *Estudis universitaris catalans*, XIV (1929), 227–58.

    Archer M. Huntington, *Catalogue of the Library of Ferdinand Columbus Reproduced in facsimile from the Unique Manuscript in the Columbine Library of Seville* (New York, 1905).

    Jeppesen, *Kopenhagener Chansonnier*, p. lxxiii.

    Dragan Plamenac, "A Reconstruction of the French Chansonnier in the Biblioteca Colombina, Seville," *Musical Quarterly*, XXXVII (1951), 501–42; XXXVIII (1952), 85–117, 245–77.

    Facsimile Reproduction of the Manuscripts Sevilla 5-I-43 and Paris n. a. fr. 4379 (*Pt. I*) with an Introduction by Dragan Plamenac (Brooklyn, N.Y.: Institute of Mediaeval Music, 1962).

    Juan F. Riaño, *Critical and Bibliographical Notes on Early Spanish Music* (London, 1887), p. 66.

    Wolf, *Notationskunde*, I, 463.

    Canti B 16

TOURNAI 94

Tournai, Bibliothèque de la Ville, MS 94 (contains the date 1511).

    Van den Borren, "Inventaire," VI (1934), 119–21.

    Adolphe Hocquet, *L'Album de musique de la Bibliothèque de Tournai* (*1511*) (Tournai and Paris, 1935), pp. 25–30.

    Amaury Louys de La Grange, "L'Album de musique du XVe siècle du musée de Tournai," *Annales de la Société d'Archéologie de Bruxelles*, VIII (1894), 114–19.

    Lenaerts, *Nederlands polifonies lied*, pp. 12–14.

    Reese and Karp, "Monophony," pp. 4–15.

    A. Wilbaux (comp.), *Catalogue de la Bibliothèque de la ville de Tournai* (Tournai, 1860), I, 35–37; 2 facsimiles in color opp. p. 35.

    Canti B 28, 34, 37; cf. *Canti B* 12

ULM 237[abcd]

Ulm, Bibliothek des Münsters, MS 237[abcd] (contains the date 1557) (four part-books).

Jeppesen, *Kopenhagener Chansonnier*, p. lxxiii.

Smijers, *Josquin des Prez: Motetten*, I, vii (Ger. trans., xi).

Wolf, *Notationskunde*, I, 463.

Wolf, *Obrecht: Wereldlijke Werken*, p. viii (Ger. trans., p. xiii).

Cf. *Canti B* 15

VERONA DCCLVII

Verona, Biblioteca Capitolare, Cod. DCCLVII (16th c.).

Albert Smijers, "Vijftiende en zestiende eeuwsche Muziekhandschriften in Italië met werken van Nederlandsche Componisten," *Tijdschrift der Vereeniging voor Nederlandsche Muziekgeschiedenis*, XIV (1935), 178.

Giuseppe Turrini, *Il Patrimonio musicale della Biblioteca Capitolare di Verona dal sec. XV al XIX* (Verona, 1952), p. 7.

Canti B 30

VIENNA 18746

Vienna, Nationalbibliothek, Cod. 18746 (five part-books) (contains the date 1523).

Josef Mantuani (ed.), *Tabulae codicum manu scriptorum praeter Graecos et orientales in Bibliotheca Palatina Vindobonensi asservatorum edidit Academia Caesarea Vindobonensis* (11 vols.; Vienna, 1864–1912), X, *Codicum musicorum Pars II., Cod. 17501–*19500*, pp. 196–200.

Smijers, *Josquin des Prez: Wereldlijke Werken*, I, vi (Ger. trans., x).

Wolf, *Notationskunde*, I, 464.

Cf. *Canti B* 16

VIENNA 18810

Vienna, Nationalbibliothek, Cod. 18810 (five part-books) (*ca.* 1524).

Mantuani, *Codicum musicorum*, pp. 219–24.

Anton Schmid, "Beiträge zur Literatur und Geschichte der Tonkunst," *Cäcilia*, XXIV (1845), No. 9, 120–22.

Smijers, *Josquin des Prez: Wereldlijke Werken*, III, vi (Ger. trans., ix).

Wolf, *Isaac: Weltliche Werke*, p. 174.

Wolf, *Notationskunde*, I, 464.

Canti B 22; cf. *Canti B* 19

WASHINGTON, WOLFFHEIM

Washington, D.C., Library of Congress, M.2.1 M 6 Case (formerly in the library of Werner Wolffheim, Berlin) (late 15th–early 16th c.).

Report of the Librarian of Congress (1929), p. 171. Extract published separately as *The Library of Congress: Division of Music, 1928–29* (Washington, 1929).

Seymour de Ricci (comp. with the assistance of W. J. Wilson), *Census of Medieval and Renaissance Manuscripts in the United States and Canada* (3 vols.; New York, 1935–40), I, p. 241, no. 153.

Versteigerung der Musikbibliothek des Herrn Dr. Werner Wolffheim (2 vols.; Berlin, 1928–29), II, no. 1262; Tafel 10, facsimile of f. 91'–92.

Wolf, *Notationskunde*, I, 446–47; facsimile of f. 91'–92 opp. p. 394, with modern edition of the same, pp. 395–97.

Canti B 16

WOLFENBÜTTEL 287

Wolfenbüttel, Landesbibliothek, MS extravag. 287 (late 15th c.).

Jeppesen, *Kopenhagener Chansonnier*, pp. xxiv–xxxvi.

Cf. *Canti B* 24

ZWICKAU 78, 3

Zwickau, Ratsschulbibliothek, MS 78, 3 (*olim* 12) (three part-books) (16th c.).

Reinhard Vollhardt, "Bibliographie der Musik-Werke in der Ratsschulbibliothek zu Zwickau," *Beilage zu den Monatsheften für Musikgeschichte*, XXV–XXVIII (1893–96), 28–30. Same published separately: Leipzig, 1896.

Wolf, *Isaac: Weltliche Werke*, p. 174.

Wolf, *Notationskunde*, I, 465.

Wolf, *Obrecht: Wereldlijke Werken*, p. viii (Ger. trans., p. xiii).

Canti B 44

B. EARLY PRINTED BOOKS

Aich [1519][5] *Lieder*

In dissem Buechlyn fynt man LXXV. hubscher Lieder myt Discant. Alt. Bas. und Tenor. lustick zu syngen. Auch etlich zu fleiten, schwegelen und an deren musicalisch Instrumenten artlichen zu gebrauchen. Cologne, Arnt von Aich (n.d.).

Modern edition: Bernoulli and Moser, *Das Liederbuch des Arnt von Aich*.

Canti B 28

Antico 1520[3] *Motetti novi e chanzoni*

Motetti novi e chanzoni franciose a quatro sopra doi. Venice, A. Antico, 1520.

Canti B 34; cf. *Canti B* 12

Antico 1520[6] *Chansons à troys*

Chansons à troys. Venice, A. Antico, L. A. Giunta, 1520.

Cf. *Canti B* 28, 41, 51

Antico 1536[1] *La Courone et fleur*

La Courone et fleur des chansons à troys. Venice, A. Antico (A. dell'Abbate), 1536.

Cf. *Canti B* 51

Antiphonarius Sarisburiensis 1520
  Antiphonarii ad usum Sarisburiensem volumen secundum: Vulgo pars estivalis nuncupata. Paris, Franciscus Byrckman, 1520.
    Cf. *Canti B* 2

Attaingnant 1529² *31 Chansons*
  Trente et une chansons musicales a quatre parties nouvellement imprimées. Paris, P. Attaingnant, 1529.
  Modern edition: Expert, *Trente et une chansons.*
    Cf. *Canti B* 6

Attaingnant 1529⁴ *42 Chansons*
  Quarante et deux chansons musicales à troys parties nouvellement et correctement imprimées. Paris, P. Attaingnant, 1529.
    Cf. *Canti B* 4

Attaingnant 1549 *Trent sixiesme livre . . . Josquin*
  Trent sixiesme livre contenant XXX. chansons tres musicales, a quatre, cinq, et six parties, en cinq livres, dont le cinquiesme livre contient les cinquiesmes et sixiesmes parties, le tout de la composition de feu Josquin des Prez. Paris, P. Attaingnant, 1549.
    Canti B 37

Berg and Neuber 1549³⁷ *Der dritte Teyl*
  Der dritte Teyl, schöner, lieblicher, alter, und newer teutscher Liedlein nicht allein zu singen sonder auch auff allerley Instrumenten zu brauchen sehr dienstlich, und ausserlesen und vormals nie gesehen. Nuremberg, J. vom Berg & U. Neuber, 1549.
    Cf. *Canti B* 19

Egenolff [c. 1535]¹⁴ *Lieder*
  [*Lieder zu 3 & 4 Stimmen*]. [Frankfurt on the Main, C. Egenolff, *ca.* 1535] (Superius only).
  Nanie Bridgman, "Christian Egenolff, Imprimeur de musique (A propos du recueil *Rés. Vm⁷. 504* de la Bibliothèque nationale de Paris)," *Annales musicologiques*, III (1955), 77–177.
    Canti B 3, 7, 9, 10, 11, 13, 15, 16, 17, 18, 19, 20, 21, 25, 28, 31, 34, 39, 40, 43, 44, 45, 46, 47, 48, 49, 50, 51

Formschneider 1538⁹ *Trium vocum carmina*
  Trium vocum carmina a diversis musicis composita. Nuremberg, H. Formschneider, 1538.
  Index in Howard Mayer Brown, *Instrumental Music Printed before 1600. A Bibliography* (Cambridge, Mass., 1965), pp. 59–62.
    Canti B 40, 44

Glareanus 1547¹ *Dodecachordon*
  Henricus Glareanus [originally Heinrich Loriti], *Dodecachordon.* Basel, H. Petrus, 1547.
  German translation: Bohn, *Glareani Dodecachordon.*
  English translation: Miller, *Heinrich Glarean, Dodecachordon.*
    Canti B 19

Lotrian 1543 *Sensuyt plusieurs belles chansons* (poetry only)
  Sensuyt plusieurs belles chansons nouvelles et fort joyeuses avecques plusieurs aultres retirees des anciennes impressions comme pourrez veoir en la table en laquelle sont comprinses les premieres lignes des chansons. Paris, Alain Lotrian, 1543.
    Canti B 12, 15, 51

Petreius 1540²¹ *Der ander Theil*
  Der ander Theil, kurtzweiliger guter frischer teutscher Liedlein, zu singen vast lustig. Nuremberg, J. Petreius, 1540.
  Modern edition: Eitner, *Der zweite Teil . . . Liedlein.*
    Cf. *Canti B* 19

Petreius 1541² *Trium vocum cantiones*
  Trium vocum cantiones centum, à praestantissimis diversarum nationum ac linguarum musicis compositae. Tomi primi. Nuremberg, J. Petreius, 1541.
    Canti B 39

Petrucci 1501 *Odhecaton*
  Harmonice musices Odhecaton A. Venice, O. Petrucci, 1501.
  Modern edition: Hewitt, *Odhecaton.*
    Cf. *Canti B* 3, 13, 16, 30, 31, 32, 42

Petrucci 1504³ *Canti C*
  Canti C. N° cento cinquanta. Venice, O. Petrucci, 1504.
    Cf. *Canti B* 1, 12, 21, 22, 41

Phalèse 1569¹¹ *Recueil des fleurs*
  Recueil des fleurs produictes de la divine musicque a trois parties, par Clemens non papa, Thomas Cricquillon, et aultres excellens musiciens. Tiers livre. Louvain, P. Phalèse, 1569.
    Cf. *Canti B* 51

Rhaw 1542⁸ *Tricinia*
  Tricinia. Tum veterum tum recentiorum in arte musica symphonistarum, latina, germanica, brabantica & gallica, ante hac typis nunquam excusa, observato in disponendo tonorum ordine, quo utentibus sint accomodatiora. Wittenberg, G. Rhaw, 1542.
    Cf. *Canti B* 51

Sensuivent plusieurs belles chansons (poetry only)
  Sensuivent plusieurs belles chansons nouvelles . . . en nombre cinquante et troys. [Paris, *ca.* 1515].
  Picot, *Catalogue*, IV, 319–22.
    Canti B 12

Susato 1545¹⁵ *Le septiesme livre . . . Josquin*
  Le septiesme livre contenant vingt et quatre chansons a cincq et a six parties, composées par feu de bonne memoire et tres excellent en musicque Josquin des Pres, avecq troix epitaphes dudict Josquin, composez par divers aucteurs . . . Antwerp, T. Susato, 1545.
    Canti B 37

Vérard, *La chasse* (poetry only)
  La chasse et le depart d'amours faict et compose par reverend pere en dieu messire Octovien de Sainct Gelaiz evesque d'Angoulesme et par noble homme Blaise d'Auriol bachelier

en chascun droit demourant a Thoulouze cum privilegio. Paris, Antoine Vérard, 1509.

Brunet, Jacques-Charles, *Manuel du libraire et de l'amateur de livres* (5th ed.; Paris, 1860–65), Vol. V, cols. 40–41.
Canti B 22, 24, 31 (T, B), 42

Vérard, *Le Jardin de plaisance* (poetry only)
Le Jardin de plaisance et fleur de rethoricque. Paris, Antoine Vérard (n.d.).
Facsimile edition: I. *Reproduction en fac-similé de l'édition publiée par Antoine Vérard vers 1501* (Paris, 1910); II. *Introduction et Notes,* by Eugénie Droz and Arthur Piaget (Paris, 1925).
Canti B 3, 24, 28, 30; cf. *Canti B* 32, 47

C. MODERN EDITIONS

Antiphonale sacrosanctae Romanae ecclesiae pro diurnis horis (Paris, Tournai, Rome: Desclée & Socii, 1949).
Cf. *Canti B* 2

Aubry, Pierre (ed.), with preface by Gaston Paris, *Huit chants héroïques de l'ancienne France (XIIe–XVIIIe siècles): poèmes et musique* (2d ed.; Paris, 1896).
Cf. *Canti B* 9

Bancel, E. M. (ed.), *Cent quarante-cinq rondeaux d'amours publiés d'après un manuscrit autographe de la fin du XVe siècle* (Paris, 1875). (After Paris 7559.)
Canti B 22 (text only)

Barbier, Pierre, and Vernillat, France (eds.), *Histoire de France par les chansons* (8 vols.; Paris, 1956–61), Vol. I.
Cf. *Canti B* 9

Becherini, Bianca, "Tre incatenature del codice fiorentino Magl. XIX. 164–65–66–67," *Collectanea Historiae Musicae,* I (Florence, 1953), 79–96.
Cf. *Canti B* 19

Bernet Kempers, K. P. (ed.), *Jacobus Clemens non Papa, Opera omnia,* II: *Souterliedekens (Psalmi Neerlandici)* (Rome: American Institute of Musicology, 1953).
Cf. *Canti B* 41

Bernoulli, Eduard, *Aus Liederbüchern der Humanistenzeit: Eine bibliographische und notentypographische Studie* (Leipzig, 1910).
Canti B 28

Bernoulli, Eduard, and Moser, Hans Joachim (eds.), *Das Liederbuch des Arnt von Aich (Köln um 1510). Erste Partitur-Ausgabe der 75 vierstimmigen Tonsätze* (Kassel, 1930).
Canti B 28

Biblia Sacra: Juxta vulgatam Clementinam divisionibus, summariis et concordantiis ornata (Rome, Tournai, and Paris: Desclée & Socii, 1956).
Canti B 40 (text only)

Bohn, Peter (translator and transcriber), *Glareani Dodecachordon, Basileae MDXLVII. Publikationen älterer praktischer und theoretischer Musikwerke,* XVI (Leipzig, 1888).
Canti B 19

Bordes, Charles (ed.), *Trois chansons du XVe siècle* (Paris, 1895).
Canti B 51

Brown, Howard Mayer (ed.), *Theatrical Chansons of the Fifteenth and Early Sixteenth Centuries* (Cambridge, Mass.: Harvard University Press, 1963).
Canti B 5, 9, 23; Cf. *Canti B* 1

Burbure, Léon de (ed.), *Étude sur un manuscrit du XVIe siècle* (Brussels, 1882). (Study of Florence 2439.)
Canti B 28 (text only)

Busby, Thomas, *A General History of Music, from the Earliest Times to the Present; Comprising the Lives of Eminent Composers and Musical Writers* (2 vols.; London, 1819).
Canti B 19

Cauchie, Maurice, "L'Odhecaton, recueil de musique instrumentale," *Revue de musicologie,* IX (1925), 148–56.
Canti B 6

Chevalier, Ulysse (ed.), *Repertorium hymnologicum: Catalogue des chants, hymnes, proses, séquences, tropes en usage dans l'Église latine depuis les origines jusqu'à nos jours* (6 vols.; Louvain, 1892–1912; Brussels, 1920–21).
Canti B 39 (bibliography for the text only)

Chilesotti, Oscar, *Sulla melodia popolare del cinquecento* (Milan, n.d.).
Canti B 1

Closson, Ernest, and Van den Borren, Charles, *La Musique en Belgique* (Brussels, 1950).
Canti B 22

Cohen, Gustave (ed.), *Recueil de farces françaises inédites du XVe siècle* (Cambridge, Mass.: The Mediaeval Academy of America, 1949).
Canti B 14 (text only)

Commer, Franz (ed.), *Collectio operum musicorum Batavorum saeculi XVI* (12 vols.; Berlin, Antwerp, Leipzig, Hamburg, and Mainz, 1840–58), XII.
Canti B 37

Danckert, Werner, *Das europäische Volkslied* (Berlin, 1939).
Cf. *Canti B* 5, 6

Disertori, Benvenuto, "Il manoscritto 1947–4 di Trento e la canzone 'i'ay prins amours,'" *Rivista musicale italiana,* XLVIII (1946), 1–29.
Canti B 30

Disertori, Benvenuto, "Una storica mistificazione mensurale di Josquin des Prés: sue affinità con Leonardo da Vinci," *Liber Amicorum Charles van den Borren* (Antwerp, 1964), pp. 49–56.
Canti B 1

Droz, Eugénie, Thibault, Geneviève, and Rokseth, Yvonne (eds.), *Trois chansonniers français du XVᵉ siècle* (*Documents artistiques du XVᵉ siècle*, IV, Paris, 1927), Fasc. I, *Bibliothèque de Dijon, Ms 517 (ancien 295), folios 1–56*.
  Cf. *Canti B* 3, 24, 30

Du Bois, Louis François (ed.), *Vaux-de-Vire d'Olivier Basselin, poëte normand de la fin du XIVᵉ siècle; suivis d'un choix d'anciens Vaux-de-Vire, de Bacchanales et de chansons, poésies normandes soit inédites, soit devenues excessivement rares* (Caen, Paris, and London, 1821).
  Cf. *Canti B* 14

Duyse, Florimond van (ed.), *Het oude Nederlandsche Lied: Wereldlijke en geestelijke Liederen uit vroegeren Tijd, Teksten en Melodieën* (4 vols.; The Hague, 1903–8).
  Cf. *Canti B* 41

Eitner, Robert (ed.), *Der zweite Teil der kurtzweiligen guten frischen teutschen Liedlein zu singen fast lustig* (comp. Georg Forster). *Publikationen älterer praktischer und theoretischer Musikwerke*, Vol. XXIX, Jahrgang XXXIII (Leipzig, 1905).
  Cf. *Canti B* 19

Expert, Henry (ed.), *Trente et une Chansons musicales* (*Attaingnant 1529*). *Les Maîtres Musiciens de la renaisssance française*, V (Paris, 1897).
  Cf. *Canti B* 6

Finscher, Ludwig (ed.), *Loyset Compère: Opera omnia* (Rome: American Institute of Musicology, 1958—), III, 20–21.
  Canti B 2

Françon, Marcel (ed.), *Albums poétiques de Marguerite d'Autriche* (Cambridge, Mass., and Paris, 1934). (After Brussels 228 and 11239.)
  Canti B 4, 7, 22, 28, 40; Cf. *Canti B* 21 (texts only)

Françon, Marcel (ed.), *Poèmes de transition (XVᵉ–XVIᵉ siècles); Rondeaux du Ms. 402 de Lille* (Cambridge, Mass., and Paris, 1938). (After Lille 402 and Moritzburg, Saxe.)
  Canti B 22 (text only)

Funck, Heinz (ed.), *Deutsche Lieder des 15. Jahrhunderts aus fremden Quellen zu 3 und 4 Stimmen. Das Chorwerk*, XLV (Wolfenbüttel and Berlin, 1937).
  Cf. *Canti B* 18

Gachet, Émile (ed.), *Albums et oeuvres poétiques de Marguerite d'Autriche, Gouvernante des Pays-Bas. Publications de la Société des Bibliophiles Belges, séant à Mons*, XVII (Brussels, 1849). (After Brussels 228 and 11239.)
  Canti B 4, 7, 22, 28, 40 (texts only)

Gasté, Armand (ed.), *Chansons normandes du XVᵉ siècle* (Caen, 1866). (After Paris 9346.)
  Cf. *Canti B* 4, 14, 34, 37, 51 (texts only)

Gérold, Théodore (ed.), *Chansons populaires des XVᵉ et XVIᵉ siècles avec leurs mélodies. Bibliotheca Romanica*, nos. 190–92 (Strasbourg, 1913).
  Cf. *Canti B* 5, 9, 34, 37

Gérold, Théodore (ed.), *Le Manuscrit de Bayeux: texte et musique d'un recueil de chansons du XVᵉ siècle* (Strasbourg, 1921). (After Paris 9346.)
  Cf. *Canti B* 4, 14, 34, 37, 51

Giesbert, Franz Julius (ed.), *Ein altes Spielbuch Liber Fridolini Sichery (um 1500) mit drei, vier und fünf Stimmen für Blockflöten oder beliebige andere Instrumente übertragen*. Edition Schott, no. 2439 (Mainz, 1936). (After St. Gall 461.)
  Canti B 28

Gillequin, Jean, *La Chanson française du XVᵉ au XXᵉ siècle. Avec un appendice musical* (Paris, n.d.).
  Canti B 4, 9, 12 (texts only)

Gröber, Gustav (ed.), "Zu den Liederbüchern von Cortona," *Zeitschrift für romanische Philologie*, XI (1887), 371–404. (After Paris 1817.)
  Canti B 5, 11, 23, 28, 32 (A, T), 34, 37 (texts only)

Hasselt, André van, *Essai sur l'histoire de la poésie française en Belgique* (Brussels, 1838).
  Canti B 7 (text only)

Hawkins, John, *A General History of the Science and Practice of Music* (5 vols.; London, 1776).
  Canti B 19

Heldt, Elisabeth (ed.), *Französische Virelais aus dem 15. Jahrhundert* (Halle/Saale, 1916). (After Paris 12744.)
  Canti B 6, 15 (texts only)

Hewitt, Helen (ed.), *Harmonice musices Odhecaton A;* edition of the literary texts, Isabel Pope (Cambridge, Mass.: The Mediaeval Academy of America, 1942; 2d ed., 1946).
  Cf. *Canti B* 3, 13, 16, 30, 31, 32, 42

Hewitt, Helen, "An Unknown Motet of the Fifteenth Century," *The Catholic Choirmaster*, XXX (1944), 56–59, 77–80, 82.
  Canti B 39

Jeppesen, Knud (ed.), *Der Kopenhagener Chansonnier: Das Manuskript Thott 291⁸ der königlichen Bibliothek Kopenhagen;* edition of the literary texts, Viggo Brøndal (Copenhagen and Leipzig, 1927).
  Cf. *Canti B* 24

Jöde, Fritz (ed.), *Chorbuch für gemischte Stimmen* (4 vols.; Wolfenbüttel and Berlin, 1927–31), III, *Alte weltliche Lieder für gemischte Stimmen*.
  Cf. *Canti B* 19

Kalff, Gerrit, "Handschriften der Universiteitsbibliotheek te Amsterdam," *Tijdschrift voor Nederlandsche Taal-en Letterkunde*, IX (1890), 161–88.
  Cf. *Canti B* 18, 41 (texts only)

Kiesewetter, Rafael Georg, *Die Verdienste der Niederlaender um die Tonkunst* (Amsterdam, 1829).
  Canti B 19

Kinsky, Georg (ed.), *Geschichte der Musik in Bildern* (Leipzig, 1929).
Canti B 51

Kottick, Edward Leon (ed.), "The Music of the *Chansonnier Cordiforme:* Paris, Bibliothèque Nationale, *Rothschild 2973*" (Ph.D. dissertation, University of North Carolina, 1962).
Cf. Canti B 3

Lenaerts, René, *Het Nederlands polifonies Lied in de zestiende Eeuw* (Mechlin and Amsterdam, 1933).
Canti B 18

Liliencron, Rochus von (ed.), *Deutsches Leben im Volkslied um 1530. Deutsche National-Litteratur*, XIII (Berlin and Stuttgart, 1885).
Cf. Canti B 19

Löpelmann, Martin (ed.), *Die Liederhandschrift des Cardinals de Rohan (XV. Jahrh.). Publikationen der Gesellschaft für romanische Literatur*, XLIV (Göttingen, 1923). (After Berlin 78. B. 17.)
Canti B 3, 24, 28, 30, 31 (T, B), 42; cf. Canti B 47 (texts only)

Lose Blätter der Musikantengilde für Jugend und Volk in Schule und Haus, III (1925).
Canti B 19

Maldeghem, R.-J. van (ed.), *Trésor musical: Collection authentique de musique sacrée et profane des anciens maîtres belges* (29 vols.; Brussels, 1865–93). ("Sacrée" or "profane" following a short title will distinguish between the two volumes published each year by Van Maldeghem.)
Canti B 1, 7, 22, 28, 40

Marix, Jeanne (ed.), *Les Musiciens de la cour de Bourgogne au XVᵉ siècle (1420–1467): Gilles de Binche (Binchois), Pierre Fontaine, Jacques Vide, Nicole Grenon, Gilles Joye, Hayne de Ghizeghem, Robert Morton: messes, motets, chansons* (Paris, 1937).
Canti B 48; cf. Canti B 1

Marsy, C. S. Lantreau de, and Imbert, B. (eds.), *Annales poétiques, ou Almanach des Muses* (40 vols.; Paris, 1778–88), II.
Canti B 24 (text only)

Miller, Clement A. (translator, transcriber, and commentator), *Heinrich Glarean, Dodecachordon* (2 vols.; Rome: American Institute of Musicology, 1965).
Canti B 19

Mincoff-Marriage, Elizabeth (ed.), *Souterliedekens: Een Nederlandsch Psalmboek van 1540 met de oorspronkelijke Volksliederen die bij de Melodieën behooren* (The Hague, 1922).
Cf. Canti B 18, 41

Osthoff, Helmuth (ed.), *Josquin des Prés, Mattheus Le Maistre, Christian Hollander, Alexander Utendal, Ivo de Vento, und Jacob Regnart: Acht Lied- und Choralmotetten. Das Chorwerk*, XXX (Wolfenbüttel and Berlin, 1934).
Canti B 19

Osthoff, Helmuth, "'Wohlauf, gut G'sell, von hinnen!': Ein Beispiel deutsch-französischer Liedgemeinschaft um 1500," *Jahrbuch für Volksliedforschung*, VIII (1951), 128–36.
Cf. Canti B 19

Paris, Gaston (ed.), music transcribed into modern notation by Auguste Gevaert, *Chansons du XVᵉ siècle* (Paris, 1875; reimpression, 1935). (After Paris 12744.)
Cf. Canti B 4, 5, 6, 9, 12, 15, 27, 51

Picker, Martin (ed.), *The Chanson Albums of Marguerite of Austria, A Critical Edition and Commentary* (Berkeley and Los Angeles: University of California Press, 1965).
Canti B 4, 7, 22, 28, 40

Picker, Martin, "The Chanson Albums of Marguerite of Austria: MSS. 228 and 11239 of the Bibliothèque Royale de Belgique, Brussels," *Annales musicologiques*, VI (1958–63), 145–285.
Canti B 7

Priebsch, Robert (ed.), *Deutsche Handschriften in England* (2 vols.; Erlangen, 1896–1901), II, *Das British Museum, mit einem Anhang über die Guildhall-Bibliothek*, 289–93 (London Add. 35087).
Canti B 18 (text only)

Quicherat, M. J. (ed.), *Les Vers de Maître Henri Baude, poète du XVᵉ siècle, recueillis et publiés avec les actes qui concernent sa vie* (Paris, 1856).
Canti B 22 (text only)

Renier, Rodolfo, "Un mazzetto di poesie musicali francesi," *Miscellanea di filologia e linguistica: In memoria di Napoleone Caix e Ugo Angelo Canello* (Florence, 1886), pp. 271–88. (After Cortona 95, 96.)
Canti B 5, 11, 23, 28, 32 (A, T), 34, 37 (texts only)

Santander, Charles Antoine de la Serna, *Mémoire historique sur la bibliothèque dite de Bourgogne, présentement Bibliothèque Publique de Bruxelles* (Brussels, 1809). (After Brussels 228.)
Canti B 7 (text only)

Schwob, Marcel (ed.), *Le Parnasse satyrique du quinzième siècle: Anthologie de pièces libres* (Paris, 1905).
Canti B 45 (text only)

Seay, Albert (ed.), *Pierre Attaingnant, Transcriptions of Chansons for Keyboard* (Rome: American Institute of Musicology, 1961).
Canti B 28

Shipp, Clifford Marion (ed.), "A Chansonnier of the Dukes of Lorraine: The Paris Manuscript *fonds français 1597*" (Ph.D. dissertation, North Texas State College, 1960).
Canti B 5, 28, 40, 46, 48

Smijers, Albert, *Algemeene Muziekgeschiedenis* (2d ed.; Utrecht, 1940).
Canti B 2

Smijers, Albert (ed.), *Josquin des Prés, Werken: Wereldlijke Werken* (4 vols.; Amsterdam and Leipzig, 1925——), II.
Canti B 34, 37

Smijers, Albert (ed.), *Van Ockeghem tot Sweelinck: Nederlandsche Muziekgeschiedenis in Voorbeelden.*
Vol. I (Amsterdam, 1939). Cf. *Canti B 1, 24*
Vol. IV (Amsterdam, 1942). *Canti B 5*
Vol. V (Amsterdam, 1949). *Canti B 1*

Stäblein, Bruno (ed.), *Die mittelalterlichen Hymnenmelodien des Abendlandes. Monumenta monodica medii aevi, Band I. Hymnen (I)* (Kassel and Basel: Bärenreiter, 1956).
Cf. *Canti B 2* (T 1 only)

Wallis, N. Hardy (trans. and ed.), *Anonymous French Verse: An Anthology of Fifteenth-Century Poems Collected from Manuscripts in the British Museum* (London, 1929).
Canti B 48 (text only)

Weckerlin, Jean-Baptiste (ed.), *L'Ancienne chanson populaire en France* (Paris, 1887).
Canti B 9 (text only)

Weckerlin, Jean-Baptiste (ed.), *Bibliothèque du Conservatoire National de Musique et de Déclamation: Catalogue bibliographique* (Paris, 1885), pp. 372–400; also published separately as *Petrucci: Harmonice musices odhecaton, avec notice* (Paris, 1885).
Canti B 1

Wolf, Johannes, *Handbuch der Notationskunde* (2 vols.; Leipzig, 1913–19).
Canti B 16

Wolf, Johannes (ed.), *Heinrich Isaac: Weltliche Werke. Denkmäler der Tonkunst in Oesterreich*, XIV/1 (Vienna, 1907).
Canti B 44; cf. *Canti B 19, 41*

Wolf, Johannes (ed.), *Jacob Obrecht, Werken: Missen* (23 vols.; Amsterdam, 1908——).
Canti B 14; cf. *Canti B 1*

Wolf, Johannes (ed.), *Jacob Obrecht, Werken: Motetten* (4 vols.; Amsterdam and Leipzig, n.d.).
Canti B 40

Wolf, Johannes (ed.), *Jacob Obrecht, Werken: Wereldlijke Werken* (Amsterdam and Leipzig, n.d.).
Canti B 3, 13, 16, 28, 35

Wolf, Johannes (ed.), *25 driestemmige Oud-Nederlandsche Liederen uit het Einde der vijftiende Eeuw naar den Codex London British Museum Add. Mss. 35087. Uitgave XXX der Vereeniging voor Noord-Nederlands Muziekgeschiedenis* (Amsterdam, 1910).
Cf. *Canti B 18*

Wolf, Johannes (ed.), *Sing- und Spielmusik aus älterer Zeit* (Leipzig, 1926). Reprinted as *Music of Earlier Times* (New York, n.d.).
Cf. *Canti B 18*

Wolff, O. L. B. (ed.), *Altfranzoesische Volkslieder* (Leipzig, 1831), p. 165.
Cf. *Canti B 14*

PLATE VII. London, British Museum, Harley MS 4425, f. 12', Illustration from *Roman de la rose*.

COMMENTARIES
ON THE COMPOSITIONS AND THEIR TEXTS

1. *L'OMME ARMÉ* Josquin 4 v. f. 2
Above the superius: . *Canon . Et sic de singulis.*

CONCORDANCES: None.

MODERN EDITIONS:
Chilesotti, *Sulla melodia popolare*, no. 6, p. 21.
Disertori, "Una mistificazione mensurale," p. 54.
Maldeghem, *Trésor musical (profane)*, Vol. XX (1884), no. 8 (text after Tinctoris, *Proportionale*, Liber III, Cap. 4) (= Reese, "Maldeghem," no. 218).[1]
Smijers, *Van Ockeghem tot Sweelinck*, V, no. 45, p. 155.
Weckerlin, *Conservatoire . . . Catalogue*, pp. 394–96 (text after Tinctoris, *Proportionale*, Liber III, Cap. 4).

RELATED COMPOSITIONS:
1. Basel F. X. 1–4, no. 114, Anon. Incipit in each of four voices. Published in Wolf, *Obrecht: Missen*, XIX, 95–96.
2a. Bologna Q 17, f. 57'–58, Anon. Incipit "Dung aultre amer" in S, A, B; incipit "Lhomme arme doyt on doubter" in T.
2b. Rome C. G. XIII, 27, f. 113'–114, Basiron. Incipit in highest of four voices. Published in Smijers, *Van Ockeghem tot Sweelinck*, I, no. 8.
3a. New Haven, Mellon, f. 44'–45, Anon. Text "Il sera pour vous" in superius; text "Lome arme" in tenor and contra.
3b. Rome 2856, f. 156'–157, Morton. Incipit "Lom arme" in each of four voices.
   Rome 2856 adds a bass to the voices in New Haven, Mellon; the melody is in the tenor of Rome 2856. Published in Wolf, *Obrecht: Missen*, XIX, 94–95, and Marix, *Musiciens de Bourgogne*, no. 63, p. 96.

[1] Gustave Reese, "Maldeghem and His Buried Treasure: A Bibliographical Study," *Music Library Association Notes*, VI (1948), 75–117.

4. Petrucci 1504[3] *Canti C*, f. 78'–79, Jo. Japart. Incipit "Il est de bonne heure ne" in S, A, T; incipit "Lomme arme" in B. Published in Brown, *Theatrical Chansons*, no. 26, pp. 79–81.

TEXT:

The text indicated by this incipit, as reproduced below, follows Smijers, *Josquin: Missen*. It appears likewise in the tenor and contra of *Il sera pour vous / Lome armé*, found in New Haven, Mellon, f. 44'–45.

The chanson is based on a seven-syllable line, with frequent repetitions, such as the repetition of "l'home armé" and "doibt-on doubter" at the beginning and at the end of the chanson. Considerable repetition of these phrases appears in both the Smijers edition and in New Haven, Mellon. The latter also inserts between lines the phrase "à l'assault," which has no meaning in the poem. Plamenac discovered the complete text (*Rapport sur le congrès archéologique et historique*, Bruges, 1925). The basic lines follow:

> L'home armé doibt-on doubter;
> On a fait partout crier
> Que chascun se viegne armer
> D'un haubregon de fer.

1. New Haven, Mellon: . . . me doibt-on doubter
3. New Haven, Mellon: Que chascun se doibt armer

MUSIC:

This short work by Josquin is an example of the puzzle canon, of which several are included in *Canti B*. It is an arrangement of the popular song *L'homme armé*, which lies in the tenor, but in such an altered form that an explanation is necessary. The old melody is set down here (p. 25) for comparison with Josquin's tenor.

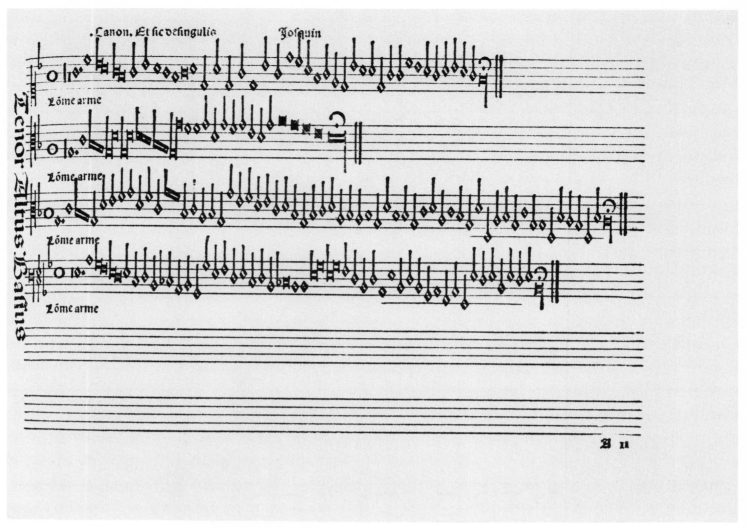

PLATE VIII.   *Canti B*, 1503, no. 1, Josquin, "L'omme armé."

Petrucci supplies the inscription *Canon . Et sic de singulis*. A dot (*punctum*) is placed directly after the first note (a *semibrevis*) of each part, but no other notes are dotted. The "period" following the word "canon" seems not to be a mark of punctuation, but a direct reference to the isolated dot appearing in each voice. A translation of the Latin inscription reads: "Canon . and thus [i.e., a dot] after each [note]." The canon thus directs the performer to place a dot, mentally, after each note of his part. With this peculiar demand, Josquin was not only playing a trick on his performers, but experimenting with the notation of his time as well.[2]

The conflict produced in a musician's mind when his eye sees the sign for *tempus perfectum*, yet his ear hears emerging a piece of music in a slow *tempus imperfectum*—this conflict can produce amusement. This was

[2] We possess no published score of this work by Ambros, but we know he was familiar with it, for he has left us his interpretation of the canon: "... because a dot is placed after the first note, all the following notes must be considered as dotted." August Wilhelm Ambros, *Geschichte der Musik* (3d ed.; Leipzig, 1887-1911), III, 57, n. 1.

precisely what Josquin was trying to do: evoke feelings of surprise, amusement, delight, through this intellectual game.

To achieve this effect the notation had to meet certain demands. Josquin could not introduce rests, for a rest could not be dotted. Hence phrases could not be set off in the usual way, nor could points of imitation. He had to make changes in the *cantus firmus*. He could write no breves having a triple value. For every note, to be capable of receiving the *punctum additionis* demanded by the canon, had to have a duple value. To achieve a note of triple value near the end he blackens the breve (tenor, mm. 13–16), reducing it to two beats; when a dot is added, the value subtracted by the coloration is restored, and the note has the three beats desired. The final phrase of the song lengthens the notes to produce a retard. Suggestions of the original melody are introduced into measures 16–18 (superius and bass), thus giving an effect of reprise.

The addition of one-half of its value to every note produces a speed one half again as slow as the normal *tempus imperfectum*. This is a new speed, for it lies

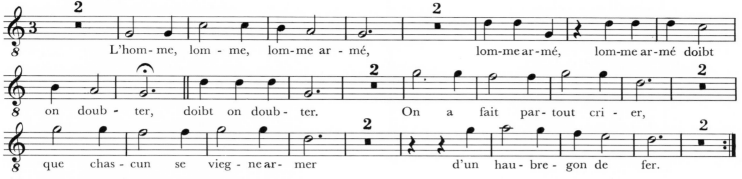

L'hom- me, lom - me, lom-me ar - mé,   lom-me ar-mé,   lom-me ar-mé doibt

on doub - ter, doibt on doub - ter.   On a fait par-tout cri - er,

que chas - cun se vieg - ne ar- mer   d'un hau - bre - gon de fer.

(After Smijers, *Van Ockeghem tot Sweelinck*, V, 155)

halfway between that of *integer valor* and that of augmentation. Thus, in contriving his musical joke, Josquin produced a notational innovation which must have been of considerable interest to the players, if not the audience.[3]

(See also Introduction, pp. xv–xvi.)

2. *VIRGO CELESTI*   Compere   5 v.   f. 2'–3

CONCORDANCES:

St. Gall 463, no. 195, Compere. Text, S, A; incipit, T 2; three of the five voices only.

St. Gall 464, no. 195, Compere. S and B only, with text.

GREGORIAN HYMN TUNE:

Antiphonale Romanum, p. [68], *Iste Confessor* (text).

Antiphonarius Sarisburiensis 1520, "Common of the Saints," f. xxvii, *Iste Confessor* (text).

Antiphonarius Sarisburiensis 1520, "Proper of the Saints," f. iii verso, *Ut queant laxis* (text).

Stäblein, *Mittelalterliche Hymnenmelodien*, pp. 94, 222, 257, and 391 for four variants of melody no. 151, with texts *Ut queant laxis*, *Quod chorus vatum*, *O pater sancte*, and eight others.

MODERN EDITIONS:

Finscher, *Compère: Opera omnia*, III, 20–21.

Smijers, *Muziekgeschiedenis*, pp. 114–15 (after *Canti B* 2).

TEXT:

     O virgin, honored by heavenly birth,
     Ever compassionate toward the human race,
     Look down upon thy servants
     Who continually dedicate themselves to thee,
     O Virgin Mary.

Exceptionally, Petrucci gave the text of *Virgo celesti*, placing the words beneath the superius and *tenor primus*; in St. Gall 463–464 they appear in alto and bass as well. This poem has a metrical structure used for many Latin

hymns of the Middle Ages: one hymn would be sung to a number of different hymn tunes; and one tune would serve as vehicle for several different hymns.[4] Although the text source of *Virgo celesti* has not been found, all other texts associated with the melody in the *tenor primus* are either complete hymns or stanzas of hymns. It seems probable, therefore, that *Virgo celesti* was also a hymn stanza.

The present edition follows *Canti B*; the text is found likewise in St. Gall 463–464. Finscher notes that there is "another composition of the same text, à 4 and without any *cantus firmus*, by frater Petrus de Ostia in Verona, Biblioteca Capitolare, MS DCCLX, f. 27'–28" (see note 6).

MUSIC:

With this setting of a stanza addressed to the Virgin Mary, Loyset Compère makes his first appearance in the Petrucci anthologies as a composer of sacred music. The compiler of *Canti B* surely intended this motet to open the collection; but, since it required two facing pages for its notation, he could not place it opposite the Index; he therefore allowed Josquin's *L'omne armé* to fill the otherwise unsightly empty staves of folio 2 recto.

Albert Smijers first recognized the hymn melody in the *tenor primus*, though he failed to identify it.[5] Ludwig Finscher[6] found the melody,[7] whose use was

---

[3] Benvenuto Disertori, "Una storica mistificazione mensurale di Josquin des Prés: sue affinità con Leonardo da Vinci," *Liber Amicorum Charles van den Borren* (Antwerp, 1964), pp. 49–56.

[4] See Gustave Reese, *Music in the Renaissance* (New York, 1954), p. 83, n. 238, for a brief development of this topic. See also Frank L. Harrison, *Music in Medieval Britain* (London, 1958), pp. 64 ff., for a discussion of the relationships between hymns and hymn tunes in the Sarum rite.

[5] Albert Smijers, *Algemeene Muziekgeschiedenis* (2d ed.; Utrecht, 1940), p. 113.

[6] See Ludwig Finscher, *Loyset Compère (c. 1450–1518), Life and Works* (Rome: American Institute of Musicology, 1964), pp. 124–27.

[7] Bruno Stäblein (ed.), *Die mittelalterlichen Hymnenmelodien des Abendlandes. Monumenta monodica medii aevi*, Band I. Hymnen (I) (Kassel and Basel: Bärenreiter, 1956). Four slightly differing variants of the melody (from different hymnals) are given here,

both widespread and long lasting. The melody is still sung today in the Roman rite to the hymn *Iste Confessor* at First Vespers of the liturgy for "Common of a Confessor not a Bishop." In the Sarum rite, also, the chant was sung to *Iste Confessor* at First Vespers on the same day, but, in addition, it was sung to *Ut queant laxis* on the day commemorating the birth of St. John the Baptist.

The reading of the Sarum chant is given above, together with Compère's adaptation.[8] In the present Roman Antiphonal, however, the "Hymn to St. John" is sung to the melody known to Guido

d'Arezzo—the union of words and melody from which he derived the solmization syllables.[9]

Both *Ut queant laxis* and *Virgo celesti* are in the form of the Sapphic stanza; but, whereas the former closes correctly with a short Adonic line (—∪∪——), "Sancte Joannes," Compère's text doubles this line to "Aspice servos, Virgo Maria" (—∪∪——, —∪∪——).

At the beginning of the motet, Compère matches the melodic setting of the first two lines of *Ut queant laxis* exactly, marking the caesura by a rest in measures 5–6. In the following line he makes a break after the second syllable, thus emphasizing the word "semper." For the closing petition he elaborates the motives of the Sarum melody to make room for the "double" invocation, thus departing from his simpler model.[10] In his first

and Stäblein lists eleven different hymns sung to this melody. One of these hymns is *Quod chorus vatum*, whose second stanza, beginning *Haec Deum caeli*, together with our melody, forms the basis of the motet *Haec Deum caeli* by Jacob Obrecht. (See Edgar Sparks, *Cantus Firmus in Mass and Motet, 1420–1520* [Berkeley and Los Angeles: University of California Press, 1963], pp. 304–6, for an analysis of Obrecht's motet and for some of its music; see p. 475, n. 68, for comments on the Gregorian melodies and texts.)

[8] This melody, in Mode 2, uses D as final in Stäblein, A in *Antiphonarius Sarisburiensis 1520*, and G in *Canti B*. The latter two are transpositions.

[9] *Antiphonale sacrosanctae Romanae ecclesiae pro diurnis horis* (Paris, Tournai, Rome: Desclée & Socii, 1949), pp. 733 ff., shows five stanzas.

[10] The short melisma on the syllable "Sol [-ve]" (line five of *Ut queant laxis*) differs in the various readings of this chant. Compère apparently felt free to write a melisma of his own.

26

approach to the final ("ser-vos") he uses the *subfinalis*, in the second ("[Ma]-ri-a"), supertonic, tonic.

The second *cantus firmus* in the *tenor secundus*—this terminology gives priority to the borrowed hymn tune (*tenor primus*)—consists of an ascending hexachord starting on F and enunciated three times: at first in perfect breves; then in imperfect breves in black notation, producing syncopation in the triple meter of the motet; and finally in semibreves, grouped in pairs by the series of binary ligatures *cum opposita proprietate*. (See also Introduction, p. xvi.)

3. *J'AY PRIS AMOURS* Obreht 4 v. f. 3'–7

CONCORDANCE:

Egenolff [c. 1535][14] *Lieder*, no. 17 a, b, c, d, Anon. Superius only, with textual incipit.

MODERN EDITION:

Wolf, *Obrecht: Wereldlijke Werken*, pp. 19–28 (after *Canti B*).

RELATED COMPOSITIONS:

See *Canti B* 30, and Hewitt, *Odhecaton*, Concordances of no. 21.

TEXT:

See Hewitt, *Odhecaton*, Note on *Odhecaton* 21.

MUSIC:

Obrecht has produced a work of extraordinary proportions—232 measures—confiding a *cantus prius factus* drawn from the original anonymous setting of the *rondeau quatrain*, *J'ay pris amours*, to each voice in turn.[11] Petrucci placed each section on a separate opening. A fermata and double bar at the end of the second section and a fresh metric signature at the beginning of the third seem to stress the division of the work into two large halves.

The opening section (mm. 1–57) uses the superius of the older work in the Hypoaeolian mode; the fourth section (mm. 177–232), the tenor, so that the work is "bounded" by Aeolian *cantus firmi*. The second section (mm. 58–119), transposing the tenor a fifth lower and placing it in the bass, assumes the Hypodorian mode.

[11] The original setting is published in Eugénie Droz, Geneviève Thibault, and Yvonne Rokseth (eds.), *Trois chansonniers français du XVᵉ siècle* (*Documents artistiques du XVᵉ siècle*, IV, Paris, 1927), Fasc. I, *Bibliothèque de Dijon, Ms 517 (ancien 295), folios 1–56*. More recently it has appeared in the dissertation by Edward L. Kottick, "The Music of the *Chansonnier Cordiforme*: Paris, Bibliothèque Nationale, Rothschild 2973" (University of North Carolina, 1962).

The third section shows a Hypophrygian version of the tenor (transposed up a fifth) in its alto.[12]

Section three (m. 150) gives us one of the three sharps found in *Canti B*; this sharp has the modern meaning of the natural sign, whereas the other sharps (found in *Canti B* 24, mm. 11 and 19) have the meaning of raising a tone which is natural according to the signature.

Some of the earliest freely composed works of Ockeghem's generation are cited as vehicles for *laude spirituali*. In 1485 the Italian poet Franceso d'Albizzo gave as *timbres* for some of his *laude*: *Iam pris amore* (see Droz, *Trois chansonniers français*, no. 2, for the original anonymous setting of this text), *Fortuna disperata* (*Canti C* 50 or 101), and *Nunquam fuit poena major* (*Odhecaton* 4). Again, an anonymous *lauda* was to be sung to either *I'a pris amour* or *Mon seul plaisir* (a setting of the latter appears in Florence 2439). In a publication of 1510 entitled *Laude vecchie e nuove*, *Le serviteur* (*Odhecaton* 35) is specified as the melody for a *lauda* by Ser Firenze.[13] Of course, many *laude* had their own melodies, or were composed as part-music. (See also Introduction, p. ix.)

4. *VRAY DIEU, QUI M'Y CONFORTERA*
Anon. 4 v. f. 7'–8

CONCORDANCES:

Brussels 11239, f. 15'–17, A. Bruhier. Text in all four voices.

Rome Vat. 11953, f. 10'–11', Anon. Bass only, with textual incipit.

[12] Other analyses of Obrecht's work may be seen in Benvenuto Disertori, "In margine all'Odhecaton: Note ed appunti," *Rivista musicale italiana*, LI (1949), 29–42 (see p. 34), and in Reese, *Music in the Renaissance*, p. 188. Reese feels that "Obrecht's settings, compared with their models, tend to reveal a more modern feeling for tonality and harmonic structure; and in his *J'ay pris amours*, transposition is employed to produce a I-IV-V-I key-relationship. . . . It is especially interesting that the feeling for tonality should become evident here in conjunction with the use of the Aeolian mode."

[13] See *Lavde spiritvali di Feo Belcari, di Lorenzo de' Medici, di Francesco d'Albizzo, di Castellano Castellani e di altri comprese nelle qvattro più antiche raccolte con alcvne inedite e con nvove illvstrazioni* (Florence, 1863). The title of the collection of 1485 reads: *Lavde fatte e composte da più persone spirituali. A onore dello omnipotente Idio e della gloriosa vergine Madona Santa Maria e di molti altri Sancti, et Sancte. . . . Et tucte le infrascripte laude ha raccolto et insieme ridocto. . . . Iacopo di maestro Luigi de' Morsi cittadino fiorentino.* The colophon reads: *Impresso già nella magnifica città di Firenze per Ser Francesco Bonaccorsi, a petizione di Iacopo di maestro Luigi de' Morsi, nell'anno MCCCCLXXXV. A dì primo di Marzo.* The *laude* cited appear on pp. 56, 56, 75–76, 103, and 228 of the edition of 1863.

MONOPHONIC VERSIONS:

Paris 9346, no. 67. Published in Gérold, *Manuscrit de Bayeux*, no. 67, p. 78.

Paris 12744, f. 83′. Published in Paris-Gevaert, *Chansons*, no. 121.

MODERN EDITION:

Picker, *Chanson Albums*, pp. 430–33, A(ntoine) Bruhier (after Brussels 11239).

RELATED COMPOSITIONS:

1. Attaingnant 1529⁴ *42 Chansons*, no. 32, p. 15′, Anon., *Hé dieu, que mi confortera* (a 4-part work based on the same popular song).
2. London Harley 5242, f. 47′–48, Anon., *Vray dieu qui my confortera* (based on the same popular song; the work is incomplete since f. 48′ is empty and f. 49 missing).

TEXT:

> Mercy, dear Lord, I am so sad,
> My jealous husband drives me mad,
> Shutting me up alone inside.
>
> A lusty gallant's my desire,
> Just thirty, full of love's sweet fire,
> Who'd sleep cool mornings by my side.
>
> Wee nightingale of the bright wood,
> Why come to me in singing mood,
> Since to this graybeard I am tied?
>
> Welcome, love, my dearest mate,
> Long for you I've had to wait.
> In this green forest oft I've sighed.

The most complete version of this text appears in Paris-Gevaert, *Chansons* (after Paris 12744), five stanzas of three lines each. Gérold, *Manuscrit de Bayeux* (after Paris 9346), shows three stanzas, Brussels 11239 two, and London Harley 5242 but one. Versions of the text found in Brussels 11239 and Paris-Gevaert are published in Françon, *Albums poétiques*; Paris 9346, as edited by Gasté, is also published in Françon, Appendix, Note V.

This edition follows Paris-Gevaert generally, but omits the second stanza as did Bruhier, composer of the *Canti B* setting. The second stanza, which points up the theme of the *mal mariée*, reads:

> Mon père m'a donné ung viellart
> Qui tout le jour crie: "Hellas!"
> Et dort au long de la nuytée.
>
> (My pa has wed me to a graybeard
> Who cries "Alas!" the livelong day,
> And sleeps the night through, come what may.)

1. Gérold, *Manuscrit de Bayeux*: Hé Dieu, qui me . . .
2. Gérold, Brussels 11239: villain
   London, Harley 5242: vieillart; m'y (superius)

3. Brussels 11239: Two voices have "esgarée"
5. Gérold: vingt
   Brussels 11239: Qui me frota(n)t la nuyt souvant. (This line is found only in Brussels 11239.)
6. Gérold: dormist grant matinée.

Gérold gives three stanzas, one and three of Paris-Gevaert, and a third which is here reproduced:

> Je ne sçay pas qui ce sera,
> Qui mon amour entretiendra
> Quant je seray despucelée.
>
> (I wonder who the man will be
> Who of my love will be empowered
> After I have been deflowered.)

The last line of each stanza is repeated in Gérold, and the first line of the chanson reappears at the end of the third stanza, probably indicating the repetition of stanza one to close the song.

MUSIC:

Bruhier's setting opens with "voice pairing." A change of meter marks the beginning of the second stanza, m. 23, but the opening meter returns for the last line of this stanza. The technique of pervading imitation is used throughout the composition. This feature, syllabic declamation of the words, repetition of phrases at will, changes of meter, etc., place this work in an advanced stage of composition for the period. (See also Introduction, p. ix.)

5. *LOURDAULT, LOURDAULT* Compere 4 v. f. 8′–9

CONCORDANCES:

Basel F. X. 1–4, no. 119, Josquin. Incipit "Lordault" in each of four voices.

Bologna Q 17, f. 60′–61, Nino petit. "Lourdeau lourdeau" in each of four voices.

Cortona 95–96, Paris 1817, no. 6, Anon. Text in S, A, T; B wanting.

Paris 1597, f. 56′–57, Anon. Text in all four voices.

Regensburg C 120, pp. 260–61, Compere. "Lordau" only in two of four voices.

MONOPHONIC VERSIONS:

Paris 12744, no. 71. Published in Paris-Gevaert, *Chansons*.

Gérold, *Chansons populaires*, no. 29 (after Paris-Gevaert, *Chansons*, and "in part after ms. fr. 1597 and nouv. acq. 1817").

MODERN EDITIONS:

Brown, *Theatrical Chansons*, no. 50, Compère (Ninot Le Petit?) (after Paris 1597).

Shipp, "Paris MS f. fr. 1597," no. 57, pp. 466-70.
Smijers, *Van Ockeghem tot Sweelinck*, IV, no. 34, pp. 119-20 (after *Canti B;* text after Paris-Gevaert, *Chansons*).

TEXT:

> O clod of clods, watch what you're doing,
> For if you marry, you'll be rueing,
> And if she's young your grief renewing.
>
> O clod of clods, you will be fleeced.
> To church, confession by the priest
> She'll often go, a dainty feast.
>
> O clod of clods, don't be so dumb.
> He'll do the job, and they'll keep mum.
> And when she's full, back home she'll come.
>
> O clod of clods, your act is mad.
> You'll raise the child, delusion sad,
> So happy when he calls you "Dad."

This *romance* appears in Cortona 95–96, Paris 1817, Paris 1597, and Paris 12744. The present edition follows the Paris-Gevaert, *Chansons*, reading of Paris 12744. The poem consists of nine one-line stanzas with a one-line refrain at the beginning of the poem and after each stanza. The entire poem is mono-rhymed, and all the lines are alexandrines. Its form is: A a_1 A; a_2 A; etc. Heldt suggests that "it can easily be brought into the form: A a_1 a_2 A; a_2 a_3 A; etc.,"[14] but in Compère's setting (shown with words beneath the notes in the Cortona manuscript and in Paris 1597) still another scheme is employed: A a_1 a_2 A; a_3 a_4 A; etc. In the first of these designs the refrain is heard ten times; in Heldt's scheme, nine times; in Compère's

setting, only five times, thus avoiding excessive repetition. Since Compère's scheme required an even number of stanzas, he had to omit one of the nine. His choice fell on stanza two. In this satirical poem the speaker advises a young man against marriage with any woman, young or old.[15] Only stanza two is devoted to the older woman: "Sy tu prens une vielle, el te rechygnera." With the omission of this line the song deals exclusively with the *jeune femme*. Textually it remains a unified whole, if losing somewhat in point: namely, that one should not marry at all. This edition also omits stanza two and has further changed the stanzaic structure to introduce the refrain after every two lines, following the music of Compère.

3. Cortona 95–96, Paris 1817, Paris 1597: Jalous tu en seras
4. Cortona 95–96, Paris 1817, and Paris 1597 stop here, the latter repeating several times: garde que tu feras.
6. merra = mènera
8. ren = rien
9. el = elle
12. hucher = crier

MUSIC:

Compère's music—of course, the work is also ascribed to Josquin and Ninot le Petit—is an arrangement of a popular melody (minor) of which there is a "major" form in Paris-Gevaert, *Chansons* (Paris 12744). Some of these popular tunes were apparently sung in both modes, with the necessary adjustments. The major version is set down here for convenience of comparison:

1. Lour-dault, lour-dault, lour-dault _____ gar-de que tu fe-ras. Car
si tu te ma-ri-es, tu t'en re-pen-ti-ras, lour-dault.
Lour-dault, lour-dault, lour-dault _____ gar-de que tu fe-ras.

(After Gérold, *Chansons populaires*, p. 40)

This melody opens with a refrain which returns at the end. In between comes a phrase to which the stanzas were sung. No *signum* is shown in Paris 12744, but Gevaert, the musical editor of this manuscript, places one at the beginning of this phrase (m. 4:4) to indicate

the alternation of refrain and stanza throughout the entire *romance*.

[15] Rabelais made capital of this song. See François Rabelais, *Gargantua and Pantagruel*, trans. Sir Thomas Urquhart and Peter Motteux (Chicago: Encyclopaedia Britannica, Inc., 1952), Book III, chap. 28, p. 184. See also Nan Cooke Carpenter, *Rabelais and Music* (Chapel Hill: University of North Carolina Press, 1954). Several references to the song of *Canti B 5* appear on pp. 5, 6, and 28-29.

[14] Elisabeth Heldt (ed.), *Französische Virelais aus dem 15. Jahrhundert* (Halle/Saale, 1916), p. 7 (after Paris 12744).

57.

PLATE IX. Paris, Bibliothèque Nationale,

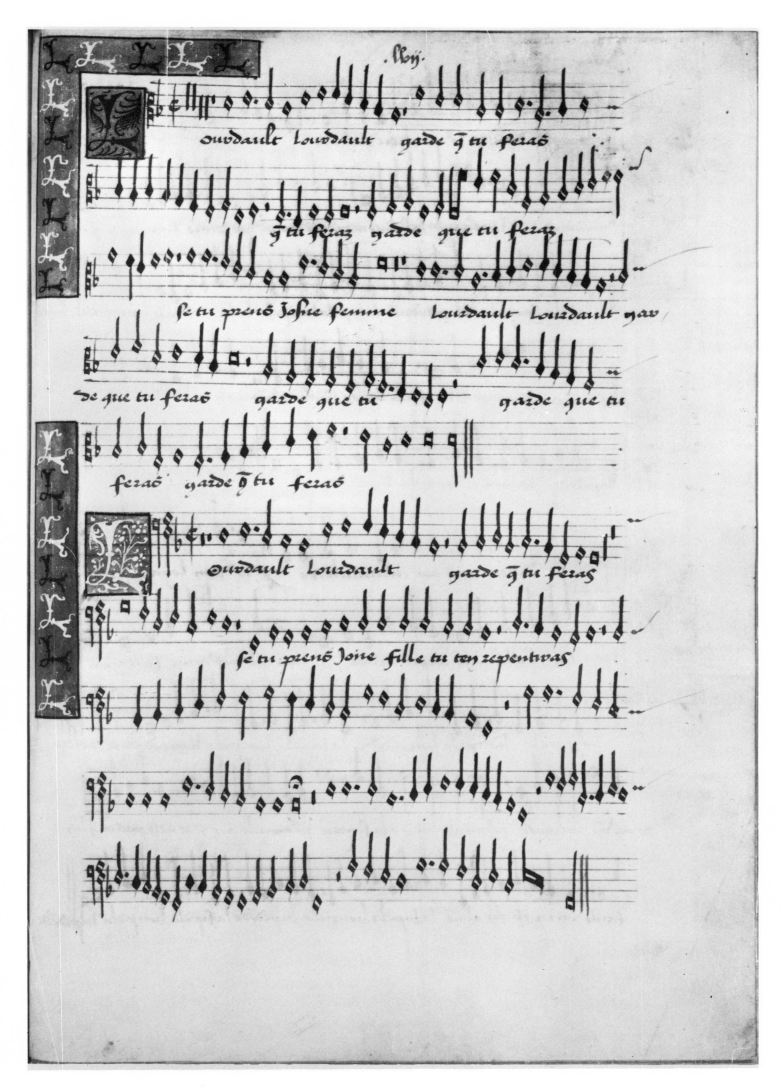

Fonds fr. 1597, f. 56'–57, "Lourdault, lourdault."

In the polyphonic setting, however, an additional phrase is found between the opening refrain and the phrase common to the two versions of the melody, thus permitting two stanzas to be sung in succession between refrains. Doubtless the popular song was also sung this way at times; there is therefore no need to assume that Compère himself invented the phrase, just because it happens not to be present in Paris 12744.[16] In Compère's setting the *signum* is placed in measure 35, that is, at the close of the setting of the stanzas; returns are made to the beginning from this point.

The *cantus firmus* appears prominently in the soprano. The first stanza is sung (mm. 20–27) to the phrase not present in the monophonic (major) version. Leisurely half notes give out the clause "Car sy tu te maries," producing a feeling of suspense. The second clause, "tu t'en repentiras," answers in quarter notes, that is, in "double quick" time, producing a very humorous effect, perhaps expressing the idea that after marriage repentance comes quickly.[17] In any event, Compère adds a cadential flourish to make this phrase the exact length it would have been if half notes had been used throughout.

The notation of this work in *Canti B* shows "conflicting signatures": ♭, ♭, ♭, 2♭. Basel F. X. 1–4 supplies a second flat in the alto: ♭, 2♭, ♭, 2♭; but Paris 1597 fails to assign a second flat, even in the bass: ♭, ♭, ♭, ♭. Cortona 95–96, Paris 1817, confirms the *Canti B* signatures in its three extant part-books (the bass is wanting), whereas Bologna Q 17 leaves the superius with a blank signature: ♮, ♭, ♭, ♭. For the fifteenth century, the Basel signature would seem the most correct, since E occurs twenty times in the bass and eighteen times in the alto and needs flatting on each occurrence; however, the superius contains only one E and the tenor only two, all three of which must be flatted according to the ordinary rules governing *musica ficta*. This bears out one of the theories advanced on the reasons for the use of conflicting signatures.[18]

The crisp rhythm, ♩. ♫♫, heard in the refrain, is shown in *Canti B* as ▪ ♪♪♪♪. In Bologna Q 17 (and occasionally, though not consistently, in Paris 1597) this rhythm is moderated—and weakened—to ♩ ♫♫ (𝅝 ♩♩♩♩).

At the close of the composition, the alto is given the third of the final chord, but then taken to the fifth. Paris 1597 assigns the fifth in both measures. Bologna Q 17 presents both notes, permitting the altos to divide and sing both notes.

Ambros noticed this tendency to omit the third in the final chord of a work. "The basis of this peculiarity lay in the 'General Rule' that Tinctoris places before all others: 'every counterpoint must begin and end with a perfect consonance.' The empty-sounding fifth at the end has a quality of its own; there is something sublime, almost awesome about it—it is like a glimpse into the depths of the night heavens, like a thought of eternity. Therefore this essentially sublime close is more suitable for sacred compositions than for secular chansons, where it is also used frequently, its effect wearing thin through continual recurrence. If the third does appear in the closing chord, it must be the major, not the minor, third—and Aron advises, where necessary, to place the sharp by the note (which, however, is done only exceptionally). The minor third above the root Papius[19] calls the worst of intervals."[20]

6. JE (SE) SUIS TROP JEUNETTE Anon. 4 v. f. 9'–10

CONCORDANCE:
Florence 176, f. 111'–113, Raulin. Textual incipit in three highest of four voices.

MONOPHONIC VERSION:
Paris 12744, f. 17. Published in Paris-Gevaert, *Chansons*, no. 22. Also published in Cauchie, "L'Odhecaton," p. 149.

[16] A possible source for the first part of this phrase is no. 88, *En venant de Lyon* (another variant of our melody), in Paris-Gevaert, *Chansons*. This melody seems to be a hybrid, for it starts in the major but ends in the minor mode. One might also compare the opening notes of the refrain of the "major" version, Paris-Gevaert, no. 71.

[17] André Pirro, in his *Histoire de la musique de la fin du XIVᵉ siècle à la fin du XVIᵉ* (Paris, 1940), p. 225, comments that Compère's "liking for the burlesque introduces a kind of sneer in *Lourdaud, Lourdaud*, and his seriousness, when he denounces the risks of marriage, is that of an informed scoffer."

[18] See Edward E. Lowinsky, "The Function of Conflicting Signatures in Early Polyphonic Music," *Musical Quarterly*, XXXI (1945), 241.

[19] Andreas Papius (1551–81) was born in Ghent, educated for the priesthood in Cologne and Louvain, and drowned while swimming in the Maas River in his thirtieth year. His most important work was his treatise *De consonantiis seu pro diatessaron libri duo* (Antwerp, 1581), in which he discusses the character of the dissonant and consonant intervals. He is perhaps best known for classifying the interval of the fourth as a consonance, approving its use even in two-part writing. See *Die Musik in Geschichte und Gegenwart*, s.v. "Papius." See also Ambros, *Geschichte der Musik*, III, 164–65.

[20] Ambros, *Geschichte der Musik*, III, 115.

MODERN EDITION:
Cauchie, "L'Odhecaton," pp. 150–52 (after *Canti B* 6).

RELATED COMPOSITIONS:
See Howard Mayer Brown, *Music in the French Secular Theater, 1400–1550* (Cambridge, Mass., 1963), "Catalogue," no. 219.

TEXT:

> Too young am I for love's delight,
> Though wanting it with all my might.
>
> Should my love appear, he'll have my heart.
> From all my kin I'll gladly part,
> And in the woods alone with him
> In beds of violet flee boredom grim.
> > Too young am I, etc.
>
> If he'll promise and surely swear
> For me alone always to care,
> No other lover will have me,
> No king, nor duke, nor grand marquis.
> > Too young am I, etc.

The text of this *virelai* is found in Paris 12744. Gaston Paris reports that the refrain and first couplet appear written by hand in the Bibliothèque Nationale copy of *Premier livre des chansons à deux parties*, published by Le Roy and Ballard (RISM [c. 1555]²⁴); the first stanza is also in Attaingnant 1529² *31 Chansons*.

E. Heldt points out in her edition (Heldt, *Französische Virelais*, no. 3, p. 60) that this is an irregular *virelai*, having the break after the fifth syllable instead of after the fourth.

Lines four (*clos*) and ten (*clos*) contain 14 syllables in place of the usual 10 (11). Since in each case the additional word is similar to another in the line, it may be that these two words are variants and that the original lines had the normal 10 (11) syllables; or it may be that popular influence extended the lines in an effort to make the meaning more inclusive. Both words in question could easily be either variants or intensifiers. Heldt omits the three syllables in line four and in line ten brackets the word in question. The music of *Canti B* calls for a line of fourteen syllables, but the same notes are repeated in each case, thus supporting the hypothesis. The original may well have had a basically ten-syllable line. Modern reading would give six syllables in the first half of each line, since the ending is in every case a neutral *e* and thus a weak ending, and five syllables in the second half which has a strong ending. The music supports this sequence.

The texts are essentially the same. This reading is based on Paris-Gevaert, *Chansons*.

1. *Canti B* incipit begins with "se." This could be the modern "si"="if" or a scribal confusion between J and S. The first word might logically be "je."
3. poste = podeste
4. Heldt, *Französische Virelais*: "mon frère " (in Paris-Gevaert) omitted to make line of 10 syllables.
5. Heldt: "M'en iray" for Paris-Gevaert "Et yray."
9. Heldt: "prisée" (in Paris-Gevaert) bracketed to show line of 10 syllables.

Paris reports variants from Attaingnant 1529² *31 Chansons* and Le Roy and Ballard, *Premier livre des chansons à deux parties*. Line five in Attaingnant reads "m'en yray jouer seullette au joly bocquet"; line six in Le Roy and Ballard reads "cueillir violette mon amy et moy."

MUSIC:

An unidentified composer, Raulin, has made a very modest arrangement of the melody, setting it forth without embellishment and without pause (except for a break of two measures between stanza and final refrain, mm. 40–41). An interesting feature is the "migration" of the *cantus firmus*. The initial refrain and the *ouvert* are assigned to the tenor (mm. 4–21); the *clos* and *tierce* to the alto (mm. 22–39); whereupon the *cantus firmus* returns to the tenor for the final refrain (mm. 42–54). The work opens with anticipatory imitations of the tenor by bass, alto, and soprano in turn. These imitations, as part of the setting of the initial refrain (mm. 1–15), are recapitulated for the final refrain (mm. 39–54); they are obscured, however, by the overlapping end of the *tierce* and some repetitions of tenor D (mm. 38–41) used to fill out the harmonies.

Raulin's work was hardly intended to be sung. Not only are rests infrequent, but the phrase structure expected by a singer is virtually non-existent in the contrapuntal voices which lack independence. The curiously static passage in the tenor (mm. 22–41) consisting either of rests or of long-held, casually placed notes on D, presents a special difficulty for a singer seeking the right words. (An editor also finds it well-nigh impossible to place text in the unthematic parts.) A soloist (preferably a tenor) could, however, sing the *cantus firmus*. A return to the beginning for the second stanza could be made at measures 39–40 (the superius completing its phrase in m. 40, and the tenor omitting mm. 40–41); after the second stanza the final refrain could be used as in measures 39–54.

The composer's name is given with this music in

Florence 176. Owing to the carelessness with which the capital initial was written, some musicologists have read the name as "Xarolin" (Jeppesen in the *Kopenhagener Chansonnier*, p. lxxii, when listing the composers represented in Florence 176) or "Xaulin" (Wolf, *Notationskunde*, I, 450) or "Xavlin [=Raoulin]" (Bianca Becherini, *Catalogo dei manoscritti musicali della Biblioteca Nazionale di Firenze* [Kassel, 1959], p. 74, MS Florence 176, where the composer is represented by three compositions).[21]

To my eye, the initial should be read "R," the name, therefore, Raulin.[22] But none of the well-known composers of the late fifteenth century is of this name. An older composer, Raulin de Vaux, is named in the famous Canonici manuscript.[23] In the Introduction, E. W. B. Nicholson states that in his attempt to identify this composer he found only that "the surname Raulin is found in the diocese of Cambrai in 1451 . . .; there is a Vaux-sous-Laons between 20 and 30 miles S. of Cambrai."[24]

Many carols were written in the sixteenth century, and frequently popular melodies of the day were cited as *timbres*. Five carols using melodies found in *Canti B* are listed by Hugues Vaganay.[25] The carol *Nouellet, nouellet viste / Chantons a Lyon* was to be sung "Sur: *Je suis trop jeunette / Pour avoir mari. / Liron, lirons, viste.*" This wording is not precisely that of the text of *Canti B* 6, but may be a variant text used with this melody. In an article on the collection containing this carol Jean Babelon gives its complete text.[26]

---

[21] See also Becherini's article "Autori minori nel codice fiorentino Magl. XIX. 176," *Revue belge de musicologie*, IV (1950), 27. Becherini identifies Xaulin and Raulin, referring to an article by Geneviève Thibault in the French *Revue de musicologie* (1929), p. 286.

[22] A similar initial may be seen in Brussels 228, f. 19'–20. No one would here question that the chanson starts *Reuenez tout regret*.

[23] *Dufay and His Contemporaries. Fifty Compositions (Ranging from about A.D. 1400 to 1440) Transcribed from Ms. Canonici misc. 213, in the Bodleian Library, Oxford*, by J. F. R. Stainer and C. Stainer. With an Introduction by E. W. B. Nicholson and a Critical Analysis of the Music by Sir John Stainer (London, 1898).

[24] *Ibid.*, p. xvi.

[25] *Les Recueils de noëls imprimés à Lyon au XVIe siècle. Essai de bibliographie suivi de quelques textes*, ed. Hugues Vaganay (Autun, 1935).

[26] "La Fleur des noels [Lyon, 1535]," *Revue des livres anciens*, I (1913–14), 369–404. The carol (19 stanzas) is found on pp. 391–94. Babelon states that Ferdinand Columbus owned a copy of this collection. See also Babelon's *La Bibliothèque française de Fernand Colomb* (Paris, 1913).

---

7. *CE N'EST PAS JEU* Pe. de la rue 4 v. f. 10'–11

CONCORDANCES:

Brussels 228, f. 5'–6, Anon. Text in all four voices.
Brussels 11239, f. 23', de la Rue. S and T only; text in both.
Rome Vat. 11953, f. 11'–12, Anon. B only; with textual incipit.
Egenolff [c. 1535][14] *Lieder*, Vol. I, no. 18, Anon. S only (with textual incipit); pitched a fifth lower than in *Canti B*.

MODERN EDITIONS:

Maldeghem, *Trésor musical (profane)*, Vol. XX (1884), no. 11, pp. 21–22 (= Reese, "Maldeghem," no. 322).
Picker, *Chanson Albums*, pp. 188–91 (after Brussels 228).
Picker, "Chanson Albums," pp. 266–69 (after Brussels 228).

TEXT:

> This kind of luck's a sorry jest,
> To have to leave what one loves best.
> Indeed I know it's not his fault,
> But fortune's wheel come to a halt.
>
> Be certain, then, that I'm distraught
> To leave the love I've always sought.
>   This kind of luck, etc.
>
> I've the reverse of all my dreams,
> And none to comfort me, it seems.
> But all this matters not a jot,
> Provided me he's not forgot.
>   This kind of luck, etc.

This *rondeau quatrain* is found in Brussels 228 and Brussels 11239. Gachet, *Albums et oeuvres poétiques*, pp. 72–73, Françon, *Albums poétiques*, no. 107, and Santander, *Mémoire historique*, p. 142, follow Brussels 228, where the complete text is given; Françon, no. 94, Gachet, p. 67, and Santander, p. 144, give the first two lines of text only after Brussels 11239. Hasselt, *Essai sur l'histoire*, p. 279, probably follows Brussels 228, as does this edition.

3. Gachet: seurs
   Hasselt: seur
   The feminine form "sceure" is grammatically correct but gives an extra syllable.
   sy = aussi
4. Brussels 11239: "me" lacking
9. Hasselt: Et s'y n'ayme qui . . .

MUSIC:

In this setting of *Ce n'est pas jeu*, Pierre de la Rue makes some radical departures from the contemporary manner of setting a *rondeau quatrain* to music. Normally the refrain is through-composed and shows a strong cadence at the close of the second line of text. La Rue observes the latter convention, but, as a setting for the last line of the refrain, recapitulates the music composed for the first line of the refrain (mm. 1–12), altering only the last three measures to give greater finality to the cadence. His polyphony thus takes on a three-part form.[27]

Equally notable is his treatment of the first hemistich of the *rondeau*. The melodic line given "Ce n'est pas jeu" is six measures in length and divides into three segments: *a*, *b*, and *c*, each of two measures. Soprano and alto start together, the alto singing segment *a* while the soprano sings *b* (mm. 1–2). In measure 3 the tenor enters with segment *a* at the fifth below, while the alto is performing *b* and the soprano *c*. Again, after two measures this combination of motives is duplicated a fifth lower as the bass enters with *a* (the tenor having *b* and the alto *c*). In measure 7 the soprano, having already sung motives *b* and *c* (mm. 1–4), presents segment *a*. Measure 8 contains the only suggestion of "double counterpoint," as the alto recapitulates the first half of *a* while the bass is starting segment *b*.

This carefully organized exposition seems to display greater interest in the music itself than in the words. Segment *a* sets the words "Ce n'est pas" to repeated notes with the values half, quarter, quarter, known as the "*canzona* rhythm."

At the beginning of Part II (mm. 32 ff.), La Rue appears to have attempted this same technique, and again employs the *canzona* rhythm. This second exposition, however, is compressed into about four measures, the setting of the complete line into nine, and Part II is some ten measures shorter than Part I.

The composition shows a mixture of melismatic and syllabic treatment of the words. The frequent use of rests to set off phrases and motives deepens the impression that repetition of portions of text was intended by La Rue, a feature not out of keeping with his obviously advanced compositional technique.[28]

(See also Introduction, p. xi.)

---

[27] This composition is analyzed in Martin Picker, "The Chanson Albums of Marguerite of Austria: MSS. 228 and 11239 of the Bibliothèque Royale de Belgique, Brussels," *Annales musicologiques*, VI (1958–63), 161–62. The "syncopated E-flat" in measure 9 (and 49) of the Brussels manuscript appears on the third beat (not the second) in *Canti B*. The dissonances mentioned by Picker as occurring on beat two are thus removed. Although *Canti B* is the earlier of the two sources we have for the alto, one would expect Brussels 228 to have the definitive reading.

[28] *Ce n'est pas jeu* (with choreography) is listed as a *basse danse* in *S'ensuyvent plusieurs Basses dances tant communes que*

---

8. *L'AUTRIER QUE PASSA* Busnoys 4 v.
f. 11′–12

CONCORDANCES: None.

TEXT: ·

Busnois' composition is probably a setting of a popular song of the day. The expression "L'autr'ier" (="L'autre jour") was a favorite beginning for popular songs relating amorous adventures. Brown, *Music in the French Secular Theater*, lists a large number of songs with beginnings of this kind under nos. 254–58 of his "Catalogue."

MUSIC:

The music divides about equally into three sections, of which the first and third are in duple meter, the second in triple meter. Triplets are used near the end of Section 1 as an anticipation of the triple meter, but they also reappear in Section 3. Busnois' harmonic style seems somewhat uneven. On the one hand, there is the "modern" and highly effective measure 12, or the fine suspension in measures 17–18; on the other hand, the weak beginning of Section 2 (m. 26) or the 6/4 chord in the second half of measure 53 (the E of the alto may be a misprint for F, but occurs in both editions of *Canti B*, our only source for this work).

Several whole notes, preceded and followed by whole rests in Section 1, were probably used merely to fill out the harmonies (see also m. 26, bass, and m. 70, alto; cf. also *Canti B* 6, tenor, mm. 28–41).

---

9. *RÉVEILLEZ-VOUS* Anon. 4 v. f. 12′–13

CONCORDANCES:
Regensburg C 120, pp. 18–19, Anon. Incipit in two of four voices.
Egenolff [c. 1535][14] *Lieder*, Vol. I, no. 19, Anon. Superius only, with textual incipit.

MONOPHONIC VERSION:
Paris 12744, no. 138. Published in Gérold, *Chansons populaires*, no. 45; Aubry, *Huit chants héroïques*, musical section, pp. 8–9; Barbier, *Histoire de France*, pp. 38–39; Paris-Gevaert, *Chansons*.

MODERN EDITION:
Brown, *Theatrical Chansons*, no. 53 (after *Canti B* 9; text after Paris-Gevaert, *Chansons*).

---

incommunes ... (Paris, Bibliothèque Nationale, Collection Rothschild). See François Lesure, "Danses et chansons à danser au début du XVIe siècle," *Recueil de travaux offert à M. Clovis Brunel* (Paris, 1955), pp. 176–84.

TEXT:

> Burgundians and Picards, awake!
> Grab each of you a good, stout stake,
> For spring is here, it is the season.
> War and blows need no more reason.
>
> Some speak of war nor could know less.
> I swear by God—a sorry mess.
> Many a soldier, pal, in strife
> Has lost his armor, goods, and life.
>
> Austria's Duke's away in Holland,
> With his Picards in Flanders' lowland,
> Who night and day to him do pray
> 'Gainst Burgundy to lead the way.
>
> Farewell, Bezançon, and you Salins,
> Farewell to Beaulnes, city of wines.
> The Picards have drunk them, the Flemish will pay
> Four pastars a pint, or they'll rue the day.

The text of this chanson appears only in Paris 12744; it has been edited by Gaston Paris.

The subject matter is not entirely clear. Paris suggests that the author was a Picard serving under Maximilian of Austria (1459–1519), singing of what he has done and hopes to do. Although a professional soldier, he sees the sordid side of war as well as the adventurous side. Aubry and Gérold have followed Paris in editing this text. Aubry speaks of "a bitter flavor and a singular power of expression which, despite the very obscurity of the piece, succeeds in interesting us." He feels that the author of the chanson was one of the soldiers. Gérold (p. 98) adds that "the primitive chanson has . . . supplied a kind of mill for a large number of later poetic improvisations."

The chanson consists of four stanzas in quatrains, without refrain. The *Canti B* melody requires a decasyllabic line for lines one, five, nine, and thirteen. It is probable that in the original form the chanson was duodecasyllabic throughout.

MUSIC:

This anonymous polyphonic arrangement is an example of the "paraphrase" technique of treating a melody. Each of the four phrases of the popular tune appears in each voice,[29] but no voice presents all four phrases in direct succession as a *cantus firmus*. Consistent imitation pervades the setting, but the "sections" are so dovetailed that this technique is obscured. In the first

[29] (Phrase) I: (m.) 1 (A), 2 (B), 6 (S), 7 (T); II: 10 (A), 11 (B), 13 (S), 14 (T); III: 19 (A), 20 (B), 24 (S), 25 (T); IV: 29 (B), 31 (A), 35 (T), 39 (S). Phrase three is transposed up a fourth, phrase four up a fifth, in alto and bass.

36

three sections the last statement of the phrase is made by the tenor; in the last section, by the soprano.

(See also Introduction, pp. xiv–xv.)

10. *EN CHAMBRE POLIE*   Anon. 4 v.   f. 13′–14

CONCORDANCE:

Egenolff [c. 1535][14] *Lieder*, Vol. I, no. 20, Anon. Superius only, with textual incipit.

MUSIC:

In the absence of the complete text of *En chambre polie* it is impossible to speak with certainty about its form. The music, however, is divided quite clearly into four sections by four points of imitation. A strong cadence occurs in measures 22–23, overlapping the first statement of the third theme; that is, in a position that may have been the middle of the refrain of a *rondeau quatrain*. No *signum* appears here, however, to give support to this conjecture.

The composer shows a liking for the interval of the third throughout this work. In the opening measures the bass accompanies the first motive of the tenor in parallel thirds for several beats. The quarter rest in the tenor (m. 3) may have marked the caesura of a metrical line of ten syllables (four plus six, as in the courtly *rondeau*). The motive following the rest is in sequence with the end of the first motive, thus allowing for more series of thirds (or tenths) as each new voice brings the subject.

In the second exposition, what might be termed a counter-subject accompanies the subject in parallel thirds (see the bass and alto, mm. 14:4 ff.; tenor and alto, mm. 17:4 ff.). The scalar fourth subject also lends itself to treatment in parallel thirds as the various entries overlap each other. A by-product of this treatment seems to be the many "chords" consisting of doubled root and doubled third (mm. 6:1, 25:1, 27:1, 39:2); or, root, fifth, and doubled third (mm. 8:4, 10:4, 20:3, 29:3, 30:1); or, root and doubled third in three-part writing (mm. 20:1, 36:3); etc. As may be expected (since they involve the leap of a third), both *cambiata* and *échappée* are found—as well as the usual passing tone, neighboring tone, and suspension.

11. *JE SUIZ AMIE DU FOURRIER*   Anon.   4 v. f. 14′–15

CONCORDANCES:

Cortona 95–96, Paris 1817, no. 9, Anon. Text in S, A, T; B wanting.

Florence 107bis, f. 11′–12, Anon. Incipit in highest of four voices.

Florence 164–167, no. 64, Anon. Text in all voices.

Rome C. G. XIII, 27, f. 111′–112, Loyset Compere. Incipit in highest of four voices.

Egenolff [c. 1535][14] *Lieder*, Vol. I, no. 21, Anon. Superius only, with textual incipit.

TEXT:

> I'm the billet sergeant's love, hey! hey!
> The army boys call me their dove.
> In the village I was caught
> Leaving one morn before I ought, hey! hey!
>
> If my pa had given me, hey! hey!
> My hundred ecus dowry,
> This outrage I'd have never done,
> To yield myself to everyone, hey! hey!

The words of this little chanson *à refrain* appear in only two manuscripts: Florence 164–167 and Cortona 95–96, Paris 1817. Of the latter manuscript, altus and superius (Cortona 95–96) were published by Renier, "Mazzetto di poesie" (no. 9); tenor (Paris 1817) by Gröber, "Liederbücher von Cortona" (no. 9).

Renier and Florence 164–167 give the refrain as one word: "orales," following lines one, four, five, and eight; Gröber divides the chanson into two stanzas of four lines each, with the refrain "Or alez" after lines one and five. This edition generally follows Gröber, but makes the refrain a separate line, thus creating a chanson of twelve lines with the refrain appearing as lines two, six, eight, and twelve. Whereas the music calls for a "changing refrain," including a full line plus the words "Or alez," the meaning of the text requires these lines to be an integral part of the poem, with only the two words as refrain.

1. fourrier, forier: a quartermaster sergeant
4. Renier: prise
   Florence 164–167: a un vilage (superius)
7. Renier: me
   Florence 164–167: mu, mes
9. Florence 164–167: . . . a mariagie (superius)

MUSIC:

Compère gives a through-composed setting of two stanzas of a popular song in the Mixolydian mode, a pleasant change from the minor modes—especially the Dorian—favored by the composers represented in the Petrucci anthologies. In the second stanza Compère achieves an increase in speed by reducing note values by half, and a section in homophony provides an effective ending.

12. *MON MARY M'A DIFFAMÉE* De Orto
4 v. f. 15′–16

CONCORDANCES: None.

MONOPHONIC VERSION:

Paris 12744, f. 75′. Published in Paris-Gevaert, *Chansons*, no. 111.

RELATED COMPOSITIONS:

1. Petrucci 1504³ *Canti C*, f. 44′–45, Anon. Incipit "Mon mari ma defamee" in each of four voices.
2a. London Add. 35087, f. 21′–22, Anon. The text occurs in all three voices.
2b. Tournai 94, f. 15–15′, Anon. Tenor only, with text. This tenor agrees with the tenor of London Add. 35087.
3. Paris 1597, f. 69′–71, Anon. Text in each of four voices.
4. Antico 1520³ *Motetti novi e chanzoni*, f. 37′–38, Adrien. Two parts, both with text, are given; two others are to be realized in performance to form a double canon.

These four polyphonic compositions are all arrangements of the same popular melody; they are different from *Canti B* 12 and from each other.

TEXT:

> Oh, how my husband slandered me
> Because to my true love I'd cleave,
> Because with him I'd rather be,
> And my love I'd never leave.
> Ah, my dear,
> To spite my husband drear,
> Who's always beating me, and more,
> Henceforth I'll do worse than before.
>
> Some have said I am to blame:
> To take a lover I would dare.
> It pleases me, I do so claim,
> It is indeed my sweetest care.
> Ah, my dear,
> To spite my husband drear,
> Who isn't worth a thin red cent,
> Far worse I'll do, on this I'm bent.
>
> When in dark of night I lie
> In the arms of him I love,
> I think that I shall faint or die
> Of love's delight—I cannot move.
> Ah, my dear,
> Would to God I need not see
> My husband for a century!
> We'd pass the time in joy and glee.
>
> —If my sweet love is so irate,
> I'm just as sad as I can be
> That he should her humiliate
> Just because of love of me.—

Ah, my dear,
To spite my husband drear,
Whose kindest word to me's a curse,
Henceforth you know I'll do much worse.

If I should now lose my good name
For love of him I truly love,
You'll know I'm not at all to blame,
For sweet and handsome is my love.
Ah, my dear,
Not half a day without a tear
Have I had with this vile man.
To him I'll do the worst I can.

The words of this chanson have been preserved in several manuscripts. The present edition follows Paris-Gevaert, *Chansons.* Tournai 94 and Paris 1597 have only the first stanza. Lotrian 1543 *Sensuyt plusieurs belles chansons,* f. 96, has three stanzas, but differs from Paris-Gevaert after the first stanza. Variants are given here from Paris 1597, Antico 1520[3] *Motetti novi e chanzoni,* Tournai 94, and Lotrian only.

E. Heldt calls this poem a chanson with a refrain of two lines, *Hé! mon amy / En despit de mon mary.* Both music and content point rather to a refrain of four lines. Although the last two lines of the refrain differ from stanza to stanza, the same may be said of the second line of Heldt's two-line refrain (compare stanzas three and five). The omission of the final two lines of the refrain in stanzas two and three of Lotrian may give the impression that the refrain has but two lines. The final two lines appear in the first stanza, however, and it is just as possible that the singer was expected to continue the refrain of four lines in the other stanzas. Furthermore, the content of the four-line refrain forms a unit quite apart from the narrative proper. There would, then, in the most complete version of the poem, be five stanzas of four lines each, with a four-line refrain after each stanza. The final line of this four-line refrain changes only in the third stanza, "Nous nous donrrions du bon temps" replacing "Je feray pis que davant."

In content the song is yet another lament of a *mal mariée,* with one stanza (the fourth) which expresses the feelings of the *amy* on the subject. Paris has bracketed this stanza as though to indicate that it did not belong in the original chanson.

2. Paris 1597: Et en despit de mon amy
3. Paris-Gevaert: De. All other sources give "pour."
5. Paris 1597: Et mon amy et mon amy
   Lotrian: O mon amy
   Tournai 94 and Antico omit this line.

7. Paris 1597: Qui m'y va ainsi batant
   Tournai 94 inserts a line between lines seven and eight of Paris-Gevaert: Car al jen seray . . .; the reading is generally poor. A miniature covering the ends of the lines makes it impossible to distinguish the letters.
8. Lotrian, Paris 1597, Tournai 94: devant
   Lotrian: J'en
   Tournai 94: J'en seray pie . . .
   Paris 1597: "pirs," confusion between "pis" and "pire"
36. Paris-Gevaert gives correct form, "coinct," as variant.

Stanzas two and three of Lotrian read:

Quand j'estaye couchée
Entre les bras de mon amy,
Je n'estoye pas fâchée
Comme je suis aujourd'huy.
O, mon amy,
En despit de mon mary.

J'ay esté mainte nuyctée
Couchée avec mon amy,
Que l'on me cuidoit couchée
En mon lict avecques mon mary.
O, mon amy,
En despit de mon mary.

(Whenever I was lying
In the arms of him I love,
Be sure I was not crying
As I do now and here.
Oh, my dear,
I spite my husband drear.

I have on many a night
Lain with my lover dear,
When all thought me tucked in right,
In bed beside my husband sere.
Oh, my dear,
I spite my husband drear.)

Two lines of the refrain are lacking in these stanzas.

MUSIC:

De Orto places the popular melody in strict canon at the fifth below in the inner parts, the alto functioning as *dux,* the tenor entering one measure later as *comes.*

The form of this song (with the cross rhyme at the beginning and the repetition of the melodic setting of lines one and two for lines three and four) resembles that of the courtly ballade. The short line "Hé! mon amy" would have no place in a ballade, but its melodic setting is merely an echo of the end of the second musical phrase, and in a later polyphonic setting of the melody by Willaert, this short line is lacking. Without it, the stanza has the normal length of a ballade. The use of the same line of words at the end of each stanza is a familiar feature of the ballade, in which this line is called the refrain. Other features, however, such as the general content of the poetry, its phraseology, and the like, prove that the song is not of courtly derivation and takes only the form of the ballade.

The phrases of the melody call for an interesting variety of modal cadences. In Paris 12744 the Dorian melody is in untransposed position; there it shows phrases ending on G and E, with the last phrase cadencing on D. In De Orto's canonic setting, two cadences occur one measure apart at the end of every line of text. The melody is transposed down a fifth for use as *dux* (alto), and down two fifths for use as *comes* (tenor), but only the bass shows a signature of two flats, the other parts having one flat. The stronger cadence is usually placed at the end of the tenor phrase (twice transposed) and the work closes in Dorian, twice transposed. A rather large number of E-flats have to be added in accordance with the rules of *musica ficta* to produce the intended modal reading. De Orto writes the expected cadences: Mixolydian (mm. 6–7 and mm. 18–19), Phrygian (mm. 10–11 and mm. 21–22), and Dorian (m. 26 and mm. 31–32)—all in transposition. The last phrase of the refrain cadences in the middle of a measure (tenor, m. 26); De Orto repeats this phrase, lengthening the first hemistich by half a measure, the remainder being shifted similarly to close on the first of the measure. Even with this extension, De Orto's work is a short one—only thirty-two measures—but it is an attractive and effective canonic chanson.

The little work opens with imitation, thus appearing perhaps deceptively as if it were meant to be sung. A closer look at the ensuing passages in soprano and bass, however, leads to the conclusion that these outer parts were not intended for voices. Although not unvocal, they seldom seem to have been contrived in reference to the lines of text. The words have been placed in the canonic voices (in the present edition) to show the complete song arranged by De Orto, and these parts could, of course, be sung if desired. A fairly strong—and suitable—cadence appears in measure 11, making possible a repeat *da capo* for the third and fourth lines of text. The notation of the work gives no sign, however, that a repeat was intended.

13. *CELA SANS PLUS*   Obreht   4 v.   f. 16'–17

CONCORDANCE:
Egenolff [c. 1535][14] *Lieder*, Vol. I, no. 22, Anon. Superius only, with incipit.

MODERN EDITION:
Wolf, *Obrecht: Wereldlijke Werken*, pp. 12–13 (after *Canti B*).

RELATED COMPOSITIONS:
See *Canti B* 16 and 24.

TEXT:

> Just that for me, and then, oh, boy!
> Sweet shepherdess so fair and nice,
> Free my heart from your prison's vise.
> Just that for me, and then, oh, boy!

Only four lines of the text *Cela sans plus* survive. They are found complete in Florence 176, f. 0'; first and last lines occur in Seville 5–I–43, f. 54'–55; the first line only appears in Florence 229, Bologna Q 17, and elsewhere.[30] In Florence 176 the lines show Italian influence in the spelling of the words. Molinet quotes line one,[31] giving it as follows: "Cela sans plus et puis hola!" The second line probably should read "Gentille bergère, belle de bon renom." Ideas similar to those expressed in the third line, "Jetes mon cueur hors de vous prison," are found in popular songs of the period; for example, "Celle qui tient mon coeur en sa prison" (Gérold, *Manuscrit de Bayeux*, no. 42, line 10); "Otez mon cueur hors de pencée" (Gérold, *Manuscrit de Bayeux*, no. 58, line 11); or, "Dame Venus tient mon cueur en prison" (Paris-Gevaert, *Chansons*, no. 84, line 1).

The rhyme scheme, *abba*, is that of the *rondeau quatrain*, so there is a slight possibility that these lines are the surviving remnant of a *rondeau*; other factors, however, argue even more forcibly against this possibility. First, the use of the same wording for the first and last lines is neither normal nor proper for the refrain of a *rondeau*; this construction seems rather to signify a stanza of two lines preceded and followed by a refrain of one line, as in a strophic song from the

---

[30] It occurs as the last line of *Si je fet ung cop* (Cortona 95–96, Paris 1817), where the tenor sings the melody of *Cela sans plus*. The three extant parts of this manuscript are identical with Japart's *Tan bien* (Odhecaton 34).

[31] As the first line of stanza 26 of *Le Débat du viel gendarme et du viel amoureux*. See *Les Faictz et Dictz de Jean Molinet*, ed. Noël Dupire (3 vols.; Paris, 1936–39), II, 616–27. In several of the long poems by this poet-musician, each stanza begins and ends by quoting the opening line of a well-known song, usually a *rondeau* or *virelai* of courtly origin.

popular literature. Second, lines one and four have essentially the same musical setting—again suggestive of a one-line refrain. Third, the words are set syllabically—the melody lies in both alto and tenor of Obrecht's setting—and this would not be the situation if this voice were drawn from a freely composed setting of a courtly *rondeau*. Fourth, the opening and closing lines are in a minor mode, whereas the inner lines move in a major framework; this dichotomy would not be suitable in a setting of a *rondeau* refrain, which must allow for a return to the beginning after the second line of text. (The *signum* usually marking this point in settings of *rondeaux* is not found in a single setting of *Cela sans plus*.)

Perhaps it was the fascination of the peculiar juxtaposition of modal phrases that attracted so many composers to this melody. Or did the appeal lie in its stanzas, of which only one has come down to us? The use of *double entendre* was a favorite conceit of the poets of the period, and it would appear that our text may have been a poem of this type.[32]

MUSIC:

Two settings of the song found their way into *Canti B*: this arrangement by Obrecht (not found complete elsewhere) and that by Colinet de Lannoy, *Canti B* 16. Lannoy places his cantus in canon at the octave between the outer parts; Obrecht chooses canon at the unison between alto and tenor. Both composers start similarly by having a non-canonic part announce the initial motive before the canon starts. Obrecht then has this voice (his superius) continue in smaller note-values against the long opening note of the *dux*, thus setting the work in motion immediately. The superius shows no other imitation of the *cantus firmus*, and the bass shows none at all. At measure 12, Obrecht starts the second phrase, but Lannoy has to wait until measure 14, since the interval of a fourth between the canonical parts involves the lowest-sounding voice of his three-part arrangement. Obrecht could place a suitable bass below this fourth (m. 12). When Obrecht reaches

measure 22 he sustains the tenor note for three measures and follows it with five measures of rest, as did Lannoy. Lannoy had to sustain the C if he wished to anticipate the next phase of the *dux* in his contra. Obrecht had no such reason for holding the C for three measures; it thus seems that it was Obrecht who borrowed his tenor from Lannoy, rather than the other way around.

Obrecht's tenor is identical with Lannoy's except at the very end, where he sustains the final tone for four measures. Lannoy maintains the interval of an octave between his voices, but Obrecht alters the interval to that of a fourth in measure 33; this shift enabled him to fill in the five measures (mm. 33–37) left empty by Lannoy, and also to repeat this final phrase in time to cadence with the tenor in measure 47. Here he writes a deceptive cadence and, surprisingly, closes in the mode of the transposed final phrase of the alto and the inner phrases of the *cantus prius factus*.

The lack of additional sources for Obrecht's work is to be regretted, for they might have thrown some light on the inscription "Obreht In missa" given with the music in *Canti B*.[33] If this means that this music is drawn from a *Missa Cela sans plus* by Obrecht, it is all that is known of this Mass today.

14. *BON TEMPS* Anon. 4 v. f. 17′–18

CONCORDANCES: None.

MODERN EDITION:
Wolf, *Obrecht: Missen*, XVI, 126.

RELATED COMPOSITIONS:
See Brown, *Music in the French Secular Theater*, "Catalogue," no. 38.

TEXT:

> Good Times, will you e'er retrieve
> The noble strength for which we grieve,
> So all those in the realm of France
> Can live in Peace's radiance?

The melody as found in *Canti B* appears elsewhere in variant forms. While no text appears in *Canti B*, sections of seemingly relevant text have been found in other sources, including a quodlibet and a drinking song. Two voices of the quodlibet (Florence 2442, no.

[32] See Helen Hewitt, *Odhecaton*. The Notes on the Literary Texts, no. 61, discuss this stanza, which seems to employ double meanings. In a Glossary appended to his article "Pièces joyeuses du XVᵉ siècle," *Revue de philologie française et de littérature*, XXI (1907), 193, Pierre Champion lists "cela" as meaning "l'amour." Several poems in *Le Parnasse satyrique du quinzième siècle: Anthologie de pièces libres*, ed. Marcel Schwob (Paris, 1905), use "cela" in this sense: nos. 4, 18, and 43, for example. They also involve the exclamation "Hola!"

[33] A similar inscription appearing with a late setting of *Fors seullement* in a manuscript at Cividale is also unexplained as yet. It reads: "Andreas *pleni*." I am indebted to Professor Lewis Lockwood of Princeton University for bringing this work, and its heading, to my attention.

49) open with what are probably deviations from the basic verses:

> (altus) Bon temps, ne viendra-tu jamaiz?
> Tu m'a donné merencollie
>
> (superius) Bon temps, je ne te puis laissier,
> Tu m'as t'amour donnée.
>
> (Good times, will you ne'er appear?
> You've made me melancholic.
>
> Good times, I cannot give you up,
> For you have given me your love.)

A close study of the settings makes it fairly certain that the following text was the one used with the *Canti B* setting:

> Bon temps, reviendras-tu jamais
> A ta noble puissance,
> Que nous puissions tous vivre en paix
> Au royaulme de France?

This quatrain is found in a stage-play of the period, "Farce Nouvelle a cinq Parsonnages" (Cohen, *Recueil de farces*, p. 379; p. 358 shows three stanzas of a *contrafactum*, "Seigneurs et dames"), and is an alternative reading to that found in Copenhagen 1848 (p. 411), where in the contra *ne* precedes the verb in the first line and the two final lines show other differences:

> Por maintenir toujours en paix
> Le réaulme de France.

It would appear that, as was often the case in this period, the various texts show considerable liberty in the development of the song, depending on the aims and attitudes of the author or the copier. An excellent example of such virtuosity is the drinking song (Gérold, *Manuscrit de Bayeux*, no. 43) beginning:

> Bon vin, je ne te puis laissier,
> Je t'ay m'amour donée.
>
> (Good wine, I cannot give you up,
> For I have given you my love.)

(The text, only, is further published in Du Bois, *Vaux-de-Vire d'Olivier Basselin*, no. 31, and Gasté, *Chansons normandes*, no. 41, both after Paris 9346; and in Wolff, *Altfranzösische Volkslieder*, pp. 61–62, after Du Bois.) This four-stanza song may well have been sung both to the melody in the minor mode appearing in *Canti B* and to a major melody found in Gérold, *Manuscrit de Bayeux*, no. 43.

For a full treatment of the settings and texts for *Bon temps*, see Helen Hewitt, "A *Chanson rustique* of the Early Renaissance: *Bon Temps*," *Aspects of Medieval and Renaissance Music* (New York: W. W. Norton & Company, Inc., 1966), pp. 376–91.

MUSIC:

The anonymous arranger of *Bon temps* places the melody in the tenor without embellishment of any kind. His compositional plan, however, is strangely uneven. For the first two phrases (AB) he requires thirty measures for his elaborate scheme of anticipatory imitations in soprano, alto, and bass; since the last two phrases (AB′) follow without pause, and imitations are lacking, this second section covers only twelve measures, the exact length of the *cantus firmus*.

Too late for inclusion in my article on *Bon temps* I discovered mention of this melody in the article by Daniel Heartz entitled, "The Basse Dance: Its Evolution *circa* 1450 to 1550."[34] In Appendix III[35] of his article, Heartz gives the choreography to fifty-eight titles "appended to the curious dance treatise of Anthoine Arena, *Ad suos compagnones*, which may have been written as early as 1519."[36] Item no. 46 in this list reads: "*Bon temps* à 20 Pi / Pi / Mi / Pi."[37] The reader is referred to Heartz's article for the dance steps indicated by these abbreviations.

15. *A QUI DIR'ELLE SA PENCÉE*   Anon.   4 v.
    f. 18′–19

CONCORDANCES:
Bologna Q 18, f. 93′, Anon. Incipit, S, T. (The work is incomplete in this manuscript.)
Regensburg C 120, pp. 22–23, Anon. Incipit, S, T, B.
Egenolff [c. 1535][14] *Lieder*, Vol. I, no. 24, Anon. Superius only, with incipit.

MONOPHONIC VERSION:
Paris 12744, f. 9. Published in Paris-Gevaert, *Chansons*, no. 11.

RELATED COMPOSITION:
1a. Copenhagen 1848, p. 129, Anon. Text, S; incipit, A.
1b. Ulm 237[abcd]: a, f. 41; d, f. 40; Anon. Incipit in both voices.
    This duo, found in Copenhagen and Ulm, places the popular melody in the upper voice. The refrain words are those of Paris-Gevaert, *Chansons*, but the stanza differs.

[34] *Annales musicologiques*, VI (1958–63), 287–340.
[35] *Ibid.*, pp. 334–36.
[36] *Ibid.*, p. 298.
[37] *Ibid.*, p. 336.

TEXT:

> Oh, whom to tell what's on her mind,
> The girl who lovers cannot find?
> The girl who lovers cannot find,
> Oh, how can she go on this way?
> She's always wide awake,
> Aroused and sleepless for love's sake.
>> Oh, whom to tell, etc.
>
> Some girls there are who've more than one.
> With two, three, four, or more they've gone.
> But I don't have a single boy
> With whom I can discover joy.
> Alas, my good years do not lag,
> And my firm breast begins to sag.
>> Oh, whom to tell, etc.
>
> This human wish I do not borrow,
> This feeling I do not deny:
> That now, tonight, and not tomorrow,
> Though I am still young and spry,
> In mortal rage I'd rather die
> Than keep on living in such sorrow.
>> Oh, whom to tell, etc.

The text of this irregular *virelai* is found in Paris 12744. Lotrian 1543 *Sensuyt plusieurs belles chansons*, f. 5, has a variant of this text, which is different after line ten. Both Gaston Paris and Elisabeth Heldt (Heldt, *Französische Virelais*, no. 33, pp. 99–100) have edited the text; the present edition follows the Paris-Gevaert, *Chansons*, reading. References to Lotrian and Paris 12744 are as reported in Paris-Gevaert.

1. Lines one and two are missing in Lotrian. dir'elle = dira-t-elle
4. Paris 12744: Vit en tristesse
5. Lotrian: Elle ne dort ne nuict ne jour
6. Lotrian: Car . . .
7. Heldt: Elle a la pucë en l'oreille
   Lotrian: Ce sont amours
8. Paris 12744: "Et" omitted
9. Lotrian: dict-elle
10. Heldt: Il en y a . . .
19. annuyt = cette nuit
22. Heldt: vivrë en tel ennuy

MUSIC:

Although textually this *virelai* must be classified as irregular, its melody (found in Paris-Gevaert, *Chansons*) is both regular and clear in its form: two musical sections, of which the second has a sign for repeat. In contrast to original settings of courtly *virelais*, which consist of two sections of music only, to which the poetry is applied according to a traditional formula, this arrangement is a continuous setting of one stanza with enclosing refrains.

A comparison of those phrases of the popular melody that occur more than once shows that the composer altered them to suit his convenience. The version of the "refrain" melody as it appears with the *tierce* is closer to the reading in Paris-Gevaert, *Chansons*, than is the opening statement in the soprano, measures 3–11.

Possibly it was intended that only one stanza be sung, but additional stanzas are at hand and could be used. After reaching measure 56, the second (or third) stanza could be started by the alto in measure 11; or, preferably, a return to measure 1 could be made after measure 46, and measures 47–56 be reserved for use with the final refrain. Whereas most of the sections overlap, sharing one measure, the composer brings all motion to a stop in measure 46 (as again in m. 51, where triple meter is exchanged for duple), thus facilitating a return to measure 1.

16. *CELA SANS PLUS* (Index) Lannoy 4 v.
f. 19'–20

CONCORDANCES:
Rome 2856, f. 153'–154, Colinet de Lannoy. Incipit, S, T, A; above B: Jo. Martinj; below B: *Si placet*.
    The three original voices by Lannoy are also found in the following sources:
Bologna Q 16, f. 50'–51, Anon. Incipit in all voices.
Bologna Q 17, f. 19'–20, Colinet de Lannoy. Incipit in all voices.
Florence 176, f. 0'–1, Anon. Text, S; incipit, C.
Florence 178, f. 39'–40, Iosquin. Incipit, S.
Florence 229, f. 100'–101, Collinet de Lanoy. Incipit in each voice.
Rome C. G. XIII, 27, f. 86'–87, Colinet. Incipit, S.
Seville 5-I-43, f. 54'–55, Anon. Text, S; incipit, T, C.
Washington, Wolffheim, f. 91'–92, "par de Lannoy" (in a later hand). Incipit in all three voices.
Egenolff [c. 1535][14] *Lieder*, Vol. I, no. 23, Anon. Superius only, with incipit.

MODERN EDITIONS:
Wolf, *Notationskunde*, I, 395–97 (after Washington, Wolffheim).
Wolf, *Obrecht: Wereldlijke Werken*, pp. 83–84 (after Rome 2856).

FACSIMILE:
Wolf, *Notationskunde*, I, opp. p. 394 (of Washington, Wolffheim).

RELATED COMPOSITIONS:

1. *Canti B*, no. 13, "Obreht In missa." Incipit, S, A. The T is identical with that of Lannoy. See no. 13 of the present edition for concordances.
2. Regensburg C 120, pp. 316–317, Anon. Incipit, S, A. S and T are identical with those of Lannoy.
3a. Florence 107, f. 15′–16, Anon. Incipit in highest of five voices. (Index: "Celansa plus del gardinale di medici.")
3b. Basel F. X. 1–4, no. 105, Leo Papa Decimus. Incipit in each of five voices.
3c. Modena IV, f. 45′–46, Leo X. Pont. Max. Incipit in each of five voices.
3d. St. Gall 463, no. 203, Leo Papa Decimus. S and A only, with incipits.
3e. St. Gall 464, no. 203, Leo Papa Decimus. S and B only, with incipits.
   The T of Pope Leo X's work is identical with Lannoy's tenor.
4a. Bologna Q 19, f. 196′–197, Rigamundus. Incipit in each of five voices.
4b. Bologna Q 19, f. 203′, Anon. Tenor only, with incipit.
   In this work by Rigamundus, a tenor not identical with Lannoy's is used twice in succession. This voice, labeled "tenor," is written out again at the foot of f. 203′ possibly because difficult to read on f. 196′. A bass voice, with incipit "O dulcis amicha dei," appears at the top of f. 203′ but has no musical relation to the "tenor" given below it.
5. Copenhagen 1848, p. 140, Anon. Incipit, T.
   This three-part piece has the popular melody in the tenor.
6. Vienna 18746, no. 17, Lebrun. Incipit in all five voices.
   This work has S of *Canti B* 24 as its S; the lower voices employ the opening motive of "Cela sans plus."
7. Petrucci 1501 *Odhecaton*, no. 61, Josquin. Incipit in each of three voices.
   See Hewitt, *Odhecaton*, for concordances and discussion.

TEXT:

See *Canti B* 13.

MUSIC:

As the Casanatense Codex (Rome 2856) states, the bass of *Canti B* 16 is an optional part added by Johannes Martini to a setting originally composed for three voices by Colinet de Lannoy. Since this arrangement and the work by Obrecht (*Canti B* 13) are based on the same popular song, words and melody have already been discussed in connection with *Canti B* 13.

Because of the modal situation, the scribes differ in their assignment of signatures to the various voices:

a 3	♮, ♮, ♮:	Bologna Q 17, Florence 176, Florence 178, Florence 229, Seville 5-I-43	
	♭, ♮, ♮:	Rome C. G. XIII, 27, Washington, Wolffheim	
	♭, ♭, ♭:	Bologna Q 16	
a 4	♮, ♮, ♮, ♭:	*Canti B*	
	♭, ♭, ♭, ♭:	Rome 2856	

Several other arrangements of this tune are known. With the exception of the five-part work by Pope Leo X[38] and Lannoy's three-part setting, these pieces are found each in a single source; Lannoy's composition, however, is extant in ten sources (two of which show Martini's added bass), which suggests that it was the original work from which the others derived. A freely composed setting of a courtly *rondeau* or *virelai* often lends one or more voices to other compositions for use as *cantus firmi*.

In my opinion, Lannoy's work is not freely composed, but borrows its tenor[39] from the repertoire of popular music. Although this song does not occur in the monophonic chansonniers extant today, other works show it in variant forms and display complete independence of Lannoy's composition—if not lack of acquaintance with it. On the other hand, a group of compositions actually seem to have derived voices from Lannoy's setting: the identity of such important details as the exact number of preliminary and medial rests and the extension of cadential tones for two or three measures (obviously having no place in the original tune) point to the dependence of these works on Lannoy's setting.

An anonymous work a 4 in the Regensburg Codex has a superius and a tenor identical with those of Lannoy's work. At this period three-part works were frequently enlarged to the newer texture of four voices, but I know of no example of the reduction of four voices to three. It therefore seems that the Regensburg Anonymous borrowed from Lannoy. The tenor of Pope Leo's five-part setting is identical with Lannoy's lowest voice, as is also Obrecht's tenor (*Canti B* 13).

In the five-part *Cela sans plus* by Rigamundus in

[38] Written before he became pope, since Florence 107bis states: "del gardinale di medici."

[39] Since the work is a 4 as it appears in *Canti B*, Lannoy's lowest voice is the tenor; his middle voice is named "contra." This terminology will be retained in the following discussion to prevent confusion.

Bologna Q 19, however, a melody approximating Lannoy's tenor is used twice in succession as tenor, but in neither section displaying "identity" with it. A still greater deviation occurs in a little three-part setting, probably by an amateur composer, in Copenhagen 1848 (p. 140). In this arrangement, after a complete statement of the melody (often with no rests whatsoever between phrases and with variant readings of some phrases which differ greatly from Lannoy's), the meter changes from duple to triple for a curious transformation of the second and third lines of text and then returns to duple meter for the final phrase, "Cela sans plus."

The conclusion seems inescapable, therefore, that the melody of *Cela sans plus* was not of Lannoy's devising but was a popular tune of the day; that Lannoy made a polyphonic setting which attracted the attention of at least four other composers (the Regensburg Anonymous, the Cardinal de' Medici, Obrecht, and Martini); and that two other composers (Rigamundus and the Anonymous of Copenhagen 1848) were acquainted with the popular song and made their own arrangements of it, possibly with no knowledge of Lannoy's arrangement.

Martini's bass tends to match the style of Lannoy's contra and thus produces a better balance between the slower- and faster-moving parts. Lannoy's pseudo-*fauxbourdon* cadence at the end prevented Martini from producing a V-I cadence; his notes, together with Lannoy's, pose many questions as to the *musica ficta* intended. At no point does this added voice imitate the *cantus firmus*, but, like the contra, contributes to the vertical sonorities and supplies rhythmical activity.[40]

Although there were several examples of the addition of *si placet* (optional) parts—usually an alto—in the *Odhecaton*, Martini's bass affords the only traceable example of this practice in *Canti B*. Since the composers of so many complete compositions of this period are unknown to us today, it is all the more remarkable that we have been told the composer of an individual voice.[41] From this information we also learn that these added parts were not written by the composers of the original works.

Other contemporary evidence concerning the addition of voices to compositions already complete is found in some documents dealing with music at the court of Mantua in the late fifteenth century. In December of 1495, Giovanni Alvise, a trombonist of Venice, wrote a letter to Francisco da Gonzaga, Marquis of Mantua, as follows:

In questi zorni passadi, nui havemo posto zerti motteti in ordine per sonar, dei quali do ne mando à la S. V., et l'uno de quei si è opera de Hobert [Obrecht], zoè le quattro voze, do sovrani et uno tenore et uno contralto; et perchè nui siamo sei, li ho azonto do voxe basse per sonar con tromboni, che viene a esser a voxe sei, et fa un bon audire, e chi'l volesse sonar anche a cinque voze, li ho facto anche un altro contra basso. Anche un altro moteto dimandase Gabrielem, è de hopera de Busnois, zoè le quattro voxe, et io li ho fato un altro contra basso, che el soniamo a zinque, che in verità tutta Venetia non vol audir altro, et nui l'havemo tribuido al nostro Serenissimo, el qual ne ha gran piacere d'esso moteto, et però ho voluto farne uno presente a la S. V. per queste feste.[42]

(During the past few days we have put certain motets in order for playing, two of which I am sending to your lordship, and one of them is a work by Hobert [Obrecht], that is to say: the four voices, two sopranos, one tenor, and one contralto; and since we are six, I have added two bass voices to be played with trombones, which makes a six-part work and sounds well; and for those who might wish to play it *a 5*, I have prepared another contrabass, also. Another motet, called *Gabrielem*, is the work of Busnois, that is, the four voices, and I have made another contrabass for it, so that we can play it *a 5*—and, in fact, all Venice does not want to hear anything else; and we offered it in tribute to our most Serene Highness, and he takes great pleasure in this motet; and therefore I wished to make a present of it to your lordship for these festivities.)

This addition of one—and even two—voices below works by Obrecht and Busnois to be played on trombones is quite in line with Martini's addition of a bass to Lannoy's original three-part work.

(See also Introduction, p. x.)

[40] Otto Gombosi made a thorough study of this work in his *Jacob Obrecht: Eine stilkritische Studie mit einem Notenanhang* (Sammlung musikwissenschaftlicher Einzeldarstellungen, IV, Leipzig, 1925). On p. 76 Gombosi characterizes Lannoy's work as "decidedly the thinnest composition I have ever encountered." On p. 77 he cites m. 45 (his source, Washington, Wolffheim, gives D, quarter, in the contra where *Canti B* shows F) as evidence that its rhythmical function was paramount.

[41] We know that an alto was added to *Odhecaton* 90 by Henry VIII of England; this voice does not appear in the *Odhecaton*, however, and was doubtless not written until some years after 1501 (see Hewitt, *Odhecaton*, p. 166, no. 90).

[42] Edmond Vander Straeten, *La Musique aux Pays-Bas avant le XIXᵉ siècle* (8 vols.; Brussels, 1867–88), VIII, 537, after Stefano Davari, "La Musica a Mantova," *Rivista storica Mantovana*, I (1885). See also Antonio Bertolotti, *Musici alla corte dei Gonzaga in Mantova dal secolo XV al secolo XVIII* (Milan, 1890), p. 17 and p. 24.

17. *MON PÈRE M'A MARIÉE* Anon. 4 v. f. 20′–21

CONCORDANCE:

Egenolff [c. 1535][14] *Lieder*, Vol. I, no. 25, Anon. Superius only, with incipit.

TEXT:

> My pa gave me away in marriage
> When I'd just left my baby carriage.
> He gave me to a patriarch
> Who soon will hit the three-score mark.
> Still shedding adolescent tears,
> Am I thus doomed to spend my years?
> You who all of this can see,
> I pray you judge both him and me.
>
> Shall I go become a nun
> In some pretty convent bright,
> Praying the god of love and fun
> That he relieve me of my plight,
> Or that I may be the wife
> Of him I love with all my might?
> So very, very sad am I,
> So sad both day and night.

One poem with this incipit has been found as a possible text for the *Canti B* setting. The only source is in the play "La Comédie de chansons" (*Ancien Théatre François; ou, Collection des ouvrages dramatiques les plus remarquables depuis les mystères jusqu'à Corneille* [10 vols.; Paris, 1854–57], IX, 99–229), at the opening of Act III, Scene 1.

MUSIC:

An unusually large amount of this music relates to what is probably a popular tune in the tenor; imitations are widely spaced, thus making for a rather thinly woven texture. Measures 1–15 are repeated immediately (mm. 16–30) and, after a brief development of a motive drawn from the ending of phrase two, this opening music is recapitulated in part (mm. 34–45). A more extended development of the theme of measures 30–34 closes the arrangement (mm. 46–55).

The poem mentioned above has been united with this music although there exists no proof that they belong together. Its presence makes possible a vocal performance of this setting even if the correct text does not exist today.

(See also Introduction, pp. vii–viii.)

18. *MIJN MORKEN GAF* Anon. 4 v. f. 21′–22

CONCORDANCES:

Bologna Q 18, f. 88′–89, Anon. Incipit in all four voices.

Rome Vat. 11953, f. 17–17′, Anon. Bassus only, without text.

Egenolff [c. 1535][14] *Lieder*, Vol. I, no. 28, Anon. Superius only, with incipit.

MODERN EDITION:

Lenaerts, *Nederlands polifonies Lied*, pp. (5)–(6) (after *Canti B*).

RELATED COMPOSITION:

London Add. 35087, f. 5′–6, Anon. Text in all three voices.

    This work is published in Funck, *Deutsche Lieder*, no. 13; Wolf, *Sing- und Spielmusik*, no. 16; and Wolf, *Oud-Nederlandsche Liederen*, no. 1. The superius of this work and superius of *Canti B* show so plainly that they are both based on the same popular tune that there can be no doubt that the text of London Add. 35087 is that required for *Canti B* 18.

TEXT:

> A young wife my mother gave me—
> No lovelier could there be.
> So well she sang in harmony
> With me: Sweet life, farewell to thee.
>
> To Andernach-on-Rhine
> A lass—such was my mind—
> Should go for wine.
> Her love's gone with the wind.

This text has survived in only one manuscript, London Add. 35087. The words appear here given completely in each of three vocal parts, with the tenor showing a closing line different from that found in the other voices. Among the four modern editions of this text, Priebsch, *Deutsche Handschriften in England* reproduces this tenor reading, making no mention of the reading of the other voices; Lenaerts, *Nederlands polifonies Lied* gives the reading as found in the other parts, making no mention of the tenor. Funck, *Deutsche Lieder*, and Wolf, *Oud-Nederlandsche Liederen*, present both readings, the former presenting the tenor line and mentioning the other line in a note.

The chanson shows Flemish treatment, in the form of a quodlibet, of the *mal mariée* theme so popular at this time. Five of the eight lines have been identified as parts of separate songs, and it is probable that the other three were similarly derived. However, this quodlibet also became a popular song in its own right. The present edition follows Wolf, *Oud-Nederlandsche Liederen*.

8. Other reading: "Den tijd moet zij oorboren," which appears alone in one voice and as an alternative line in the tenor.

Related texts existed, for the theme was a popular one:

Kalff, "Handschriften . . . Amsterdam," p. 179: "Mijn vader gaf my enen man."

Mincoff-Marriage, *Souterliedekens*: "Mijn moerken gaf my eenen man." The melody of this song was indicated for a setting of Psalm 58.

MUSIC:

Mijn morken gaf, one of two arrangements of a Dutch song, is regrettably anonymous. It is a quodlibet in both text and music. The soprano melody, occurring also in the anonymous three-part arrangement in London Add. 35087, seems to be only partially new. As in the bar form, the first two phrases are repeated for the third and fourth lines of poetry. The same phrases, altered rhythmically to accommodate better the fifth and sixth lines of text, appear again at the beginning of the second division of the music; two new phrases bring the song to a close. The *cantus firmus*, then, comprises only four different phrases; of the four, two may be drawn from songs cited in the text. Phrase two is identical with the first phrase of Colinet de Lannoy's setting of *Adieu naturlic leven mijn*, and these words are sung to this phrase on the repeat of the first two phrases of our song. The seventh phrase is reminiscent of one of the phrases of *Het soude een meisken gaen om wijn* and accompanies these words in the quodlibet.

There are several points of resemblance between the arrangements in London Add. 35087 and *Canti B*. In both works the popular melody lies in the soprano; both works start out with consistent imitation; after the double bar, all three voices in London Add. 35087, and the three lower voices in *Canti B*, set out together and with the same rhythm, thus creating a homophonic effect; in both works a brief point of imitation occurs at the beginning of the seventh phrase. The London setting is for only three voices, whereas that in *Canti B* is for four, and separating its phrases by longer intervals it reaches thirty-nine measures as against the twenty-seven of the London arrangement. In *Canti B*, also, the tenor shows anticipatory imitations of the phrases of the soprano and then extends them by melismatic approaches to their cadences. Alto and bass function primarily as non-thematic counterpoints except when they participate in the points of imitation.

The setting in *Canti B* is the more sophisticated; yet, while it conforms to the various requirements of polyphony, the harmonic element seems somewhat stronger than usual. This effect may be due to the placement of the *cantus prius factus* in the soprano.

19. COMMENT PEULT AVOIR JOYE Josquin 4 v. f. 22'-23

CONCORDANCES:

Bologna Q 17, f. 58'-59, Josquin. Incipit in three notated parts; above S: *Fuga duorum temporum dyapason*.

Florence 178, f. 7'-8, Josquin. "O men potauer yoye" in highest of three voices; a *signum* in S marks the entry of a canonic voice.

Rome C. G. XIII, 27, f. 11'-12, Josquin despres. Incipit "Ne come peult" in highest of three voices; a *signum* in S marks the entry of a canonic voice.

Egenolff [c. 1535][14] *Lieder*, Vol. I, no. 27, Anon. Superius only, with incipit.

Glareanus 1547[1] *Dodecachordon*, pp. 356-57, Iodocus Pratensis. Text "O Iesv, fili David" in all voices.

Glareanus substituted a Latin sacred text for the French secular one; in this form the work passed into many publications.

MODERN EDITIONS:

Bohn, *Glareani Dodecachordon*, pp. 316-18.

Busby, *History of Music*, I, 463-70 (after Glareanus).

Hawkins, *History of Music*, II, 467-69 (after Glareanus).

Kiesewetter, *Verdienste der Niederlaender*, pp. 30-32 (after Hawkins, *History of Music*).

Lose Blätter, pp. 37-39, "O Jesu, fili David."

Miller, *Heinrich Glarean, Dodecachordon*, II, 434-36.

Osthoff, *Josquin des Prés . . . Chorwerk* XXX, no. 1, pp. 5-7, "O Jesu, fili David." (This edition adds a German translation to the Latin which is after Glareanus.)

RELATED COMPOSITIONS USING THE FRENCH WORDS:

1. Bologna Q 18, f. 68'-69, Anon. Incipit in all three voices.
   The melody appears in the contra.

2. London Add. 35087, f. 36'-37, Jo. de Vyzeto. Text in each of three voices (see Plate X).
   The direction "In dyatessaron" and a *signum* in S indicate a fourth, canonic, voice. A variant of the melody lies in the superius.

3. Rome C. G. XIII, 27, f. 117'-118, Ysach. Incipit in the highest of three voices.
   This arrangement by Isaac shows the melody in the contra. It is published in Wolf, *Isaac: Weltliche Werke*, E 6, p. 66.

4. Egenolff [c. 1535][14] *Lieder*, Vol. III, no. 50, Anon. Superius only.
   This voice shows the opening notes of the melody.

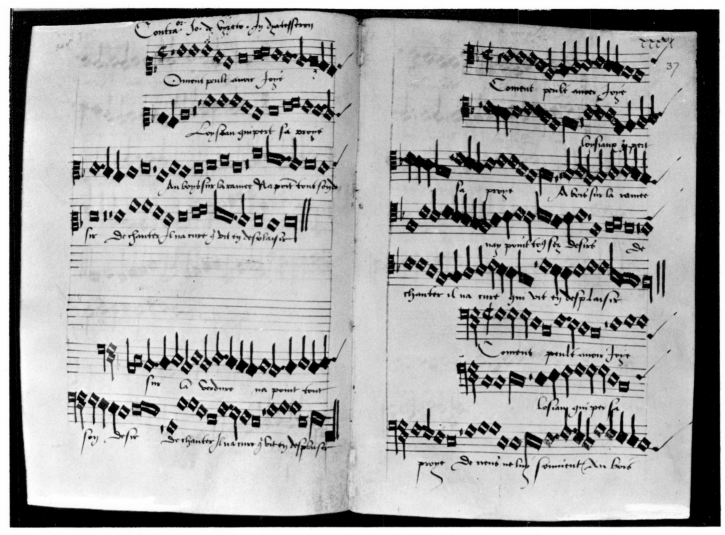

PLATE X. London, British Museum, Add. MS 35087, f. 36'–37, Jo. de Vyzeto, "Coment peult avoir joye."

RELATED COMPOSITIONS USING THE GERMAN WORDS:

1. Vienna 18810, no. 16, Henricus Isaac, "Wolauff gut gsell von hinnen." Incipit in highest of three voices.

   A variant of the melody lies in the superius. This arrangement by Isaac is published in Wolf, *Isaac: Weltliche Werke*, E 40, p. 110.

2. Berg and Neuber 1549[37] *Der dritte Teyl*, no. 65, G. Othmayr, "Wolauf gut gsell von hinnen." Text in each of four voices.

   This arrangement is published in Liliencron, *Deutsches Leben im Volkslied*, pp. 351–54, with four stanzas of text; also in Jöde, *Chorbuch für gemischte Stimmen*, no. 38. Othmayr's work uses a late variant of our melody.

3. Petreius 1540[21] *Der ander Theil*, no. 18, Anon., "Wolauf! gut gsel, von hinnen." Text in each of four voices.

   This arrangement is published in Eitner, *Der zweite Teil ... Liedlein*, no. 18, pp. 28–30.

TEXT:

How can anyone be gay
Who finds misfortune in his way?
The bird whose prey is lost and gone
Now has happy thoughts of none.

He, in woods of leafy green,
Of what he wants has not a thing.
He whose life is sad and mean
Cares not at all to sing.

The most nearly complete French text of this chanson appears in London Add. 35087, used for the present edition. Two parts (superius and tenor) present a chanson of six lines. The third part (contra) inserts a line between lines two and three of the other parts and gives a variant of line three of superius and tenor. Neither version seems complete. If it is a chanson of six lines, line three of the contra would be omitted. If it is a chanson of eight lines, line three of the contra must be kept and another line added. A study of the rhyme scheme shows that a line added after line one would complete the rhyme *abab* of the first four lines.

Helmuth Osthoff ("Wohlauf, gut G'sell," p. 136) and Bianca Becherini ("Tre incatenature," p. 94) cite four lines of this chanson as part of a quodlibet found in Florence 164–167. Since the manuscript gives a poor reading, with many Italianisms, it is difficult to state exactly that these lines are those of our chanson as found in London Add. 35087. There is no doubt, however, that they include the missing second line:

1. Come put auor ioie
2. ch(e) fortuna co(n)trent
3. Ieseu ch(e) p(ert) sa proie
4. de neus de li souie(n)t

The articles by Osthoff and Becherini present variant readings. Since these four lines are the only bit of French in a text otherwise completely Italian, it is not strange that an Italian scribe gave a highly distorted reading. If the French equivalent is substituted for "che fortuna" this line will read "Qui fortune contrent."

If the reading for line three is now taken from the contra, the rhyme of the last four lines becomes *cdcd*. We now have one complete stanza of eight lines, with rhyme scheme *abab cdcd*.

2. Line missing in London Add. 35087
   Florence 164–167: che fortuna contrent
3. oysiaux (tenor)
4. "De neus de luy souuient," appearing only in contra (as line 3); this would rhyme with line 2 (missing from London Add. 35087).
5. A bois (tenor)
   Superius and tenor (line 3) read: sur la ramee.
   This is undoubtedly a variant, since the word "verdure" (contra), very similar in meaning, rhymes with "cure" of line 8.
6. N'ay point tous sez desirs (tenor)

MUSIC:

In spite of its auspicious debut—publication as a chanson in the *Canti B* of 1502—this work by Josquin has enjoyed so successful a career as "motet" that its true nature has remained obscured and has only recently been brought out into the light.

In 1547 Henricus Glareanus published Josquin's work in his *Dodecachordon* with the Latin text, "O Jesu, fili David" (Matt. 15: 22, 26, 27), that has been associated with Josquin's music right down to the present. Republished as a "motet" by Hawkins (1776), Busby (1819), and Kiesewetter (1829)—all after Glareanus—it was brought out in our own day by Helmuth Osthoff with the comment that it "embodies the peculiar and rare case of the association of a Gospel text with a folk song."[43] This observation was correct

enough, but it carried the implication that Josquin himself combined the two.

No other contemporary source shows the Latin text, and the conclusion seems inevitable that Glareanus substituted the Latin words (as he is known to have done with other compositions) to make his treatise more international in its appeal and usefulness. He himself states that he derived this example "from the German and French languages."[44] There exists, then, no evidence that Josquin himself did not arrange a popular song with French words. Glareanus knew that the song was sung on both sides of the Rhine. Whether Josquin also knew this we do not know, but Isaac wrote two settings of the tune, one calling for the French words; the other, the German (see the Related Compositions above).

Recently Osthoff investigated this matter further and in an impressive article reviewed the vast amount of material, both French and German, sacred (Masses based on this melody) and secular, from around 1480 to 1622.[45] He concludes:

We do not hesitate, therefore, to strike out the word "motet" and simply hold to the much better documented instrumental setting [*Canti B* 19] as the original. Its "device" points to a Burgundian-French chanson, whose complete text I have till now been unable to locate.[46]

Osthoff devotes considerable attention to the popular song as such. He extracts the melody from the Gloria of Isaac's *Missa Wol auff*, Isaac's chanson *Coment peult*, Josquin's *Comment peult* (*Canti B* 19), and Othmayr's late setting of "Wolauf." Comparison of these four melodies proves conclusively that French and German words were sung to one and the same melody.

Osthoff feels the German song should not be classified as a folk song: "Lines . . . from the second strophe . . . bring it closer to the courtly-patrician lyric. . . ."[47]

The first stanza reads:

> Wohlauf, gut G'sell, von hinnen!
> Meins Bleibens ist nimmer hie,
> Der Mai der tut uns bringen
> Den Veiel und grünen Klee.

[43] Helmuth Osthoff (ed.), *Josquin des Prés, Mattheus Le Maistre, Christian Hollander, Alexander Utendal, Ivo de Vento, und Jacob Regnart: Acht Lied- und Choralmotetten (Das Chorwerk*, XXX [Wolfenbüttel and Berlin, 1934]), "Vorwort," p. 2.

[44] *Heinrich Glarean, Dodecachordon*, translation, transcription, and commentary by Clement A. Miller (Rome: American Institute of Musicology, 1965), II, 263. See below for the complete passage from which this phrase is taken.

[45] "'Wohlauf, gut G'sell, von hinnen!': Ein Beispiel deutschfranzösischer Liedgemeinschaft um 1500," *Jahrbuch für Volksliedforschung*, VIII (1951), 128–36.

[46] *Ibid.*, p. 132.

[47] *Ibid.*, p. 128.

Vor'm Wald da hört man singen
Der kleinen Vöglein G'sang,
Sie singen mit heller Stimme
Den ganzen Sommer lang.

(Come on! from hence, good fellow!
I can no longer bide;
With violets and green clover
May dots the countryside.
At forest's edge one hears it—
The little birdlings' song—
They sing with bright, clear voices
Throughout the summer long.)

Osthoff believes that the song hailed from Germany because of the "ideal agreement between words and music" and the use of the repeat-barform, a favorite form of the minnesingers and the later master singers.[48]
On the other hand,

From the outgoing Middle Ages on, many melodies traveled the road from west to east by the agency of art music and courtly dances. Germanized melodies and song-settings from the Burgundian-French domain are encountered in Oswald von Wolkenstein, in the Lochamer Liederbuch, in the Rostocker Liederbuch, the Trent codices, the Glogauer Liederbuch, etc. The opposite is very much rarer. Examples of it are primarily the German folksong melodies and 'court-tune'-tenors, which Jacobus Clement (Clemens non Papa) borrowed for his three-voiced 'Souterliedekens' (Antwerp, 1556–1557).[49]

In Josquin's arrangement, the popular melody appears in canon at the octave between soprano and tenor, and these canonic voices seem in augmentation in comparison with the other voices. Like many other arrangements in *Canti B*, Josquin's composition was probably written for instrumental performance. The soprano begins the canon in measure 6. At the end of the work, after the popular melody has been completed, the final phrase is repeated in an elaborated form. Attention might be called to the bass progression in measures 42–46; contemporary sources indicate that the B, which alternates with a C several times, should be flatted, thus producing perfect fifths in these measures. In a clear Ionian that heralds the coming of the major mode, these transposed Mixolydian cadences[50] are the most audible reminders of the modal past.

[48] *Ibid.*, p. 136.
[49] *Ibid.*
[50] Cf. Lowinsky, "The Function of Conflicting Signatures," pp. 242–44, where these cadences were identified for the first time. See also the same author's *Tonality and Atonality in Sixteenth-Century Music* (Berkeley and Los Angeles: University of California Press, 1961), pp. 3 and 80, n. 3.

In conclusion we may quote Glareanus' comments on Josquin's canon, made with obvious affection for the work of this master.

After this we have added two examples by Josquin, the first of which [*Comment peult*], taken from the German and French languages, is exceedingly lovely. In it the *cantus* and tenor are separated by two *tempora*, and have been bound together as if under a yoke; likewise, they have been divided very beautifully through ten *clausulae* for each, and thus they move along with the same mien and the same adornment so that they seem to be coupled, a bridegroom leading his bride, as it were. The alto and bass sing delightfully before them and with them, and play together so much that they might be considered as players who have been called to a wedding. Then one should also consider with what beauty the sixth *clausula* of the *cantus* and tenor falls obliquely [i.e., each *clausula* in its turn], into the fourth of the Dorian, but not without a wonderful charm.[51]

(See also Introduction, p. xv.)

20. *COMMENT PEULT* Anon. 4 v. f. 23'–24

CONCORDANCE:
  Egenolff [c. 1535][14] *Lieder*, Vol. I, no. 28, Anon. Superius only, with incipit.

RELATED COMPOSITION:
  Although both *Canti B* 19 and 20 show the same textual incipit, there is no musical relationship between the two, and the text of *Canti B* 19 does not have the form required by the music of *Canti B* 20.

TEXT:
  For discussion of a text beginning "Comment peult," see *Canti B* 19. There seems to be nothing in this composition to indicate that the words of *Canti B* 19 could be used with it. It is perhaps only coincidence that these two texts begin with the same words.

MUSIC:
  The music of *Comment peult* is divided into four almost exactly equal sections by strong cadences in measures 11, 23, 34—and 44, the final measure. These four cadences are all shaped similarly and have an interesting tonal relationship: in modern terms they are in G minor, D minor, B-flat major, and G minor. In all three internal cadences the bass rests at the point

[51] *Heinrich Glarean, Dodecachordon*, ed. Clement A. Miller, II, 263. Dr. Miller has written me as follows: "Glarean's phrase 'the fourth of the Dorian' refers, I think, to the melodic contour of the sixth *clausula*, which begins on high G and closes on D. I suppose it might also be related to *re sol*, the first fourth-species, which Glarean discusses in Book I of his tome."

of resolution and then starts up again, thus bridging the end of one section and the beginning of the next.

Small use of imitation, together with the general awkwardness of style, its frequent parallel fifths (mm. 3–4, 8, 29–30, 36), inelegant dissonance treatment (see especially mm. 16–17, 26, 32, 41), crowded texture, and numerous voice crossings may indicate an early work and a limited talent.

The four motives, one for each of the four sections, are predominantly scalar and lack interest. The little work may have been a freely composed setting of a *rondeau quatrain*, although no *signum* appears at the cadence in m. 23 to confirm this conjecture.

21. *HÉLAS, HÉLAS, HÉLAS*   Ninot   4 v.
f. 24′–25

CONCORDANCES:
Regensburg C 120, pp. 24–25, Anon. Incipit in all voices.
Egenolff [c. 1535][14] *Lieder*, Vol. I, no. 29, Anon. Superius only, with incipit.

RELATED COMPOSITION:
Petrucci 1504[3] *Canti C*, f. 42′–43, Anon. The incipit "Helas helas fault il" occurs in each of four voices.
Thematic resemblances between this work and *Canti B* 21 suggest their being based on the same popular melody.

TEXT:
No satisfactory text for this *Canti B* setting has been found. *Canti C* contains a setting of a text beginning "Helas helas fault il"; Brussels 228 (f. 38′–39) provides a composition that is thematically unlike either the *Canti B* or the *Canti C* settings, but whose text may be that required. Gachet, *Albums et oeuvres poétiques*, p. 84, and Françon, *Albums poétiques*, no. 40, have published this text, here reproduced:

> Hélas! fault-il qu'à vous priser je cesse
> Qui tant ay mis mon cueur à vous servir
> En cuidant bien, en servant, déservir
> Que me fussiez une bonne maistresse?

> (Alas, must I cease to adore
> You whom my heart so long has served,
> Believing, thus serving, I deserved
> Your faith and love for ever more?)

1. Other voices have: penser
2. déservir = mériter

These four lines are all that remain. Although the stanzaic structure may be that of a *rondeau quatrain*, and

the subject is one familiar in the *rondeau*, there is no way of ascertaining. As it exists in this manuscript, it is a four-line decasyllabic stanza, rhyming *abba*.

MUSIC:
The music of this setting is written in a very modern vein. Its frequent use of the voices in pairs, duet fashion, with one pair imitating the other, passages suggesting hocket, the use of the quarter as beat note, all are characteristic of this style. The setting is in three-part form, for the opening section, measures 1–18, is recapitulated, measure 48 to the end.

If this work is based on a popular song, nothing has been found in the monophonic chansonniers or in related polyphonic compositions to prove it. *Helas helas fault il* from *Canti C* starts with a motive greatly resembling that of *Canti B* 21; later motives, however, show less resemblance to those of Ninot's work. The latter is also solidly in a major mode (Mixolydian), whereas the *Canti C* work closes in the minor (Aeolian mode).

22. *TOUS LES REGRETZ*   Pe. de la rue   4 v.
f. 25′–26

CONCORDANCES:
Basel F. X. 1–4, no. 109, Pirson alias Pe. de la Rue. Incipit in each of four voices.
Brussels 228, f. 3′–4, Anon. Text in all voices.
Brussels 11239, f. 9′–11, de la Rue. Text in all voices.
Florence 2442, no. 43, P. de la Rue. Bassus wanting; text in remaining voices.
Regensburg C 120, pp. 264–65, Josquin. Incipit, S, A, and T.
Rome Vat. 11953, f. 8′–9, Rue. Bassus only, with incipit.
Vienna 18810, no. 64, Petrus de La Rue. Incipits in all voices.

MODERN EDITIONS:
Maldeghem, *Trésor musical (profane)*, Vol. XX (1884), no. 9, pp. 16–17 (after Brussels 228) (= Reese, "Maldeghem," no. 320).
Picker, *Chanson Albums*, pp. 180–83 (after Brussels 228).

FACSIMILE:
Closson, *Musique en Belgique*, p. 472 (of Brussels 228).

RELATED COMPOSITION:
Petrucci 1504[3] *Canti C*, f. 164′–165, Anon. Incipit "Tous les regrets" in each of three voices.
This work, not found elsewhere, has nothing in common, musically, with *Canti B* 22.

> All sorrows, you who hearts torment,
> Now strike at mine, do not relent.
> Cut short my life, for lost is she
> In whom all virtues perfectly
> Were found and merits excellent.
>
> Come, do not be reticent.
> My senses, ready, confident,
> Do welcome you. Pray come to me.
>   All sorrows, etc.
>
> I pray you, be not negligent.
> Take pleasure, joy—to this consent—
> That once kind Fate did lend to me.
> Now sad care's victim I must be,
> So come in haste. Be diligent.
>   All sorrows, etc.

The text of this *rondeau cinquain* appears in many sources: Paris 477, f. 81; Paris 1158, f. 37; Paris 1719, f. 111; Paris 7559, f. 21; Paris 19182, f. 111; Bancel, *Cent quarante-cinq rondeaux*, p. 120 (after Paris 7559); Françon, *Albums poétiques*, no. 82 (after Brussels 11239), no. 105 (after Brussels 228), App., note V (after Lille 402, f. 253, and Moritzburg, Saxe, no. 253); Françon, *Poèmes de transition*, no. 253 (after Lille and Moritzburg); Gachet, *Albums et oeuvres poétiques*, p. 63 (after Brussels 11239) and p. 71 (after Brussels 228); Quicherat, *Vers d'Henri Baude*, p. 41, Henri Baude (after Paris 1717, f. 55′); Vérard, *La Chasse*, f. B v′. All readings are fundamentally the same, with differences in spelling and at times in the wording of a line. Brussels 228, Brussels 11239, and Florence 2442 offer only the refrain; Quicherat, Bancel, Paris 1158, Vérard, and Moritzburg, Saxe, present the entire *rondeau*. This reading follows Quicherat.

2. Brussels 11239: Venes a moy
   Florence 2442: Venez sur moy
3. Gachet (Brussels 11239): aberger
5. Bancel: Estoit en meurs et parfaicte en bonté
   Moritzburg, Saxe: bontez
   Florence 2442: parfaicte bonté
6. Paris 1158, Vérard: rien plus
10. Bancel, Moritzburg, Saxe: Et si vous prise que d'avec moy oustez
11. Moritzburg, Saxe: Joye plaisir . . .

MUSIC:

Although Pierre de la Rue was active for more than fifteen years after the publication of *Canti B*, his compositional technique and his personal style were at their height around 1500. In his setting of *Tous les regretz*—a *rondeau cinquain*—he has given us a classic example of the manner in which this generation of composers set one of the *formes fixes* to music: the clear division of the *rondeau* into its two parts (m. 31), the division of a line of words at the caesura (soprano, m. 6, for example), and everywhere the fine balance between the longer notes at the beginnings of phrases and the shorter ones as the lines continue in gracefully flowing curves. Note his use of the harmonic diminished fifth which occurs several times (mm. 38–40); he has treated it with elegance by placing it on the unaccented beat and by having its tones progress in stepwise motion. Characteristic is the low bass range with the rare "great C" in measure 41.

(See also Introduction, p. ix.)

23. *VECI LA DANSE BARBARI* Vaqueras 4 v. f. 26′–27

CONCORDANCES:

Florence 107[bis], f. 13′–14, Anon. Incipit, S. (Index: Vesila d. b.)

Segovia, f. 125′–126, Loysette Compere. Incipits in all voices.

MODERN EDITION:

Brown, *Theatrical Chansons*, no. 58, pp. 178–80 (after Florence 107[bis]).

RELATED COMPOSITION:

Cortona 95–96, Paris 1817, no. 5, Anon. Bassus wanting; text in remaining voices.

This composition is based on the same popular song as is *Canti B* 23.

TEXT:

> This is the dance of Barbary.
>
> It happened in Barbary the other day,
> This startling event.
> Three daughters of a city gent
> Went to the green to play.
> Said the youngest of the three, "It's evident,
> My span is no doubt quite superior
> From navel down to my posterior."
>
> This is the dance, the dance, the dance,
> The dance of Barbary.

This chanson consists of nine lines, including a one-line refrain appearing at the beginning and again at the close. The chanson does not seem complete in this version. There may once have been other stanzas.

Gröber ("Liederbücher von Cortona," no. 5, after Paris 1817) and Renier ("Mazzetto di poesie," no. 5, after Cortona 95–96) have edited the text. The present edition follows Renier. The language shows dialectal traits.

2. l'altrier = l'autre jour
4. troes = trois
5. yoent, from the verb "jouer"
6. yone = jeune
8. Renier notes in one voice: . . . in chanon bril

A Spanish manuscript (Segovia) shows the same music and incipit, "Veci la dancha barberj." Two voices continue with "L'autre jour."

MUSIC:

In the original notation, a single bar in *Canti B*, a double or triple bar in the various voices of the Segovia manuscript, separates the opening refrain from the stanza that follows. It seems probable that later stanzas would have started after this bar, so that stanza and refrain would alternate. The popular melody lies in the tenor throughout. The refrain melody enters in measure 6, after alto, bass, and soprano in turn have anticipated its opening motive. After the double bar the device of "voice pairing" is used extensively; at measure 44 the meter changes from duple to triple for the fifth line of text, returning to duple meter only for the final refrain. From the double bar to measure 61, bass and tenor move in canon at the fifth; the phrases are so separated by rests, however, that the two voices overlap by only a note or two. Usually the alto forms a counterpoint to the bass, the soprano to the tenor; only where the duets overlap does one hear all four voices together. The final refrain uses all four voices in a homophonic passage.

The fabric of most of the work is very loosely woven. The thinness resulting from this manner of writing is also noticeable in *Canti B* 21. In *Veci la danse*, the tenor melody ceases to be "tuneful" during the 3/4 section, merely oscillating between the notes A and B. Counting the phrases in the canonic bass part, six of these "oscillating" phrases occur, each helping with the narration. The triple meter and this pendulant movement seem to suggest the twirling of dancers. As the speed increases—when the 3/4 sets in and once more at the change to 2/2, which now seems more like 4/4 since the quarter assumes the role of beat-note—the little work seems to reflect the excitement aroused when dancers move faster and faster.

The name of Vaqueras, sometimes with "Bern." (for Bernardus), sometimes with "Bertr." (for Bert-

randus) as Christian name, occurs in the lists of the singers in the papal chapel for the first time in 1483.[52] In that year he was given the number 24. He seems to have been a member of the chapel continuously from this date to 1507, when his name is listed for the last time. By then he had risen to the position of no. 2; presumably he was the second oldest member in point of years of service.

The papal archives in Rome contain two Masses attributed to Vaqueras, two settings of the Credo (one for four voices, one for five), and several motets. Glareanus has two *partes* of a motet, each for two voices, in his *Dodecachordon*, citing its composer as merely "Vaqueras," and adding no biographical data. The Swiss humanist Egidius Tschudi listed him in the Index of St. Gall 463 as "Vaqueras Gallus." But it was the Chevalier de Theux who discovered in his study of *Le Chapitre de Saint-Lambert* [Liége][53] that he was a native of Liége, who was offered a canonry at Saint-Lambert as successor to Pierre de Holey—an offer he did not accept. Thus, Vaqueras was yet another Franco-Flemish composer who might have found employment at home, but found his position in the papal chapel so congenial that he felt no urge to return to his homeland.

24. *D'UNG AULTRE AMER* De orto 4 v. f. 27'–28

CONCORDANCES: None.

RELATED COMPOSITIONS:

See Howard Brown, *Music in the French Secular Theater*, "Catalogue," no. 85, for full information on the original setting of *D'ung aultre amer*, from which *Canti B* 24 borrows its soprano, and on many other related compositions.

TEXT:

Another love would shame my heart.
Think not from him I'd be seduced
And have my honor thus reduced,
Or from this purpose ever part.

[52] Fr. X. Haberl, "Die römische 'schola cantorum' und die päpstlichen Kapellsänger bis zur Mitte des 16. Jahrhunderts," *Vierteljahrsschrift für Musikwissenschaft*, III (1887), 189–296. (This article also appeared as Vol. III of Haberl's *Bausteine für Musikgeschichte* [Leipzig, 1888].)

[53] Liége and Brussels, 1871, Vol. II, pp. 328–29. Antoine Auda refers to the book of De Theux in his work on *La Musique et les musiciens de l'ancien pays de Liége: Essai bio-bibliographique sur la musique liégeoise depuis ses origines jusqu'à la fin de la Principauté (1800)* (Brussels, Paris, and Liége, 1930), p. 73.

I love him so there is no art
By which to change I'd be induced.
Another love, etc.

Lord, I'd gladly feel Death's dart
Before my love would be misused.
Let no one think I'd be abused
And cause my faith to fall apart.
Another love, etc.

The text of this *rondeau quatrain* appears in many collections of the period. Paris 15123 has only parts of the refrain, and those in poor readings; Paris, Bibliothèque de Geneviève Thibault, Nivelle de la Chaussée Chansonnier; Vérard, *Le Jardin de plaisance*; Löpelmann, *Liederhandschrift des Cardinals de Rohan* (Berlin 78. B. 17); Paris 2245; Paris, Rothschild 2819; Smijers, *Van Ockeghem tot Sweelinck*, I (after Florence 2794); and Wolfenbüttel 287 give readings that vary in detail only. The present reading follows Smijers.

1. Vérard: s'esbahiroit
2. Vérard; Paris, Chaussée: Il ne fault ja penser . . .
3. Paris 2245: Ne que pour riens propos ne change
4. Paris 2245, Wolfenbüttel 287, Löpelmann: s'en
6. Vérard: a moy possible de consentir leschange Löpelmann; Paris, Chaussée: possible a moy de consentir la change
   Paris 2245: "don" for "d'en"; "La change" for "l'échange"
8. Vérard, Löpelmann: desferoit
   Paris 2245: desseroit
11. Paris 2245: messeroit
    Paris, Chaussée: Ma loyaulté trop en amainderoit

MUSIC:

This second work in *Canti B* by Mabriano de Orto[54] is an unusually interesting example of the puzzle canon. It is also a *cantus-firmus* work, for it borrows for its highest voice—without change in values or pitches of notes or rests—the superius of the freely composed setting of *D'un autre amer* by Johannes Ockeghem.[55] The work is accompanied by two canonic instructions.

The first canon applies to both alto and bass and reads: *Obelus quinis sedibus ipse volat*. Without the aid of this instruction these two voices would be quite

unintelligible, for each consists of just half as many measures as does either the soprano or the tenor. Both show at correspondingly irregular intervals single lines drawn completely through the staff, an unusual feature in the notation of the period.[56] These lines are related to the canon, as will be shown.

A partial translation of this canon might read: "The *obelus* itself flies by five places." The choice of the Greek word *obelus* is interesting. The word has more than one connotation: it can mean a sharp point of land jutting out into a body of water; or, it can mean the mark or sign used in medieval manuscripts to indicate a spurious or doubtful reading. Combining these two meanings, we may interpret it as referring to any stretch of the vocal part extending from one of the lines through the staff to the next, about the reading of which there is something spurious. The purpose of the lines, then, is to mark off the segments to be dealt with.

The verb *volare*, "to fly," may connote speed, but here must be interpreted in its primary meaning of soaring to a height. The extent of this height is revealed in the words *quinis sedibus*—"five places"—or, in musical parlance, "the interval of a fifth." The word *ipse* may now provide the solution to the puzzle. Meaning "itself" or "the very same," it stresses that the transposition must be applied to "the very same" segment, and thus implies that the segment has already been used once. There is, then, something "spurious" about these segments of music: their notation is correct for a first use, but is incorrect (that is, transposition is required) for their second use. The full meaning of the canon is now clear. Each segment marked off by lines through the staff must be performed first at the pitch level indicated by the notation, and then immediately afterwards at the fifth above.

The second Latin expression (appearing with the tenor) is quite superfluous, since the notation is correct as given. It might be rendered as "[a] supporting fourth [voice]";[57] that is, a voice providing support for the structure.

Since the soprano part was drawn directly from a vocal setting of the *rondeau*, it could, of course, be sung.

[54] *Canti B* 12, *Mon mary m'a diffamée*, is also by De Orto.

[55] Ockeghem's setting may be seen in a modern edition in Droz, *Trois chansonniers français*, no. 36 (after Dijon 517); Knud Jeppesen (ed.), *Der Kopenhagener Chansonnier: Das Manuskript Thott 291⁸ der königlichen Bibliothek Kopenhagen*; edition of the texts by Viggo Brøndal (Copenhagen and Leipzig, 1927), no. 28; or Albert Smijers (ed.), *Van Ockeghem tot Sweelinck: Nederlandsche Muziekgeschiedenis in Voorbeelden*, I (Amsterdam, 1939), no. 3 (after Florence, Biblioteca Riccardiana, MS 2794).

[56] Howard Mayer Brown, *Music in the French Secular Theater*, "Catalogue," no. 73 e, p. 205, cites one work in which similar lines through the staff indicate that the preceding notes are to be repeated. See also *Canti B* 23, where a line through the staff has a completely different meaning.

[57] Charles Du Cange, *Glossarium mediae et infimae latinitatis*, II (1883), 500, gives "confortatio" = "corroboratio."

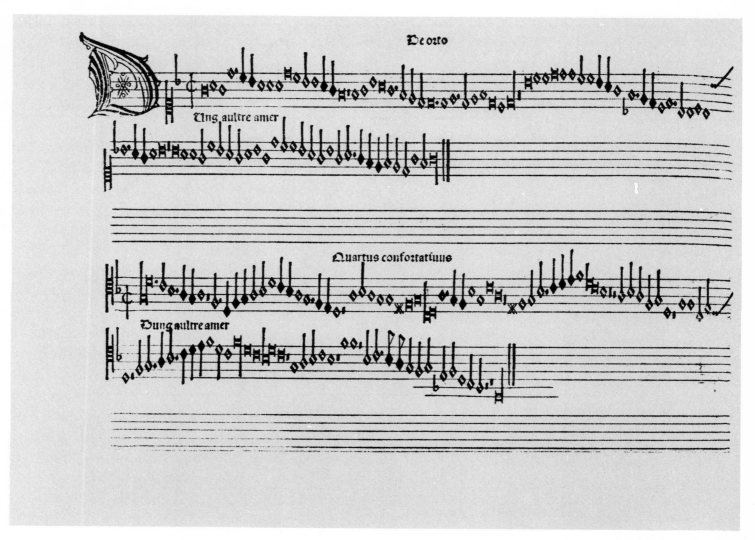

De orto

Ung aultre amer

Quartus confortatiuus

D'ung aultre amer

PLATE XI.   *Canti B*, 1503,

For the other parts, particularly the alto and bass with their unusual construction, only instrumental performance suggests itself. The work is a *tour de force*, and the composer must have taken pride in the success of his unusual and original accomplishment, as well as pleasure in the compliments that doubtless came his way.

This piece appears to be a unique example of the rapid and continuous alternation of melodic sections and their transpositions, but the thought processes that evolved this idea, fantastic as it may be, must still be admitted to be typical of what Ambros calls "die Künste der Niederländer."[58]

Jean Molinet quotes the complete first line of *D'un autre amer* in his poem, *Collaudation à Madame Marguerite*,[59] and again in his *Oroison à Nostre Dame*,[60] while its incipit appears in a morality play written by

Nicholas de la Chesnaye, physician to Louis XII, for the diversion of the king and his queen.[61]

(See also Introduction, pp. xiv and xv.)

25. *NOÉ, NOÉ, NOÉ*   Brumel   4 v.   f. 28'–29

CONCORDANCES:

Bologna Q 18, f. 22'–23, Anon. Incipit in S only.
Greifswald E^b 133, no. 5, Antonius Brummer. The text *Bonus et rectus dominus* is found in each of four voices.
Egenolff [c. 1535][14] *Lieder*, Vol. I, no. 30, Anon. Superius only, with incipit.

TEXT:

No French text has been found to accompany the music of *Canti B*. In Greifswald E^b 133, however, some verses from the Psalms, in Latin translation, accompany this music. These words correspond in meaning to

---

[58] See Ambros, *Geschichte der Musik*, III, 62–82, a section with this title, for a survey of the types of canon used by this school of composers.
[59] *Les Faictz et Dictz de Jean Molinet*, I, 265–68.
[60] *Ibid.*, II, 468–75.

[61] *La Condamnacion de Bancquet*, in *Recueil de farces, soties, et moralités du quinzième siècle*, ed. Paul Lacroix (Paris, 1876), p. 314. The passage in which this quotation occurs, along with incipits of many other texts of pieces in the Petrucci anthologies, may be seen in Brown, *Music in the French Secular Theater*, p. 93.

54

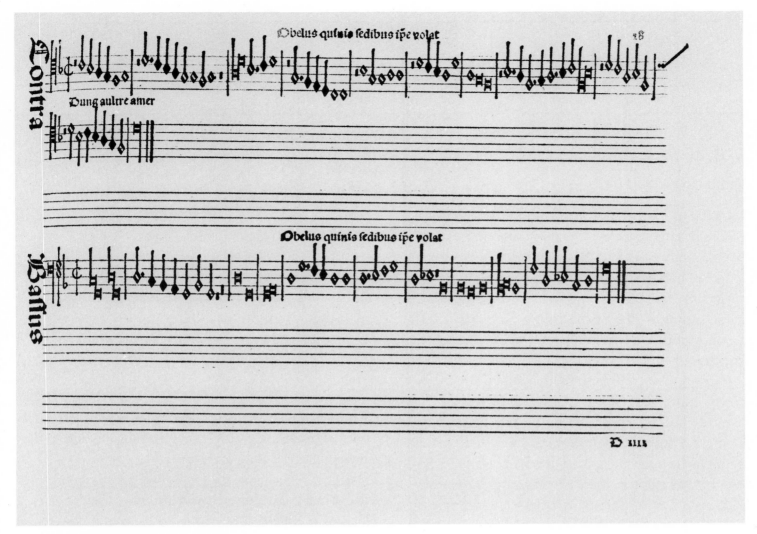

no. 24, De Orto, "D'ung aultre amer."

Psalm 24: 8–11 of the Vulgate, but do not follow precisely the wording of Jerome's version. It has been impossible to identify this particular translation.

Music:

The music begins homophonically and moves rather slowly during the first twenty measures (halves and wholes predominating); this same style returns for the last six measures of the composition (mm. 51–56). From measure 21 to measure 50 the pulse seems to quicken, for the quarter note asserts itself.

In measures 21–22 a six-note figure is stated in the soprano and imitated by the tenor, bass, and alto in quick succession. This figure then appears sequentially a third higher (m. 23), and then another third (m. 26), and again is treated in imitation. Brumel then interrupts this interweaving of patterns by inserting some repeated chords (mm. 29–30) leading into a conventional cadence (mm. 31–33).

In measures 33–34 a new figure appears and again is treated in imitation. Each voice then reproduces this figure sequentially, beginning on four successive tones

of the ascending scale. The sequence is diatonic, so that the interval of a third is now minor, now major. When the sequence reaches its climax (m. 39), Brumel extends the motive to cover a fifth by adding another third below the first. He now treats this longer motive in a descending sequence, all voices taking part in the sequences and imitations.

Since, in the sources available (Greifswald E^b 133 and Bologna Q 18), no flats beyond E-flat are inserted as accidentals, it might appear that the sequence was intended to remain diatonic within the transposed Dorian mode. Performed in this way, the few intervals that are not "perfect" may seem unobjectionable.[62] Such extensive use of sequence comes as a surprise among the works of *Canti B*,[63] and one regrets only

[62] The "dead" intervals of a fourth in the soprano (m. 45) and the tenor (mm. 44–45); the interval of a fifth between the extremes of the motive in the alto (mm. 44:4—46:1) and the bass (mm. 44:2—45:3). See, however, the General Editor's commentary in the Introduction, pp. xi–xiv.

[63] Cf., however, as an isolated example, the strikingly similar treatment of the same words, "Noel, noel," in Nicole Grenon's *Nova vobis gaudia*, published by Jeanne Marix in *Les Musiciens*

the loss of the carol text to which Brumel's interesting music was once sung.

(See also Introduction, pp. xi–xiv.)

26. *UNA MOZA FALLE YO* Anon. 4 v. f. 29′–30

CONCORDANCES: None.

MUSIC:

The arrangement of *Una moza falle yo*, probably a popular *villancico*, bears a strong melodic resemblance to *Je suis trop jeunette* (*Canti B* 6), a setting of a popular *virelai*. In both pieces the melody migrates between tenor and alto. The Spanish song, beginning "I am a young girl," also reminds one of the French "I [a young girl] am too young. . . ." Unfortunately, no continuation of the Spanish song could be found, so no proof exists that both songs developed the same subject. The return of the initial refrain at the end, unfamiliar in the *villancico*, makes one wonder whether the French song could have made its way to Spain, undergoing great musical alteration on its journey.

Analyzed as a *villancico*, its form would seem to be as follows. The initial refrain, or *estribillo*, occurs in the tenor, measures 3–9, and is imitated in the alto, measures 9–16. The text for this section may have consisted of one long line or two unequal shorter ones. The tenor now presents the first *mudanza*, measures 17–20, while the alto answers with the second *mudanza*, measures 21–24. Then follows a tenor phrase whose closing measures (29–33) are identical with the close of the *estribillo*, but whose opening measures (25–28) read differently than the corresponding measures of the initial refrain; this would have been called the *vuelta*. The melody closes with an exact recapitulation of the opening refrain or *estribillo*.

27. *ET LA LA LA* Anon. 4 v. f. 30′–31

CONCORDANCES:
Florence 164–167, no. 53, Anon. Text in all voices.
Florence 2442, no. 18, Ninot le petit. Bassus wanting; text in remaining voices.

TEXT:

La, la, la, la, la, la, la, la,
Shower her with kindness.

Early one day up was I
In the cool morn I love.
To our garden I did fly
To gather up some clove.

La, la, la, la, la, la, la, la,
Welcome the lovely shepherdess
And shower her with kindness.

To our garden I did fly
To gather up some clove.
I found it gathered far and nigh
By none other than my love.

La, la, la, la, la, la, la, la,
Welcome the lovely shepherdess
And shower her with kindness.

This text is found in two Florentine manuscripts, of which Florence 2442 gives the better reading throughout. Florence 164–167 shows Italianisms and is less consistent in spelling and forms.

A chanson *à refrain*, this composition consists of two stanzas of four lines each and a refrain which has two lines at the beginning of the chanson and three lines after each of the stanzas.

There is a chanson of thirteen stanzas in Paris-Gevaert, *Chansons* (no. 130), of which this text is probably a variant. The same stanzaic structure and subject matter appear in the first two stanzas of both chansons. Another chanson in the same collection (no. 104) has similar subject matter, with a mixture of French and Provençal forms. The theme was a popular one.

2. Florence 164–167: "Faytes le bonne chiere," in some voices
3. Paris-Gevaert gives "m'y" in two related poems (nos. 104 and 130).
4. Florence 164–167: "matin," in two voices
5. no = notre
Florence 164–167: en un jardin (bassus)
6. giroufflés, gironsflée, gironfflés; cf. Paris-Gevaert: la girouflade (no. 104)
9. Florence 164–167: "ale," Italian influence
12. Florence 164–167: luy mon amy, le mon amy, la mon amy; cf. Paris-Gevaert: le myen amy (no. 130)
13. Florence 164–167: amassés
14. "Et" appears in the superius of each manuscript.
16. Florence 164–167: alle belle bargère

de la cour de Bourgogne au XVᵉ siècle (1420–1467): Gilles de Binche (Binchois), Pierre Fontaine, Jacques Vide, Nicole Grenon, Gilles Joye, Hayne de Ghizeghem, Robert Morton: messes, motets, chansons (Paris, 1937), pp. 233–36, mm. 19 ff., mm. 43 ff., and mm. 67 ff.

MUSIC:

Three features give this little work a very "modern" air: the prevalence of the quarter note, its use of the Ionian mode, and the appearance of the melody in the soprano—a comparatively new practice around 1500. Although anonymous in *Canti B*, it appears in Florence 2442 under the name of Ninot Le Petit. Since all works of Ninot are in this same modern vein, the attribution is probably correct. No related compositions have come to light, nor has a monophonic version of the melody survived. It seems doubtful, however, that Ninot composed every note of *Et la la la*; he was probably making a polyphonic arrangement of a popular song of the day.[64]

The composition is a continuous setting of two stanzas separated and enclosed by refrains. Ninot's refrain does not occur in the song found in Paris-Gevaert, *Chansons*, nor was it found elsewhere in connection with any music. Two references to this refrain in the contemporary literature, however, lead one to believe either that a popular song with this refrain did once exist—or else that these citations refer specifically to Ninot's composition. We have no sources to prove either conjecture to be true, but the former is the more likely to be so.

In a collection of Noels of the sixteenth century, one carol beginning *Chantons nau nau nau nau nau / A gorge desployée nau* was to be sung "Sur: *La la la la la la / Faictes luy bonne*."[65] The second reference occurs in an interesting context. Jean Molinet, poet and musician of the late fifteenth century, produced a prose version of the medieval *Roman de la rose*, which he called *Roman de la rose moralisé*. The original *Roman* was a very long

poem of 21,780 lines. The first part was written about 1230 by Guillaume de Lorris and dealt with the love philosophy of the troubadours; the latter part was added by Jean de Meun(g) about forty years later, and its story is subsidiary to all sorts of poetic digressions. Molinet not only "de-rhymed" the entire poem, he brought its language up to date; he also divided his prose text into one hundred and seven chapters and added a moral or religious commentary at the end of each chapter.[66] He followed an established tradition when he "de-rhymed and moralized" the *Roman*.[67]

At the end of chapter 86, in the "Morality,"[68] Molinet describes the vicissitudes of fortune, using musical terms of his day. A translation of the passage follows the original French:

S'il vous samble que Dandenare face plus que le possible ou miroer de ce monde par son art magicque, je vous dis bien que Fortune fait encoire plus fort es choses quasi incredibles, par sa fainte musique,[69] car souvent advient qu'elle eslieve une povre minime de petite valeur, sy le fait monter en pou d'espace, par regles, degrés et joinctures de la main, tellement qu'elle se treuve au plus hault de la game, tant augmentee et de sy grant value que ceste povre note qui n'estoit que simple minime devient une grande maxime, portant une bien longue queuwe et illec chante a haulte voix: le serviteur hault guerdonné. Et quant Fortune voit qu'il se degoise et glorifie en son estat, qui n'est point de majeur parfait,[70] elle dit a ses chambourieres:

[64] 1502, the date of publication of *Canti B*, is probably too early a date for composers to have been writing in imitation of the popular song. In discussing this matter, Howard Brown comments ("The *Chanson rustique*: Popular Elements in the 15th- and 16th-Century Chanson," *Journal of the American Musicological Society*, XII [1959], 16–26; 24): "Familiarity seems to have bred imitation. In the first quarter of the [sixteenth] century popular tunes were borrowed by serious composers; in the second quarter serious composers were writing their own."

[65] See Vaganay, *Les Recueils de noëls*, pp. 35 ff. This carol is no. 6 in *La Fleur des Noelz nouuellement imprimez faictz et composez à l'honneur de la nativité de Jesuchrist et de la Vierge Marie sa benoiste mere lesquelz sont moult beaulx et de nouueau composez* [Lyons, "before December, 1535"]. Vaganay gives this title in 1935; Babelon, writing in 1913, gives a title with the same meaning, though differently worded. Babelon stated ("La Fleur des Noels [Lyon, 1535]," *Revue des livres anciens*, I [1913–14], 369–404, 371) that only one copy of this collection was known (1913). Perhaps some other edition had different contents, for Babelon's *Fleur des Noels* does not contain *Chantons nau nau nau*.

[66] *Encyclopaedia Britannica* (Chicago, London, Toronto, 1959), XIX, 430–31, *s.v.* "Roman de la Rose."

[67] Noël Dupire, *Jean Molinet: La Vie—Les Oeuvres* (Paris, 1932), p. 79. An entire subsection under this heading (pp. 79–89) is devoted to proof of this assertion.

[68] Molinet's first twenty chapters correspond to Lorris' part of the poem, chapters 21–107 to the part by Meun.

[69] The interpretation of *musica ficta* as a symbol of Fortune's quality of being subject to change has been given by Edward E. Lowinsky in "The Goddess Fortuna in Music: With a Special Study of Josquin's *Fortuna dun gran tempo*," *Musical Quarterly*, XXIX (1943), 45–77. It is corroborated in this passage by Molinet in an unexpected fashion—not only the aspect of *musica ficta*, but also those of augmentation, diminution, ascending and descending, and so on.

[70] Since Molinet is speaking of the note when it was a *maxima*, this expression may have reference to the mensuration of a *maxima*. The contemporary theorist Johannes Tinctoris defines it: *Maxima est nota in modo maiori perfecto valoris trium longarum, et in imperfecto duarum* ("The maxim is a note with the value of three longs in the *perfect major* mode, and two in the imperfect"). See Johannes Tinctoris, *Dictionary of Musical Terms* (*Terminorum Musicae Diffinitorium*), Latin and English edition, translated and annotated by Carl Parrish (London: The Free Press of Glencoe, Collier-Macmillan Limited, 1963), pp. 40–41. A note with this mensuration would be the largest note known to mensural notation. Molinet uses a corresponding expression to characterize the note after its downfall. He speaks of *deschanter*

la, la, la, faictes luy bonne chiere. Mais la fine gaupe, cognoissant les tampz, les modes, les couleurs, les imperfections, les prolations, les proportions et les tons de musicque, soudainement le fait descendre de hault en bas par soubtilles muances,[71] dont elle scet les tours, sy qu'elle le boute jus du nit, se l'apprend a deschanter son petit mineur et a diminuer tant legierement et sy bas que sa voix n'est plus oye. . . .[72]

(If it seems to you that Dandenare does more than the possible in the mirror of this world by his magic art, I tell you that Fortune, indeed, does still greater and almost incredible things by her feigned music,[69] for it often happens that she elevates a poor minim of little value, so makes him rise a small interval by lines, degrees, and joints of the hand, that he finds himself at the very top of the scale, so augmented and of such great value that this poor note that was only a simple minim has become a big maxim, bearing a very long tail, and there he sings in a loud voice: *Le serviteur hault guerdonné* [cf. *Odhecaton* 35]. And when Fortune sees that he is boasting and glorying in his estate, which is not at all of the perfect major [mode],[70] she says to her chambermaids: *La, la, la, faictes-luy bonne chière* [cf. *Canti B* 27]. But the shrewd trollop, knowing the times, the modes, the colors, the imperfections, the prolations, the proportions, and the tones of music, suddenly makes him descend from top to bottom by subtle mutations,[71] of which she knows the tricks, so that she throws him down from his high nest and teaches him to go back to his humble minor [prolation] and to diminish so lightly and so softly that his voice is heard no more. . . .)[72]

Molinet selected his songs carefully to strengthen his symbolism. *Le serviteur* is indeed a song of a person who is happy with his lot: "Assovy et bien fortuné, l'eslite des eureux de France" ("satisfied and very fortunate, select of the lucky ones of France"—refrain, line two). Molinet's reason for citing *E la, la, la* seems to be twofold. First, Fortune tells her maids to lull him into a state of carelessness by giving him "bonne chière." Then, as the "poor minim" in the guise of "a big maxim, bearing a very long tail," glorifies himself "at the very top of the scale," Fortune decides to "take him down a peg," and what would be more suitable for this purpose than the melodic setting of the refrain of *E la, la, la*—the complete descending scale, from top to bottom! Although he sang *Le serviteur* in a loud voice, his voice now diminished, along with his size, until "it was heard no more."

Ninot's work opens with a polyphonic setting of the refrain. The next refrain is treated homophonically, and the pedal point (mm. 18–20) sounds as natural as if its use were an everyday occurrence in Franco-Flemish polyphony.[73] The same setting is used for the final refrain. The refrain melody (soprano, mm. 1–5, for example) is not an independent phrase but is borrowed from the setting of the second half of the stanza (soprano, mm. 15–18).

The first stanza places the melody in the superius; the second stanza gives the melody to the tenor for the first two lines, then to the soprano for the last two. The passage connecting the two sections starts with a kind of "false entry" in the tenor (mm. 32–33), in which the phrase is compressed into two measures. The bass imitates exactly, and the remaining voices enter in ascending order. The climactic entry of the soprano brings the melody, which remains in this part to the end of the work.

The extensive use of the quarter note, the Ionian mode, the insistence on the diatonic scale, the melody in the soprano, the V-I cadences, coupled with 4-3 suspensions, the tonic pedal-points—all contribute to an amazingly modern and "tonal" sounding composition.

(See also Introduction, p. xv)

---

son petit mineur. Now, according to Randle Cotgrave, *A Dictionarie of the French and English Tongues* (London, 1611; facs. ed., University of South Carolina Press, Columbia, 1950), *deschant* means not only "Descant (of Musicke;)" but "also, a Palinodie, recantation, or contrarie song to the former," and likewise *deschanter*, therefore, means "also, to recant, or unsay what one hath formerly delivered." It is in this second meaning that Molinet uses the term, making it perfectly clear that the "povre minime de petite valeur," first elevated by Fortuna to the status of "une grande maxime," finds himself suddenly, by the Goddess' wily maneuvers, thrown down from his high estate to become small and insignificant as before.

[71] "Muances" must be a reference to the mutations of the hexachordal system, the means of changing from one hexachord to another as one sang up or down the scale. It is also the old equivalent of modern "modulation" and thus further corroborates the equation between the Goddess Fortuna and *musica ficta* (see the study cited in note 69, pp. 67–69).

[72] Dupire, *Jean Molinet*, pp. 23–24.

---

28. *FORS SEULLEMENT*   Pe. de la rue   4 v.
      f. 31′–32

CONCORDANCES:

Basel F. X. 1–4, no. 118, Mathias Pipilari. Incipit "Forseulement" in each of four voices.

Bologna Q 19, f. 1′–2, Pipelare. Incipit in all voices.

Brussels 228, f. 17′–18, Anon. Text in all voices.

Florence 164–167, no. 61, Anon. Text in all voices.

Paris 1597, f. 60′–61, Anon. Text in all voices.

[73] See Lowinsky, *Tonality and Atonality*, musical examples 13 and 15; see also pp. 95–96 for other examples of pedal points.

Regensburg C 120, pp. 336–37, Pipelare. Incipit in two of four voices.

Segovia, f. 92, Matheus Pipelare. Text "Exortum est in tenebris" in all voices.

St. Gall 461, pp. 8–9, m. pipelare. A capital F only in tenor (of four voices).

Tournai 94, f. 22–22', Anon. Tenor only, with text.

Aich [1519]⁵ Lieder, f. 74, Anon. Incipit in highest of four voices.

Egenolff [c. 1535]¹⁴ Lieder, Vol. I, no. 31, Anon. Superius only, with incipit.

MODERN EDITIONS:

Bernoulli, *Aus Liederbüchern der Humanistenzeit*, Beilage XII, pp. 98–99, M. Pipelare (after St. Gall 461).

Bernoulli, *Liederbuch des Arnt von Aich*, no. 72, pp. 126–27 [Matthaeus Pipelare].

Giesbert, *Ein altes Spielbuch*, pp. 8–9, M. Pipelare (after St. Gall 461).

Maldeghem, *Trésor musical (profane)*, Vol. I (1865), no. 6, Matthaeus Pipelare (= Reese, "Maldeghem," no. 555).

Maldeghem, *Trésor musical (profane)*, Vol. XXI (1885), no. 12, Matthieu Pipelare (= Reese, "Maldeghem," no. 557).

Picker, *Chanson Albums*, pp. 233–36 (Matthaeus Pipelare) (after Brussels 228).

Seay, *Pierre Attaingnant, Transcriptions*, no. 10 [Pipelare] (after Florence 164–167).

Shipp, "Paris MS f. fr. 1597," no. 61, pp. 485–89 (Pipelare).

Wolf, *Obrecht: Wereldlijke Werken*, Beilage, no. 3, pp. 88–90, Pipelare (after Florence 164–167).

RELATED COMPOSITIONS:

See H. Hewitt, "*Fors seulement* and the *Cantus Firmus* Technique of the Fifteenth Century" (to be published in a volume of essays honoring Dr. Dragan Plamenac) for more than thirty compositions related to *Canti B* 28 both textually and musically.

TEXT:

Save waiting only till I die,
In my sad heart no hope have I.
For my ill fate torments me so,
No sorrow not from you I know.
On losing you I can rely,
Your cruel darts intensify
My woe. No comfort from this tie
Nor satisfaction can I show.
　　Save waiting, etc.

In sadness all alone I cry,
Cursing, when I do not sigh,
This loyalty which pains me so.
Alas, this life I would forego
When you all succor me deny.
　　Save waiting, etc.

This *rondeau cinquain* appears in many manuscripts of the period. Several sources give only the refrain: Brussels 228 (f. 17'–18), Florence 2439 (f. 52'–53), Wolfenbüttel (Landesbibliothek, MS 287 extravag., f. 43'–45), and Antico 1520⁶ *Chansons à troys* (no. 19) are substantially the same; Paris 1597 (f. 60'–61), Florence 164–167 (no. 61), Cortona 95–96, Paris 1817 (no. 22), and Tournai 94 (f. 22–22') give poorer readings. The entire *rondeau* is found in Paris 1597 (f. 36'–37), Paris 1719 (f. 34), Paris 1722 (f. 72'), Berlin 78. B. 17 (f. 69), and Vérard, *Le Jardin de plaisance* (f. 115). This edition follows the Löpelmann (*Liederhandschrift des Cardinals de Rohan*) reading of Berlin 78. B. 17.

2. Vérard: A mon . . .
3. Paris 1597, f. 60'–61: Car mon las cueur . . .
　Brussels 228: sy fortune tourmente
4. Vérard, Paris 1719, Paris 1722, Brussels 228, Cortona 95–96, Paris 1817: "Qu'il . . .," a better reading
　Brussels 228: pour vous
　Antico 1520⁶ *Chansons à troys*: que n'est
5. Florence 2439, Paris 1597, f. 36'–37: je suys
6. Paris 1722: m'y
7. Vérard: "se" for "ce"; n'a
　Paris 1597, Paris 1722: Qu'en ce parti il fault que je m'asseure
8. Paris 1597, Paris 1722: Dont je n'ay bien qui en rien me contente
13. Vérard omits this line, needed to complete the *rondeau*.
14. Paris 1597: n'est
　Paris 1722: rien

Another text (found in St. Gall 463 and Antico 1520⁶ *Chansons à troys*) exists, having the same incipit but with different words thereafter. Five lines have been found.

Fors seulement la mort sans nul aultre attente
De reconfort soubz doloreuse tante
Ay pris se jour despitieuse demeure
Comme celuy qui, désolé, demeure
Prochain d'enuy et loing de son attente.

(Awaiting only death so dire,
Have I, in sorrow's tent, in hopeless ire
Begun this day my cruel stay,
Like him whose constant, desolate way
Leads but to woe and far from his desire.)

MUSIC:

Although both editions of *Canti B* name Pierre de la Rue as composer of this work, four manuscripts attribute it to Matthaeus Pipelare. Jozef Robyns

59

PLATE XII. Brussels, Bibliothèque Royale de Belgique,

MS 228, f. 17'–18, "Fors seulement."

ascribes the work to La Rue.[74] Since he names only *Canti B* as source, one wonders what his opinion would be in the face of the many attributions to Pipelare. Ronald Cross, who claims the work for Pipelare,[75] thought that the attribution to La Rue in the 1502 edition was withdrawn in the 1503 edition. In actuality, La Rue's name is present in both editions.

As is well known, the chanson is but one of a large number of compositions (thirty to forty) bearing the name of this *rondeau cinquain*. I have dealt with this family of chansons in my article mentioned above.

29. *ET DUNT REVENIS VOUS* Compere   4 v.
f. 32'–33

CONCORDANCES: None.

MUSIC:

Even in the absence of its text, this work is recognizable as an example of the "new style" of setting words to music. One may assume that the text was a free chanson, for nothing in the form or style of this music suggests an association with one of the *formes fixes*. One need only compare this work by Compère with Hayne van Ghizeghem's *De tous biens* (*Odhecaton* 20), a beautiful example of the earlier, melismatic style of writing, to observe the changes that have taken place in the manner of musical composition.[76]

In the more extensive use of the quarter note these new works acquire a quickness and lightness, an air of gaiety and abandon, that is in marked contrast to the serene, detached—even somber—mood of the older works. Shorter phrases and more rests accompany the quicker pace. A delightful effect of light and shade is created as the voices enter and disappear in quick succession. Hayne's four-part *De tous biens*, for example, in sixty measures has twenty-five rests; Compère's *Et dunt revenis vous* in fifty-nine measures has sixty-nine rests. The opening phrase of Hayne's

soprano is fifteen measures long (or see the alto, mm. 1–16, of his *La Regretée, Canti B* 48), that of Compère's, three measures.

The repeated note as an effective compositional device has now come into its own. Hayne also repeated notes, but in one of two ways: either as an anticipation in a syncopated, melodic cadence (*Canti B* 48, soprano, m. 37) or in the old under-third cadence (*Canti B* 42, soprano, m. 14); or as a means of extending a melodic tone when new syllables had to be sung (*Canti B* 48: tenor, mm. 47–48; soprano, mm. 51–52 or 64–65). Both uses are unobtrusive. Quite different is Compère's treatment in measures 25–27 of the soprano of *Et dunt*. Here repetition is employed for its rhythmical and declamatory effect; it is perhaps even intended to amuse. Pirro felt that "often, moreover, Loyset recites his texts rather than sings them, observing this narrating tone that the French musicians adopt when they have an amusing anecdote to tell. In *Et dont revenez-vous*, the soprano declaims ten syllables on the same *la*. This tendency to speak is observed also in *Une plaisante fillette* [*Canti C* 6], in *L'autre jour* [*Canti C* 47], in *Je suis amie du fourrier* [*Canti B* 11], in *Allons faire nos barbes* [*Odhecaton* 26], in *Des trois la plus*, in *J'ai un sion*."[77]

Another feature of the new style is the frequent employment of homophonic passages in which the chord takes precedence over the individual vocal part. This may occur in half notes, as in *Canti B* 15 (mm. 47–50); or, more frequently, in quarters (*Et dunt*, mm. 25 ff.); or in a mixture of the two (*Et dunt*, mm. 50–53). (Here all four voices join in presenting two chords alternately four times in succession.)

Another modern feature, paired imitation, is found in *Et dunt* (mm. 28–32). (Note the final "comment" by the lower voices [mm. 33–35] in augmented values, which must have had a relation to the words of the song.) The medieval hocket is revived as an amusing device: in measures 48–49, soprano and tenor are paired against alto and bass, each pair singing a single quarter note and then resting for a quarter while the other pair answers.

All these features are intimately linked with the new text treatment. In the earlier style only the general mood of a text (usually that of grieving) was reflected in the music. In the newer style more thought is given to the declamation of the text; even a single word may receive individual attention. Along with this greater

---

[74] Jozef Robyns, *Pierre de la Rue (circa 1460–1518): Een bio-bibliographische Studie* (Brussels, 1954), p. 172 (no. 18).

[75] Ronald Cross, "Matthaeus Pipelare: A Historical and Stylistic Study of His Works" (Ph.D. dissertation, New York University, 1961), p. 99.

[76] In a valuable study of "Changes in the Literary Texts of the Late 15th and Early 16th Centuries, as Shown in the Works of the Chanson Composers of the Pays-Bas Méridionaux" (*Musica disciplina*, XV [1961], 145–53), Margery Anthea Baird touches on the observable changes in the attitude of the composers toward the words of the songs and how this is reflected in their musical settings.

[77] Pirro, *Histoire de la musique*, p. 225.

interest in texts, which are now more frequently of a light, gay, amusing content, goes a new tendency to repeat words: this may be an entire phrase, or it may be a single word or syllable. In *De tous biens*, for example, Hayne writes a phrase of fifteen measures for a line of verse of only nine syllables. Ninot Le Petit in *E la la la* (*Canti B* 27), on the other hand, repeats a line of seven syllables (making fourteen syllables in all) within a phrase filling only five measures (tenor, mm. 34–38).

With the older settings, the generally plaintive mood of one piece of music suits one *rondeau* as well as another of the same size. The new treatment of the poetry[78] makes substitution of a different text difficult, if the original has been lost. Should another be substituted, the effects originally planned by the composer, and dependent on the words, would inevitably be spoiled.

(See also Introduction, pp. x–xi.)

30. *J'AY PRIS AMOURS* Japart 4 v. f. 33'–34

CONCORDANCES:

Florence 178, f. 4'–5, Japart. Incipit, S only. Above S: *Antiphrasis baritonat.*

Florence 229, f. 158'–159, Jannes Japart. Incipit, S, A. Above S, *Canon: Ne sonites a mese—Lycanosipathon summite.* In the margin: *Antiphrasis baritonat.*

Rome C. G. XIII, 27, f. 66'–67, Jo. Japart. Incipit "Je pris amorus," S. Above S: *Canon Vade retro sathanas.*

Verona DCCLVII, f. 48'–49, Anon. Without text.

MODERN EDITION:

Disertori, "Il manoscritto 1947-4 di Trento," p. 15 (after *Canti B* 30).

RELATED COMPOSITIONS:

See *Canti B* 3 and Hewitt, *Odhecaton*, no. 21, for additional related material.

MUSIC:

The present work is an example of the practice of "borrowing" one voice from another composer's work and using it as the basis of a new work. Jean

Japart borrows for use as his bass the soprano part of the anonymous setting of *J'ay pris amours*, also drawn upon by Obrecht in *Canti B* 3.[79] In the original notation of *Canti B* 30 the borrowed voice appears in the usual place of the superius, the upper part of the folio verso; accompanying the notes, however, there is a canon which reads: *Fit aries piscis in licanos ypathon.* According to Tinctoris, "a canon is a rule showing the purpose of the composer behind a certain obscurity."[80] The present canon is no exception. *Aries* ("the Ram") is the first sign of the zodiac; *Pisces* ("the Fishes"), the last. In requiring that *Aries* become *Pisces*, therefore, the composer is directing that "the first shall be last; and the last shall be first,"[81] that is, the part is to be performed in retrograde motion. *Pisces* is the twelfth sign distant from *Aries*, which implies that the part must be transposed by a twelfth, obviously downward, for an upward transposition would carry the part beyond the upper limits of the gamut. Yet, to leave nothing to chance, the canon concludes: *in licanos ypathon*, a note precisely a twelfth below the opening tone, a', of the borrowed *cantus firmus*. When this transposition is made, the superius becomes the actual bass of the work. In astrology, *Aries* is said to govern the head; *Pisces*, the feet. Musically, the part that was the "head" or highest member of the printed parts becomes the "foot" or lowest member in performance.[82]

At the beginning, the alto sings the first four notes of the original superius (see the bass, mm. 55–57), while, two measures later, the soprano quotes the first four notes of the tenor of the original three-part setting of *J'ay pris amours*.[83] Since the *cantus prius factus* in the bass could hardly be recognized, these brief quotations were designed to identify the arrangement for the connoisseur as belonging to the family of compositions based on *J'ay pris amours*.

The poem is a *rondeau quatrain*, and in the original setting each line of the refrain had its own musical

---

[78] Baird, "Changes in the Literary Texts of the Late 15th and Early 16th Centuries," p. 153, comments that the "difference in text setting lies just here. In the 15th century chanson there is a meandering, indecisive quality in the setting—an unconsciousness, not of the structure of the text, but of the rhythm; in the 16th century chanson there is a clarity and precision—the result of a conscious consideration, not only of the formal structure of the poem, but of its rhythmic structure also. It is a difference in conception and style which separates the two centuries. . . ."

[79] *Odhecaton* 21 is another arrangement of the same *cantus firmus* by Japart; see Droz, *Trois chansonniers français*, no. 2, for the original setting of the *rondeau.*

[80] *Tinctoris, Dictionary of Musical Terms*, ed. Parrish, p. 13.

[81] Matt. 19:30.

[82] In an article devoted to several *cantus firmus* treatments of *J'ay pris amours*, Benvenuto Disertori publishes Japart's arrangement and discusses the canon ("Il manoscritto 1947-4 di Trento e la canzone 'i'ay prins amours,'" *Rivista musicale italiana*, XLVIII [1946], 1–29; see pp. 12–18).

[83] A comparison may be made with *Canti B* 3: tenor, mm. 177–79.

phrase. A short rest marked the caesura in each line, thus creating eight possible cadential points. In Japart's bass these melodic cadences now fall in measures 1, 11; 14, 21; 27, 36; 44, 50. Japart managed to produce some of his polyphonic cadences at these same points (see mm. 21, 36, and 44, in particular). The work never comes to a full stop, since the bass tones of the cadences are beginning notes of new phrases in Japart's arrangement.

The new voices imitate not the opening notes of Japart's bass phrases but those of the original phrases of the *cantus firmus*: (1) after the caesura of line one the original *cantus* read C, D, E, F, in half notes (see the bass, mm. 51:3—53:2); the soprano anticipates (mm. 51–52) with C, D, E, F; (2) the third phrase of Japart's bass closes with three half notes on E (mm. 19–20); three half notes on A open the soprano and alto phrases (mm. 23–24). Stylistically, Japart matches his borrowed *cantus firmus* well throughout the work.

The presence of the *cantus firmus* in the bass gives this part an unusually melodic cast. Since no attempt would have been made to sing the words backward, it becomes doubtful whether any of the parts would have been sung—although they are never "unvocal." It would seem, rather, that many of these arrangements of *cantus prius facti* were considered by their composers as problems in composition *per se* and were thus not necessarily written with vocal performance in mind.

31. *JE CUIDE* (S, A) / *DE TOUS BIENS* (T, B) Japart 4 v. f. 34′–35

CONCORDANCE:
Egenolff [c. 1535][14] *Lieder*, Vol. I, no. 32, Anon. Superius only, with incipit.

RELATED COMPOSITIONS:
See *Canti B* 42 and Hewitt, *Odhecaton*, Concordances to nos. 2 and 20, for other material.

TEXT:

Although the text of *Je cuide* has not been found, it was doubtless a *rondeau quatrain*. In Florence 229, a *corona* is placed in measure 33, indicating that a return to the beginning could be made after completion of the cadence (mm. 33–34). In *Canti B* 31, however, no *signum* appears at this point. A stop would be possible in measure 33; singing an F-sharp in the soprano would make a smooth transition to measure 1.

MUSIC:

This is the first example in *Canti B* of the simultaneous use of two *cantus prius facti* within the same composition. Japart employs the superius of an anonymous setting of *Je cuide se ce tamps me dure* (occurring as *Odhecaton* 2 and possibly by Japart himself) and the tenor of Hayne van Ghizeghem's *De tous biens* (*Odhecaton* 20).

Hayne's work was written in the Dorian mode once transposed, and Japart retained this mode. The original setting of *Je cuide* was in the Ionian mode. Some modal adjustment was therefore necessary. Japart transposes the borrowed superius down a fourth and adds one flat to the signature. This voice, which originally had a major flavor, now takes on minor characteristics and blends modally with Hayne's tenor. Furthermore, Hayne's tenor had to be changed to accommodate contrapuntally the unchanged superius melody of *Je cuide*. Since Hayne's *De tous biens* was several measures longer than the original *Je cuide*, Japart started the notes of *De tous biens* ahead of those of *Je cuide* and diminished the original note values at times (a sudden change occurs at m. 14:1). Elsewhere he cut a phrase into two segments (the rests in mm. 11–12 divide the very first phrase into two shorter ones) or varied the reading of a phrase for a few beats (mm. 19–24).

At the beginning of the work, the added parts (alto and bass) are reminiscent of Hayne's composition: compare the bass (mm. 1–4) with the superius of *Odhecaton* 20 (mm. 1–5); or the alto (mm. 1–6) with Hayne's tenor (*Canti B* 31, tenor, mm. 4–13). Elsewhere the added voices move independently of either *cantus firmus*.

32. *FRANC COEUR, QU'AS TU* (S) / *FORTUNA D'UN GRAN TEMPO* De Vigne 5 v. f. 35′–36

CONCORDANCES: None.

RELATED COMPOSITIONS:
See Hewitt, *Odhecaton*, no. 74, Concordances, for other compositions based on the melody of *Fortuna d'un gran tempo*.

TEXT:

> Dear, noble heart, why do you sigh?
> Do you not in pleasure lie?
> Take and have your joy in me,
> Be as a lover ought to be.
>
> – – –

Fortune long to me has been
My kindly, gracious, lovely queen.
But this one favor that I ask,
For it she dons her cruel mask.

We are dependent on purely literary sources for the poem *Franc coeur qu'as tu*. A number of the poems of the period begin with the favorite epithet, *Franc coeur*, but continue differently from the incipit in *Canti B*.[84] We do, however, find a few references to a song having the correct continuation, *qu'as tu*, but as *timbres* for carols.[85]

One or more lines of *Franc coeur, qu'as tu a soupirer* occur in three different French farces.[86] The most extended quotation appears in *Le Médecin et le badin*, when "La Chamberière chante":

Franc coeur, qu'as tu a soupirer?
Es tu poinct bien en ta plaisance?
Prens en moy toñ esiouyssance,
Ainsy c'un amoureulx doibt avoir.[87]

Every known reference to *Franc coeur, qu'as tu* continues *a soupirer*. The carols show stanzas of six lines, so that the original text must have been strophic and therefore not one of the *formes fixes*. The longest textual quotation that we have found consists of only four lines. Words and melody are nowhere found together.

The text of *Fortuna d'un gran tempo* has been published by Gröber, "Liederbücher von Cortona," no. 20 (after Paris 1817), and by Renier, "Mazzetto di poesie," no. 21 (after Cortona 95–96). It is a *canzona a dispetto* with four stanzas of two lines each.[88]

[84] For example, the *rondeau quatrain*, *Franc cueur gentil sur toutes gracieuse*, found in Vérard, *Le Jardin de plaisance* (poetry only), f. 74–74', or (f. 98') the *rondeau cinquain*, *Franc cueur gracieux*. The former was set to music by Dufay (*Guillelmi Dufay, Opera omnia*, ed. H. Besseler, VI, 89); it also became an Italian dance, *Francho cuore gentile*, which was danced *à deux*. In this form it appears on f. 73'–74 of MS L. V. 29 of the Biblioteca Comunale of Siena (see *Bibliofilia*, XVI [1914–15], 204).

[85] In a collection of carols, *Nouelx faitz a lonneur de Ihesucrist* (Lyons, *ca.* 1506), no. 28, *Nouel nouel nouel nouel* is headed by the *timbre* "Sur: *Franc ceur quas tu à suspirer*." Other carols sung to this melody are listed in Brown, *Music in the French Secular Theater*, "Catalogue," no. 135.

[86] Brown, *Music in the French Secular Theater*, "Catalogue," no. 135 a–c.

[87] Adrien J. V. Leroux de Lincy and Francisque Michel (eds.), *Recueil de farces, moralités et sermons joyeux* (4 vols.; Paris, 1837), II. In the copy I have seen, each play has its own pagination. This text appears on p. (6) of the tenth (unnumbered) item in this volume.

[88] Cf. Hewitt, *Odhecaton*, the concordance of *Odhecaton* 74. This is an unusual setting of *Fortuna d'un gran tempo*, in which the basic melody is not shown so clearly as in some other settings. See Lowinsky, "The Goddess Fortuna in Music."

MUSIC:

This work is unusual in its use of five voices and its simultaneous employment of two secular poems: one, French; the other, Italian. A number of settings of the melody *Fortuna d'un gran tempo* survive,[89] but no source is known for the melody of *Franc coeur, qu'as tu*.

De Vigne's tenor presents a straightforward reading of the melody *Fortuna d'un gran tempo*. De Vigne treats the melody as two phrases separated by six measures' rest (mm. 22–27). The *cantus firmus* is in augmentation.

The composer used in a free way the technique of the "mensuration canon." Starting together with the tenor melody, the alto (labeled "contra," meaning "contratenor altus") sings the same *cantus firmus* two times, but twice as fast. Although the tenor melody is in the Mixolydian mode—the prevailing mode of the composition—the first alto statement (m. 10:1—m. 20:1) is in the Dorian mode (at the fifth above), whereas the second alto statement is in the Ionian mode (at the fourth above). Since the alto phrases proceed without pause, they come to an end at measure 30:2. De Vigne thus had to add two short phrases of his own to make this voice equal in length to the tenor.

In his study of "The Goddess Fortuna in Music, with a Special Study of Josquin's *Fortuna dun gran tempo*," Edward Lowinsky drew De Vigne's arrangement into the circle of compositions symbolizing Fortune in some way:

There are variations in the literary and pictorial representations of the wheel. "In the *Roman de Fauvel* good and bad Fortune are symbolized . . . by two wheels, one fast and the other slow, within each of which is another small wheel that has a contrary movement." To reproduce this in music, one voice would have to give the *Fortuna* melody at a fast pace, another at a slow pace—or "augmented," as music theory terms it—, a third voice would have to accompany the first melody at its own brisk rate but in contrary movement, while a fourth voice would move slowly but again in contrary movement.

Such a technical feat would be almost impossible of achievement. Yet this is precisely the plan of *Fortuna dun gran tempo* by De Vigne. . . . To be sure, the assignment is too difficult to be carried out all through the work. But while, from meas. 10 to the end, the two larger wheels are perfectly symbolized by the simultaneous slow and fast singing of the *Fortuna* melody, the two smaller wheels are at least recognizable in the form of the pair of fast and slow voices that begin at the same time and invert the theme, thus moving in contrary motion with the first pair.[90] [See the

[89] See Hewitt, *Odhecaton*, discussion of the text of *Odhecaton* 74.
[90] Lowinsky, "The Goddess Fortuna in Music," p. 75.

superius, m. 10:1—m. 11:1, and the bass, m. 10:1—m. 11:4.]

This interpretation, though bold, now appears corroborated by Molinet's astonishing commentary on Fortuna's musical presentation (see above, pp. 57–58). The voice below the tenor (also labeled "contra," but with the meaning "contratenor bassus") starts with an imitation of the tenor, thus stressing the importance of *Fortuna d'un gran tempo* as the basic *cantus firmus*. The bass, however, serves mainly a harmonic function. It shows only three rests; of these, the first two are quarter rests, but the third, in measure 30, is a half rest and is followed by D twice repeated, probably in imitation of the opening of the second phrase of *Fortuna*.

The soprano has an unusual structure. The *Fortuna* melody unexpectedly appears in the soprano (mm. 22–32); since the tenor is resting during measures 22–27, the canon shifts to the two highest voices during these measures. If the soprano was sung, what words were sung to the closing phrase (mm. 33–37)? And are the phrases found in measures 1–20 those to which *Franc coeur* was sung—or were they freely composed by De Vigne? At present, insufficient material is at hand to answer these questions with certainty. The text has been inserted in the soprano to make a vocal rendition possible, and if there is no contemporary authority for doing so, neither is there any against it.

Petrucci gives the name "De Vigne" with the music of *Canti B* 32; in the index we find "Devigna." Glareanus in his *Dodecachordon* assigns a motet, *Ego dormio*, to "Antonius a Vinea" and later comments, "est Traiectensis in Belgis."[91] Tschudi calls him "Antonius de Vinea Germanus."[92]

In a study of music in Antwerp, Léon de Burbure relates that "an old Belgian composer, Antoine van den Wyngaerde, became *chapelain* of the church of Notre Dame in 1483. According to the usual custom of the time, his name was Latinized to 'de Vinea.' When he took possession of his benefice Ant. de Vinea was already qualified as *Magister*; he took a place in the

choir on the left, beside a chaplain by the name of Comperis, whose Christian name we have been unable to discover. He assisted at the execution of the Offices by the large choir up to 1498–99, the date of his death. He was buried in the church of Notre Dame with all the honors due himself and the rank of his family in Antwerp."[93]

Vander Straeten found mention in the registers of the University of Louvain (in its "matricules") of an "Antonius de Vinea, cameracensis diocesis," who was listed as having matriculated as a student "XXX^a augusti" (the year not being given by Vander Straeten).[94] Since Antwerp was in the diocese of Cambrai,[95] this was doubtless our composer.

Like many other composers of the day, he was known under several "disguises," but the French "Vigne," the Latin "Vinea," and the Dutch "Wyngaert" all mean "vine" or "vineyard" in English.

Beside *Canti B* 32, only one other composition is known to be by De Vigne: the motet *Ego dormio & cor meum vigilat* ("I am sleeping, and my heart is awake"), which Glareanus published in the *Dodecachordon* with the comment:

The whole song, moreover, has a natural grace in all voices, so that you see a person who is sleeping, yet really awake; the song is simple, not in the least artificial, and quite without elaboration; and therefore it should deservedly have a greater reputation among all the most eminent persons; and, indeed, prove alluring to the reader by virtue of this charm.[96]

(See also Introduction, p. vii.)

33. *AMOURS ME TROCTE PAR LA PANCE*
Lourdoys   4 v.   f. 36'–37'

CONCORDANCE:
   Florence 2442, no. 26, Lourdault. Bassus wanting; text in the remaining voices.

TEXT:
Through my loins Love does his dance
As foxes chase a hen.
He has strewn coins all over France
To entertain the girls again.

[91] Henricus Glareanus, *Dodecachordon* (Basel: H. Petrus, 1547), p. 253.
[92] St. Gall 463, f. 103. It should be added that the designation "Germanus" at that time meant no more than that the person so named came from the German Reich, which then included the Netherlands. Glareanus (*Dodecachordon*, p. 460) calls Heinrich Isaac, who is a Fleming, "Germanus." (See also Hans Albrecht, *Die Musik in Geschichte und Gegenwart*, VI, s.v. "Isaac," cols. 1417–34; 1418.)
[93] "La Musique à Anvers aux xive, xve, et xvie siècles (Extrait des archives de l'église Notre-Dame d'Anvers)," Copie du manuscrit de M. le Chevalier Léon de Burbure par Louis Theunissens, *Annales de l'Académie Royale d'Archéologie de Belgique*, LVIII (1906), 252.
[94] Edmond Vander Straeten, *La Musique aux Pays-Bas*, IV, 8.
[95] *Ibid.*
[96] Glareanus, *Dodecachordon*, p. 253.

Just one double-banded billiard cue,
My bells' two spurs, jingling true,
Sound clear as a trumpet up in the blue.
Press on the assault with all good speed. Spur on the steed
Both front and back.
The steed's expired.
No, he's not, but now he's tired.
Quick, on in to the flag,
Spur on the horse, plunge in without fear,
Launch the attack right from the rear.
Our trouble's for naught, the barn's full and taut. Ho! Ho!
Sound trumpets and clarions and spinets inspired!
Tattoo on the drums, for the steed has expired!
Thus in the game of love we do.
Thus in the game of love we do.

The present chanson is also found in Florence 2442 of which the bass part-book is wanting. It is one of many chansons of the time containing words and phrases that have a double meaning. For a discussion of such songs, consult P. Champion, "Pièces joyeuses du XVᵉ siècle," in *Revue de philologie française et de littérature* (XXI [1907], 161–96).

The text has no definite stanzaic pattern although certain sections show an attempt at a precise rhyme or meter. It may be that the composer borrowed sections from other texts, which he then elaborated.

The voices vary somewhat in the presentation of the text. Soprano and alto take the line "Le courtault est mort"; tenor and presumably bass follow with "Non est mai s'il dort." A few lines farther, soprano and alto take "Jouez du testu," tenor and presumably bass the following, "Laschez tost les cu."

Two voices and the *Canti B* incipit read "trotent," while the other voices give "trocte." The verb "sema" (two lines below) is likewise dependent on "amours" and is singular in all voices. Such confusion in endings, common to the period, is again seen in the terminals *s* and *z* of this text.

> *Canti B* incipit: sur
> Florence 2442: par

MUSIC:

The entire composition—both words and music—seems to be a completely original one, and the music a continuous setting of its elaborate text. In its form the work has no parallel in *Canti B*; the stylistic techniques employed, however, are not uncommon in the setting of popular songs. There is much use of paired imitation at the distance of an octave to either the same words or the other half of a couplet. Homophonic writing

alternates with a simple polyphonic style. The setting is for the most part syllabic.

Imitation is used most effectively in the closing section (mm. 85 ff.). A theme of six measures appears successively in all four voices in the order of their pitch from lowest to highest, each new statement coming one measure after the preceding one. This eight-measure passage, unique in *Canti B*, produces the same climactic effect as does the stretto in a fugue. A decidedly humorous effect, undoubtedly inspired by the text, results as the word "ainsi" is enunciated four times: "Ainsi [ainsi . . . ainsi . . . ainsi] va le jeu d'amourettez."

"Lourdoys," as in *Canti B*, or "Lourdault," as in the part-books in Florence, was a nickname given Jean Braconnier, the composer of *Amours me trocte*. Both words had essentially the same meaning;[97] only "lourdaud," however, survives in modern French.

André Pirro has compiled all the information we have on this composer in his concise "Notes sur Jean Braconnier, dit Lourdault,"[98] so that only a brief résumé need be included here. In 1478 Braconnier was in the service of René I, Duke of Lorraine. From 1496 to 1506 he was a member of the "Grande Chapelle" of Philip the Fair of Burgundy, accompanying Philip on his trips to Spain in 1501 and 1506; he then passed into the service of Louis XII of France as "chapelain." He died in January, 1512. Braconnier was a "ténoriste" at the Burgundian court, and his voice, described as "silvery," must have had a beautiful quality. He was apparently a favorite of Philip, who once referred to him as "nostre bien amé Johannes Braconnier."

Guillaume Crétin wrote a very touching "Plainte sur le trépas de Lourdault, chantre nommé proprement Maistre Jehan Braconnier"—a poem running to some nineteen stanzas. This lament survives today in two different manuscripts at the Bibliothèque Nationale[99] and over the years has been published at least three times.[100] It is the source of our information concerning his nickname: he was named Lourdault "after a song that was sung," namely, *Lourdault, lourdault,* an

[97] Randle Cotgrave, *A Dictionarie of the French and English Tongues,* s.v. "lourdois" and "lourdaut."

[98] *La Revue musicale,* IX (April, 1928), 250–52.

[99] Fonds fr. 24315, fols. 96–99; fonds fr. 12406, fols. 53–56.

[100] In *Esprit des journaux* (May, 1779), pp. 279 ff.; again in an article by J. Peyrot, "Une poésie de Guillaume Crétin (vers 1500) sur la mort d'un chanteur de la Chapelle royale," *Tribune de Saint-Gervais,* XXI (1919), 4–7, 35–38; and more recently in *Oeuvres poétiques de Guillaume Crétin,* ed. Kathleen Chesney (Paris, 1932), no. 43.

arrangement of which, by Compère, appears in *Canti B* as no. 5.

Here is the stanza, as printed in the Chesney edition, p. 212 (after fonds fr. 12406), referring to his nickname:

> Lourdault eut nom par ung epitethon
> Qu'on luy donna d'une chanson chantee.
> Tousjours fut prest quand on disoit "chanton"
> Et n'eust on sceu prendre en si meschant ton
> Que ayr ne fendist de sa voix argentee.
> Sa voix rendoit toute oreille enchantee
> Et de l'ouyr chascun avoit envye.
> Helas! pourquoy n'est demeuré en vie,
> Veu qu'il donnoit au roy tant de liesse?
> O dur regret, quel chantre aboly esse!
>
> (They gave him as a nickname "Clod"
> From a song he once had sung.
> So prompt when they said "Sing, by God!"
> You couldn't give him words so odd
> That he'd not pierce the air with silver tongue.
> To his voice all charmed ears clung,
> To hear him was all hearts' desire.
> Alas, why did he of this life tire,
> Since to the king he gave such joy?
> Sad fate this singer to destroy!)

The lament contains references to several other contemporary composers: the "gentil Musicien Maistre Anthoine Févin," "Nostre bon père et maistre, Prioris," "Longueval, et Mouton," and "Josquin des Préz."

(See also Introduction, p. ix.)

34. *BAISÉS MOY* Josquin 4 v. f. 38

CONCORDANCES:

Cortona 95–96, Paris 1817, no. 2, Anon. Bassus wanting; text in remaining voices.

Tournai 94, f. 22'–23', Anon. A tenor voice, with text.

Antico 1520[3] *Motetti novi e chanzoni*, f. 17'–18, Anon. Text in the two notated voices. The words "In dyatessaron" and a *signum* in each voice direct that two additional parts are to be realized in performance.

Egenolff [c. 1535][14] *Lieder*, Vol. I, no. 33, Anon. Superius only, with incipit.

MONOPHONIC VERSIONS:

Paris 9346, no. 102. Published in Gérold, *Manuscrit de Bayeux*, and *Chansons populaires*, no. 20.

This melody is virtually identical with the bass of *Canti B* 34.

MODERN EDITION:

Smijers, *Josquin des Prez: Wereldlijke Werken*, no. 20a, p. 53 (after *Canti B* 34).

RELATED COMPOSITION:

See *Canti B* 37.

TEXT:

> "A kiss, a kiss!
> Again a kiss, my own sweet miss,
> For love I pray. 'Tis not amiss."
> "No, no."
> "Why so?"
> "Such folly'd grow,
> To my ma's woe."
> "And now I know, and now I know."

The present edition of the text follows Gérold, *Manuscrit de Bayeux*. Smijers, *Josquin des Prez: Wereldlijke Werken*, Tournai 94, and Gröber, "Liederbücher von Cortona" (Paris 1817), offer the text with slight variations. Renier, "Mazzetto di poesie," gives separate readings of Cortona 95 (altus) and Cortona 96 (superius) showing a different stanzaic structure in each.

This chanson *à refrain* consists of seven lines: two two-line stanzas and lines one, four, and seven which are in the nature of a refrain, although all are different. Renier does not recognize the refrain in either of his readings.

1. Cortona 95–96 and Gasté, *Chansons normandes* (Paris 9346), omit the first line.
4. Gröber: E no feré
   Renier: seray
   Smijers: et non feray (in contra and bass)
6. Smijers: morrie = marrie = fâchée
   Gérold omits "en," found in all other readings.
7. Tournai 94 does not repeat.

MUSIC:

A comparison of the first part of *Baisés moy* from Gérold's edition and my parallel transcription of the same bars demonstrates that the reading from the Bayeux manuscript is closer to Josquin's quotation than Gérold's transcription suggests.

Three notable facts concerning *Baisés moy* may be mentioned. First, it appears *twice* in *Canti B*: as a double canon on folio 38 and as a triple canon on folio 40 verso. (Here the third canon appears beneath the two found on f. 38.)

Second, whereas *Canti B* 37 shows only the *dux* of each of the three canons, with a *signum* indicating where the *comes* should begin, *Canti B* 34 gives all four voices completely written out.[101] Possibly the full

---

[101] *Canti B* 34 shows conflicting signatures: soprano and tenor have one flat; alto and bass, a blank signature. These signatures seem to reflect the transposition involved in canons at the fourth above. This, too, confirms one of Lowinsky's theories on the

As transcribed by H. Hewitt:

As transcribed by Gérold in *Le Manuscrit de Bayeux*, p. 120:

(sic)

notation was supplied to improve the appearance of the printed page—for a *signum* would have sufficed. Minute, but insignificant, differences crept in as both canonical voices were written out.[102] A comparison of the four voices of *Canti B* 34 with the corresponding voices of *Canti B* 37 also discloses slight differences. The four-part version has the less elaborate readings, also in the Cortona manuscript and Antico.

Third, although the double canon is attributed to "Josquin" by Petrucci, the triple canon was published as an anonymous work, but ascribed to Josquin in later sources (see commentary to no. 37). Doubts have been raised as to the authenticity of the third canon, however, more on stylistic than documentary grounds.

(See also Introduction, pp. ix–x.)

35. *VA UILMENT* (INDEX: *UA VILMENT*) (SEGOVIA: *WAT WILLEN WIJ*) Obreht 4 v. f. 38′–39′

CONCORDANCES:
Rome C. G. XIII, 27, f. 26′–27, J. Obrech. The incipit "Maule met" is found in the superius only.
Segovia, f. 120′–121, Jacobus Hobrecht. Incipit in each voice, beginning "Wat willen wij."

MODERN EDITIONS:
Wolf, *Obrecht: Wereldlijke Werken*, pp. 29–33 (after Rome C. G. XIII, 27).

Wolf, *Obrecht: Wereldlijke Werken*, pp. 38–42 (after *Canti B*).

TEXT:

No complete text of this poem was discovered. However, an extended incipit found in Segovia shows that the *Canti B* composition was undoubtedly the setting for a Dutch poem. Smijers, in "Twee onbekende Motetteksten van Jacob Hobrecht," *Tijdschrift der Vereeniging voor Muziekgeschiedenis*, XVI (1941), 129, n. 1, speaks of two unintelligible French incipits which are but a corruption of good Dutch. These incipits are "Vanilment," found with the *Canti B* music in Wolf, *Obrecht: Wereldlijke Werken*, and "Maule met," found with the *Canti B* music in Rome C. G. XIII, 27.[103]

The incipit of the Dutch piece, apparently a gambling song, reads "Wat willen wij metten budel spelen, ons ghelt es uut," which means something like "What shall we use for chips, our money is gone."

MUSIC:

Obrecht's arrangement of *Wat willen wij*, with its regrettably incomplete text, shows the features commonly found in arrangements of French popular songs: voice pairing, changes of meter, a final section in homophonic style, and the like.

36. *OR SUS, OR SUS, BOVIER* Bulkyn 4 v. f. 40

Above the superius: *In subdiatessaron*

CONCORDANCES: None.

function of conflicting signatures ("The Function of Conflicting Signatures," pp. 240 and 254). In spite of these differences in signature, only four flats need to be supplied: in measures 17 (bass), 32 (bass), and 36 (bass and alto). Cortona 95–96, Paris 1817, which shows only the three highest parts, gives each a blank signature. Tournai 94, which shows the tenor only, also puts no flats in the signature.
[102] Cf. alto, m. 19:1–2, with superius, m. 20:1–2; bass, m. 29:4, with tenor, m. 30:4. Note also the repetition of D in the alto (mm. 37–38), which probably should have been a single note (double whole) as in the six-part version.

[103] Perhaps it was these widely differing spellings which misled Wolf, who published *Maule met* as a separate work just a few pages before *Vanilment* in his edition of Obrecht's works. See the Concordance above.

PLATE XIII. Paris, Bibliothèque Nationale, Fonds fr. 9346 (Le Manuscrit de Bayeux), no. 102, "Baisés moy."

MUSIC:

Only three of the voices are notated, the fourth to be derived by observing the canon *In subdiatessaron* placed above the superius. The piece starts quite normally, if somewhat stiffly, with the non-canonic voices showing anticipatory imitations of the canonic parts. The first motive is not distinctive, consisting entirely of a series of half notes; this motive ascends, but the remaining motives or phrases all descend and seem more like approaches to cadences than "themes" or "motives." At measure 20 a cadence on D overlaps the start of a repeat, note for note, of the first nineteen measures. One final phrase—an upward transposition by a fourth of the penultimate phrase (mm. 40–43)—brings the composition to a close in the Mixolydian mode. Except for one brief anticipatory imitation in the bass (m. 11), the lower voices merely provide a non-thematic support for the canon.

Every effort to identify Bulkyn has been fruitless. His name was not unknown around 1500, however, for a motet, *Ave virginum gemma Catherina*, in Petrucci's *Motetti libro quarto* (Venice, 1505) is attributed to "bulkin," and the beautiful double canon, *En l'ombre d'un buysonnet*, attributed to Josquin in *Canti C* (no. 111) and elsewhere, is found in Rome 2856 under the name "Bolkin." Vander Straeten wrestled with the meaning of the name: "*Bulkyn* or *Bulkin* is a Flemish surname, perhaps become a patronymic name. Its meaning is: *petit taureau* [little bull]; in a figurative sense: *petit brutal* [little bully]. If, as we hardly think, a *t* had been omitted by Italian euphony, so as to form, with the help of this consonant, the word *bultkin*, we would then have, as an exact translation: *petit bossu* [little hunchback]."[104] Later he returns to this subject, inquiring tentatively, "Genesio Bulten ... perhaps to be assimilated to the enigmatic *Bulkyn* of the Venetian *Odhecaton*?"[105]

37. *BAISÉS MOY* (INDEX: *A SEI*) Anon. 6 v.
f. 40'

Above the superius: *Fuga In diatessaron*
Above tenor and bassus: *Fuga*

CONCORDANCES:
Copenhagen 1848, p. 133, Josquin. Incipit, S; text, bassus. Above S and T: *Canon in epidiatessaron.*

[104] Edmond Vander Straeten, *Les musiciens néerlandais en Italie du quatorzième au dix-neuvième siècle* (Brussels, 1882), p. 295.
[105] Vander Straeten, *La Musique aux Pays-Bas*, VIII (1888), 544. Vander Straeten means specifically the *B* volume of Petrucci's series.

Resolutions of these two canons are written out at the bottom of pp. 132 and 133 respectively. Curiously, there is no *signum* in the bass voice to mark the start of the third canon, nor is any resolution given of this third canon.

Attaingnant 1549 *Trent sixiesme livre* ... *Josquin*, f. xii, Josquin des Prez. Text in each of six voices.
Susato 1545[15] *Le septiesme livre* ... *Josquin*, f. xii, Josquin de Pres. Text in each of six voices.

MODERN EDITIONS:
Commer, *Collectio operum musicorum*, Vol. XII, no. 17, pp. 53–55 (source not given).
Smijers, *Josquin des Prez: Wereldlijke Werken*, Vol. II, no. 20, pp. 51–52 (after Susato).

RELATED COMPOSITION:
See *Canti B* 34 which gives the middle and top canons only.

TEXT:
For material on this text, see note on *Canti B* 34.

MUSIC:

In this arrangement of *Baisés moy* a third canon has been added below the two given in *Canti B* 34. In measure 3 of the lowest voice the composer creates a brief figure, borrowing the ideas of repetition in quarters and the leap of a third from the first motive of the first stanzaic line (tenor, mm. 8–9). This figure becomes the most important motive of the lowest canon. At the very end of the work (mm. 32 ff.) this motive is used as an *ostinato* and on each appearance is treated slightly differently in its rhythmic values. As the idea is carried out logically, a six-four chord develops in measure 38. The reading in Susato's publication of 1545 (republished by Smijers) apparently seeks to correct this passage. The three highest voices read as in *Canti B* 37, as does also the antecedent of the lowest canon. The consequent of the lowest canon, however, lacks the final "Vela de quoy!," showing a rest (m. 37) and a G, *longa* (mm. 38–39). The lower voice of the central canon descends to great G instead of ascending to small G, thus dipping below the lowest canon and converting the six-four chord into an eight-five. But why the omission of the final notes of the consequent of the lowest canon? Was this done to allow the use of the leading tone in the top voice? If so, the F in measure 37 of the lowest canon would have had to be sung F-sharp also.

Friedrich Blume questioned the authenticity of the six-part setting of *Baisés moy* (and of other chansons for six voices attributed to Josquin). In an article entitled

"Josquin des Prés" (*Der Drachentöter*, 1929, pp. 52–69; 68) he refers to "... the two settings of the chanson *Basiez moy* (for four voices, 1501; for six voices, 1545), of which the earlier shows the purest Josquin style, whereas the later is nothing other than a setting thickened and obscured by two added voices."

(See also Introduction, pp. ix–x.)

38. *AVANT, AVANT* Anon. 4 v. f. 41

Above the superius: *In subdiatessaron*

CONCORDANCES: None.

TEXT:

The correct text for this setting has not been found. A number of texts exist that begin with a single "avant." None of these fits the musical setting, however.

MUSIC:

As in *Canti B* 36, canon at the fourth below is indicated by the rubric *In subdiatessaron* placed above the superius. Again the composition shows much evidence of form not dependent on words. Two musical ideas permeate the work: an ascending series of four tones, first heard in the canonic voices (m. 3:4— m. 5:4), and the upward leap of a fourth (alto, mm. 6:4 ff., for example). Both ideas are treated in the passage, measure 3:4 to measure 12, which is brought back later (m. 32:4 to the end). The work may then be analyzed as a miniature three-part form, with the first three measures serving as an introduction.

39. *AVE, ANCILLA TRINITATIS* Brumel 3 v. f. 41'–42

CONCORDANCES:

Munich 322–325, no. 17, Anon. Trium Ad Aequales. Text in all voices.

Segovia, f. 156'–157, Anthonius Brumel. Text in all voices.

Egenolff [c. 1535][14] *Lieder*, Vol. III, no. 14. Superius only, with incipit.

Petreius 1541[2] *Trium vocum cantiones*, no. 46, Io. Mouton. The text "Ave Maria" is in each voice.

(Although both composer and text given are incorrect in Petreius, the music is that of *Canti B* 39.)

TEXT:

Chevalier, *Repertorium hymnologicum*, Vol. I, no. 1692, Beata Maria, salutatio. "Ave, Ancilla Trinitatis" (text not given). See also Vol. V, p. 45, for three sources

of this text that were not available to me: *Diurnale Vapincense* (1534), *Missale Viennen.* (1519), Avignon, MS 2595, f. 125. In regard to the last, L.-H. Labande, *Catalogue sommaire des manuscrits de la bibliothèque d'Avignon (Musée-Calvet)* (Avignon, 1892), states that this text is found in a section of MS 2595 entitled "Propres des saints."

The text is found in many Books of Hours of the period, usually in a section near the end called "Miscellaneous Prayers."

MODERN EDITION:

Hewitt, "An Unknown Motet," pp. 77–80 (after *Canti B* 39).

TEXT:

> Hail, handmaiden of the Trinity.
> Hail, daughter of the eternal Father.
> Hail, bride of the Holy Spirit.
> Hail, mother of our Lord Jesus Christ.
> Hail, sister of the angels.
> Hail, foretold of the prophets.
> Hail, queen of Heaven.
> Hail, teacher of the apostles.
> Hail, comforter of the martyrs.
> Hail, fountain and plenitude of the confessors.
> Hail, honor of the widows.
> Hail, crown of the virgins and of all the saints.
> Be thou with me in all my tribulations.
> Amen.

This version of the text in honor of Our Lady is taken from Munich 322–325. Many variants appear scattered through the Books of Hours of the period.

For further material concerning this composition, both text and music, see H. Hewitt, "An Unknown Motet of the Fifteenth Century," *The Catholic Choirmaster*, XXX (1944), 56–59, 77–80, 82.

MUSIC:

Nos. 1–38 of *Canti B* were written for four or more voices. Brumel's motet now opens the final section of the anthology, which is devoted to three-part works. It is written *ad aequales voces*, that is, for voices of equal range, as is also his *Mater patris* in the *Odhecaton* (no. 62), both works having rather similar opening themes. Each of the dozen salutations is provided with its own distinctive motive, and its close is marked by a cadence. Consistent imitation is frequent, and occasionally imitations are at the unison; each section overlaps the next, however, so that the music never hesitates in its forward progress. The setting is in the main syllabic, but brief decorative melismas keep it from becoming stiff.

Brumel changes from duple to triple meter at the point where the salutations cease and the final petition begins (m. 68). At the words "in omnibus tribulationibus" a two-measure motive is treated in ascending sequence. This motive is initiated in the middle voice and is imitated at the fifth above by the top voice one measure later; each of these voices makes three statements of the motive, the top voice finally reaching the height of a′. The lowest voice makes only two statements, moving in parallel thirds with the last statements of the middle voice. In the Segovia manuscript this voice is altered so that from measure 76 to measure 83 the lowest voice moves in parallel tenths with the top voice. Since either effect is quite satisfactory, a performance today could follow either reading.

Three other composers set this text, though these works bear no musical relationship to Brumel's composition. A four-part setting by "Yzac" occurs in the Florentine manuscript, Biblioteca Nazionale Centrale, II, I, 232 (*olim* Magl. XIX, 58), f. 150′–152. The alto has the familiar text of the "Ave Maria." Another four-part setting by Andreas de Silva is found in Antico's *Motetti novi libro II*, where it appears at the beginning of the publication, provided with a *secunda pars*, *Ave cuius conceptio*. The third work is a five-part setting by Willaert, found in a manuscript in the Biblioteca Vallicelliana in Rome, but also available in two contemporary prints.[106] The *quinta pars* "carries as *ostinato* the beginning of the famous Gregorian *Ave Maria* . . . starting alternately on c and g."[107] The remaining voices begin "Ave maria ancilla sancte trinitatis" and continue as does Brumel's text.

40. *SI SUMPSERO* Obrecht 3 v. f. 42′–44

CONCORDANCES:

Augsburg 142ᵃ, f. 31′–32, Anon. Without text.
Augsburg 142ᵃ, f. 34′, Anon. Superius only, without text.
Brussels 11239, f. 33′–35, Anon. Text in all voices.
Greifswald Eᵇ 133, no. 11, Anon. Incipit, S, T, C. (In the tenor part-book, no. 10.)
Heilbronn X. 2, no. 8, Obrecht. Contra only, with incipit.
Paris 1597, f. 5′–6, Anon. Text, S; incipit, T, C.

St. Gall 463, no. 24, Anon. Superius only, with incipit.
Egenolff [c. 1535]¹⁴ *Lieder*, Vol. III, no. 15, Anon. Superius only, with incipit.
Formschneider 1538⁹ *Trium vocum carmina*, no. 12. (In the copy at Jena "Jacobus Obrecht" is written in by a later hand.) Without text.

TEXT:

Biblia Sacra, Ps. 138:9 (English Version, Ps. 139:9) and Ps. 22:4 (English Version, Ps. 23:4).

MODERN EDITIONS:

Maldeghem, *Trésor musical (sacrée)*, Vol. XIX (1883), no. 6, Petrus de la Rue, "Muteta" Tertia Pars (= Reese, "Maldeghem," no. 304 iii).
Picker, *Chanson Albums*, pp. 467–71 (after Brussels 11239).
Shipp, "Paris MS f. fr. 1597," no. 6, pp. 254–60.
Wolf, *Obrecht: Motetten*, Vol. IV, no. 19, pp. 175–78 (after *Canti B* 40).

TEXT:

The Latin text appears with the music of *Canti B* in Brussels 11239 and Paris 1597. The text includes sections from two verses of the Psalms as found in the Vulgate.

Ps. 138:9 Si sumpsero pennas meas diluculo, et habitavero in extremis maris.
Ps. 22:4 (middle section): non timebo mala, quoniam tu mecum es.

Paris 1597 gives only the section from Psalm 138.
Brussels 11239: tu mecum est.

In the King James version this text reads: "If I take the wings of the morning, and dwell in the uttermost parts of the sea . . ." " . . . I will fear no evil: for thou art with me."

MUSIC:

Si sumpsero confronts us with the recurrent problem: vocal or instrumental? The thirty-seven syllables of the Latin verses are strung in a haphazard manner over the hundred and four measures of the work. Was Obrecht's intention that they be sung? If not, why was the text given at all?

Johannes Wolf, editor of Obrecht's complete works, does not discuss this matter, but one may infer that he accepted the work as a "motet," for he not only included it in the volume of Obrecht's motets, but inserted the words, following his own judgment as to their placement, and introduced a great deal of textual repetition not indicated by the manuscript sources. Martin Picker refers to this problem, feeling that "the

---

[106] Edward E. Lowinsky, "A Newly Discovered Sixteenth-Century Motet Manuscript at the Biblioteca Vallicelliana in Rome," *Journal of the American Musicological Society*, III (1950), 173–232; 210. The signature of the manuscript is "Vall. S. Borr. E. II. 55–60," and Willaert's motet appears in it as no. 30.

[107] *Ibid.*, p. 210.

6

PLATE XIV.   Paris, Bibliothèque Nationale,

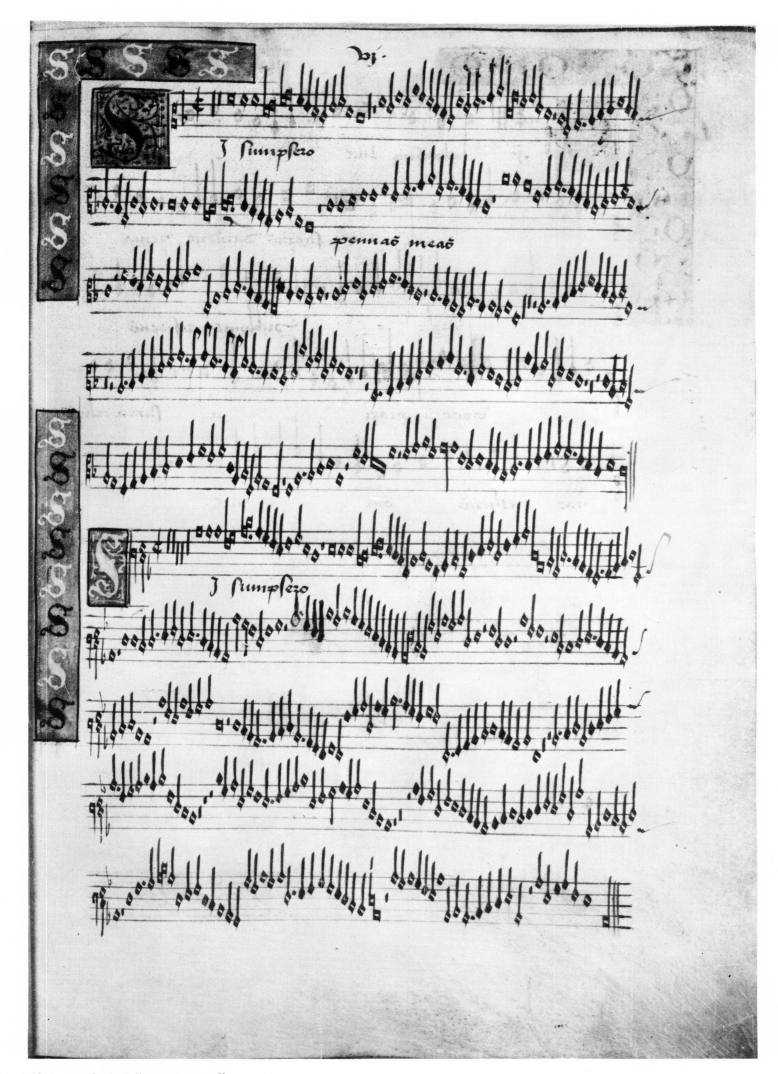

Fonds fr. 1597, f. 5'–6, "Si sumpsero."

text fits so loosely that the practicability of vocal performance is open to question."[108]

Both Picker and Wolfgang Stephan[109] feel that this music, with its own "form" clearly delineated by motives, repetitions, and so forth, anticipates the later instrumental fantasia.

The results of a search for a *cantus firmus*—a plainsong setting of a text beginning *Si sumpsero*—were negative. Although such a setting of *Si dedero* (*Odhecaton* 56) appears in both the Roman and Sarum rites, none of *Si sumpsero* was found. My search did disclose how few chants begin by descending a third and then ascending a second followed by another second. If even this opening is "un-Gregorian," the continuation by shaping one of the cadential approaches common in polyphonic music of the period makes it seem even less likely that Obrecht was treating a plainsong melody.

41. *MON PÈRE M'A DONNÉ MARI*   Anon. 4 v. f. 44'–45

CONCORDANCES: None.

RELATED COMPOSITIONS:

1. Copenhagen 1848, p. 441, Anon. Text, S; incipit, T, C.

    This work is based on the same popular melody as is *Canti B* 41.

2a. Florence 2442, no. 34, L. Compere. Bassus wanting; text in remaining voices.

2b. Segovia, f. 127'–128, Loysette Compere. Incipit in each of four voices.

2c. Petrucci 1504³ *Canti C*, f. 66'–68, Compere. Incipit in each of four voices.

    This work, found in *Canti C* and the two preceding sources, treats *Mon père* in its first section, a different song in its second section.

3. Florence 229, f. 3'–4, Henricus Yzac. Incipit, S, A. Published in Wolf, *Heinrich Isaac: Weltliche Werke*, E 30, p. 96.

[108] Martin Picker (ed.), *The Chanson Albums of Marguerite of Austria, A Critical Edition and Commentary* (Berkeley and Los Angeles: University of California Press, 1965), p. 94. Edgar H. Sparks, *Cantus Firmus in Mass and Motet: 1420–1520* (Berkeley and Los Angeles: University of California Press, 1963), p. 307, thinks that "like most motets of this class [song motets], *Si sumpsero* is probably not based on *cantus firmus*."

[109] Picker, *The Chanson Albums of Marguerite of Austria*, p. 94; Wolfgang Stephan, *Die Burgundisch-niederländische Motette zur Zeit Ockeghems* (Heidelberger Studien zur Musikwissenschaft, VI [Kassel: Bärenreiter, 1937]), p. 59.

4a. St. Gall 463, no. 33, Anon. Superius only, with text.

4b. Antico 1520⁶ *Chansons à troys*, no. 24, Anon. Superius and contra only, with text.

    This incomplete work shows no musical resemblance to *Canti B* 41; after the first two lines of text the poem continues differently also.

Dutch counterpart of the French popular song *Mon père*:

1. Kalff, "Handschriften ... Amsterdam," pp. 179–80, *Mijn vader gaf my enen man*. Melody and text after a late fifteenth-century manuscript in the University Library, Amsterdam.

2. Mincoff-Marriage, *Souterliedekens*, no. 145, pp. 265–66. Psalm 58 was to be sung to the melody of *Mijn moerken gaf my enen man*. (The melody is from the edition of 1540; the text is after Kalff, "Handschriften ... Amsterdam." Also published in Duyse, *Oude Neder-landsche Lied*, II, 937; the text is from Kalff, the melody from Mincoff-Marriage.)

TEXT:

My pa has wed me to a relic
Whose beard has long been hoary.
Wed thus at fifteen's not idyllic,
Graybeards are not my glory.
    Now he's so sage,
    But I do rage
For lack of love's sweet game.
And that's why Ill-Wed is my name.

This text has survived somewhat illegibly in Copenhagen 1848, more clearly in Florence 2442, where it forms the first part of a quodlibet. The musical setting of the quodlibet is also found in *Canti C*. The first eight lines may be a stanza of the chanson needed for the *Canti B* setting; the other half of the quodlibet is a different poem in both structure and content. It would seem that parts of two poems were joined to make the quodlibet, the first eight lines sung by the "mal mariée" and the second section (also of eight lines) by a young man.

Florence 2442 preserves only one stanza of text, but there is evidence that other stanzas existed and that the final line of our text is a refrain, "Mal maridade, c'est mon nom."

A Dutch version of this poem shows the same refrain line appearing at the end of each of the five stanzas, "Meshouwet, soe is den name mijn." The content shows a variation on the familiar theme of the *mal mariée*.

There is evidence of Provençal influence in the text.

4. "mi," for "m'y" or "me"
5. sade = maussade
6. rade = impétueuse
8. maridade = mariée

Two other sources, Antico 1520[6] *Chansons à troys* and St. Gall 463, give eight lines, but differ from the text in Florence 2442 after the first two lines:

Mon père m'a donné mari
A qui la barbe grise point
Mauldit soit-il qui la nourit
Car de plaisir il n'y a point.
　　Il est infâme,
　　Il me veult blasme,
Il est jaleux, comme l'on dit,
De ce mignon qui va de nuit.

(My pa has wed me to a hubby
Whose beard has long been hoary.
May he who smooths it have but worry,
For in it there's no joy or glory.
　　This wretch for shame
　　E'er me does blame,
Jealous fool he, so goes the story,
For this sweet young lad's nightly foray.)

The last two lines are repeated in Antico.

Since the two poems have identical metrical construction, the second text could also be sung to the *Canti B* music. However, the melody in St. Gall 463 and Antico is not that of *Canti B* 41.

MUSIC:

Research on *Mon père m'a donné mari* uncovered such a wealth of material that I have dealt with it in a separate article, in which it was shown that the popular tune forming the basis of our composition was sung to both a French text and a Dutch one.[110] The Dutch poem survives and runs to several stanzas, each closing with a one-line refrain, "Meshouwet. . . ." By analogy one may say that the French poem also closed with a refrain, "Malmaridade . . .," even though only one stanza seems to have come down to us.

This melody occurs, with slight changes, in the *Souterliedekens* of 1540, attached to Psalm LVIII, indicating perhaps that the melody was "arranged" for this use. Clemens non Papa used a simpler form of

the melody when arranging it for his three-part settings of the *Souterliedekens* published in 1556. For comparison, reference is made to Henry Bruinsma's dissertation on the *Souterliedekens*[111] and Bernet Kempers' edition of the settings by Clemens.[112]

Various attempts to fit the text to the chanson were finally abandoned. Not only was there no text whatever for the final section (mm. 52–71), no convincing and consistent way could be found of providing the main melody in the tenor with words.

(See also Introduction, p. ix.)

42. *DE TOUS BIENS* Ghiselin 3 v. f. 45'–46

CONCORDANCES: None.[113]

RELATED COMPOSITIONS:
See *Canti B* 31 and Hewitt, *Odhecaton*, no. 20, Concordances.

MUSIC:

This composition, the only one by Johannes Ghiselin in *Canti B*, is an arrangement of the soprano voice of Hayne van Ghizeghem's celebrated setting of *De tous biens*. The poem, in the form of the favorite *rondeau quatrain*, was originally given a three-part setting by Hayne, but it appears with an optional alto in the *Odhecaton* (no. 20). In Ghiselin's arrangement, Hayne's soprano is given a completely new accompaniment. Mode and note values of Hayne's superius are retained with minor variants. In measures 5–6, for example, Hayne had written three half notes (one syllable to be sung to each); Ghiselin, however, combines the three into one long note: a hint that the words were not to be sung. At the end of several phrases, Hayne had used the old under-third cadence; when Hayne's setting was "brought up to date" by the

[110] "Malmaridade and Meshouwet," *Tijdschrift voor Muziekwetenschap*, XVII (1951), 181–91.

[111] Henry A. Bruinsma, "The *Souterliedekens* and Its Relation to Psalmody in the Netherlands" (Ph.D. dissertation, University of Michigan, 1949).
[112] K. P. Bernet Kempers (ed.), *Jacobus Clemens non Papa, Opera omnia*, II: *Souterliedekens (Psalmi Neerlandici)* (Rome: American Institute of Musicology, 1953).
[113] In the Concordances, I have kept within the limits set for my edition of the *Odhecaton*; that is, I have made no mention of Masses based on *cantus firmi* drawn from the chansons, later instrumental arrangements, etc. Clytus Gottwald, editor of Ghiselin's *Opera omnia* for the American Institute of Musicology, finds two later lute arrangements of Ghiselin's *De tous biens*. One is in Hans Newsidler's *Lautenbüchlein* (Nuremberg, 1536), no. IX. The other is in Otto Gombosi's edition, *Compositione di Meser Vincenzo Capirola, Lute-Book (circa 1517)* (Neuilly-sur-Seine, 1955), p. 31.

addition of a fourth voice, the interval of a third was "smoothed out" by the insertion of the leading tone. Ghiselin, however, retains Hayne's original cadence formula.

The style of Ghiselin's added voices contrasts strikingly with that of Hayne's graceful placid melody in the superius. These parts differ in range from that of Hayne's superius (a thirteenth as opposed to an eleventh for the superius); they are also more fragmentary in their construction: whereas the *cantus firmus* rests only four times, the tenor has thirteen rests, the contra seventeen. They move at a much faster speed, causing the *cantus firmus* to stand out as if in augmentation. The contrast seems to reflect the difference between a vocal setting and an instrumental arrangement. The way in which the range is covered differs also: notice how the contra (mm. 42–45) leaps down an octave and then continues a downward course with a leap of a third, and, after a second, another third; the vocal soprano makes no leap greater than a fourth in either direction. An ascending scalar motive (contra, mm. 22:2—23:4) is put to incessant use. It is heard more than two dozen times, appearing at various pitch levels, sometimes treated in imitation at the distance of two, or even one beat, and, less often, sequentially (mm. 36 ff.). The strong contrast here between the *cantus firmus* and its accompaniment is reminiscent of Josquin's arrangement of the two upper voices of the same work by Hayne (*Odhecaton* 95). Both works appear to be designed for instrumental performance.

The lower voices are thematically connected with each other, but make no reference whatsoever to the *cantus prius factus*. They do join with it in forming cadences—one deceptive (m. 28), others authentic (mm. 15 and 41)—at the points where the lines of the *rondeau* come to an end. The *cantus firmus* reaches its last tone in measure 60; the lower voices rest for one beat and then enter on the second beat to form the subdominant triad. The tenor proceeds with a motive filling the interval of a minor sixth in two measures; the contra then imitates this motive at the octave below and closes on the tonic in measure 64—a favorite device for "tapering off" a composition: the instruments seem to drop out, one by one, until only a full-sounding tonic (in octave or double octave) remains.

Clytus Gottwald places *De tous biens* in Ghiselin's early period of composition. He believes that works such as this (with one voice borrowed from a vocal setting, but with instrumental parts added) led directly into the sphere of instrumental music. He also feels that the motive in the tenor (mm. 19—21:2) is an anticipation of the opening motive of Ghiselin's *La Alfonsina* (*Odhecaton* 80), which he places in the composer's middle period.[114] Essentially the same motive occurs again (mm. 39—40:1), where the leading tone may be used, as in *La Alfonsina*.

The difficulty in distinguishing between instrumental and vocal works in this period is highlighted by the history of this motive in other works of the sixteenth century. First of all, it occurs in *Réveillez-vous* (*Canti B* 9, alto, mm. 41—43:2), that is, in the very heart of a vocal composition. At the end of the century it turns up as head motive of a keyboard fantasia by Giles Farnaby:[115]

Finally, it occurs at the beginning of a three-part *canzonetta* in Monteverdi's *Opus* 1:[116]

Rag - - - gi (dov'è il mio ben

A situation like this illustrates the precariousness of assuming too dogmatic a position concerning the instrumental nature of this or that melodic configuration.

43. *POUR QUOY FU FAIT CESTE EMPRISE*
Anon.   3 v.   f. 46′–48

CONCORDANCE:
Egenolff [c. 1535][14] *Lieder*, Vol. III, no. 17, Anon. Superius only, with incipit.

[114] *Johannes Ghiselin—Johannes Verbonnet* (Wiesbaden: Breitkopf & Härtel, 1962), pp. 100–102: "Fifths and octaves are frequently found filled in by 'passage work,' which leads to a very interesting anticipation of the opening motive of Ghiselin's famous 'Alfonsina' which occurs twice.... This relationship with *L'Alfonsina* confirms in retrospect from a purely instrumental piece the instrumental conception of the work."
[115] *The Fitzwilliam Virginal Book*, edited from the original manuscript, with an introduction and notes, by J. A. Fuller Maitland and W. Barclay Squire (2 vols.; New York: Dover Publications, Inc., 1963), II, 270 [no. CCVIII].
[116] Monteverdi, *Tutte le opere*, ed. G. F. Malipiero (16 vols.; Asolo, 1926–42), X, 6.

MUSIC:

When Christian Egenolff published his three volumes of songs, he included twenty-eight works from *Canti B*. With one exception, the pieces occur in the same order as in the Petrucci volume: Vol. I, nos. 17–22, 24, 23, 25–33; Vol. III, nos. 14–15, 17–25. Of the three-part works, he took all except Ghiselin's arrangement of *De tous biens* (*Canti B* 42). Of the remaining thirty-nine four- (five- or six-) part works (*Canti B* 1–38, 41) he selected seventeen. The reason for his omission of *Virgo celesti* (*Canti B* 2) and the six-part arrangement of *Baisés moy* (*Canti B* 37) was that they had more than four parts. His reason for omitting *L'omme armé* (*Canti B* 1), *D'ung aultre amer* (*Canti B* 24), or *J'ay pris amours* (*Canti B* 30), probably lay in their difficult canons. It would be interesting to know his reason for excluding *De tous biens* (*Canti B* 42) or for including *Pour quoy fu fait* (*Canti B* 43).

Although stylistically this work is of its period, its form is difficult to determine in the absence of the complete text. There appears to be no *cantus firmus*, and its style indicates that it was not a setting of a popular song. No freely composed *rondeau* of the time shows as complete a division into two parts as is found, with double bar and repetition of the metric signature, at measure 38. The *virelai* comes to mind, but the second part of *Pour quoy* shows no repetition of material such as would be required for *ouvert* and *clos* of a *virelai*. It is possible that two *rondeaux* were added together, but the style of the two parts is so uniform that one is forced to discard even this hypothesis. The close of part one is quite charming in its treatment of a simple repetition in descending sequence and in imitation between superius and contra as the tenor provides a more flowing figure (mm. 34–38). All three parts descend through an octave before coming to rest each on a different member of the tonic triad.

One can learn from this one composition many ways of forming cadences in this period, either in two parts (mm. 41, 79) or three (*passim*): with the leading tone in the superius (mm. 8–9), tenor (mm. 19–20), or contra (mm. 17, 18, or 27–28); the authentic cadence on the tripled tonic (mm. 86–87) or doubled tonic (one voice dropping out, mm. 21–22); a cadence with the fifth present in the tonic chord (mm. 41–42) or the third (mm. 11–12); the Phrygian cadence (mm. 72–73); or the deceptive cadence (mm. 15–16).

44. *ADIEU, FILLETTE DE REGNON*   Anon.
   3 v.   f. 48′–49

CONCORDANCES:
   Zwickau 78, 3, no. 24, Isaac. Without text.
   Egenolff [c. 1535]¹⁴ *Lieder*, Vol. III, no. 18, Anon.
      Superius only, with incipit.
   Formschneider 1538⁹ *Trium vocum carmina*, no. 33, Anon.
      Without text.

MODERN EDITION:
   Wolf, *Isaac: Weltliche Werke*, E 52, pp. 120–21 (after Zwickau).

MUSIC:

It is doubtful whether *Adieu, fillette* was intended to be sung. Various features give it the stamp of the instrumental *tricinium*. It begins with a theme or motive that is rhythmically interesting, and in its descent from dominant to tonic it calls to mind the opening of the same composer's *Hélas* (*Odhecaton* 50). Following imitations of this motive (in fact, of the entire phrase, mm. 1–5) by tenor and contra in succession, the work takes an almost improvisatory course. There are cadences, both melodic and polyphonic, in abundance; but one notes the lack of regular formal structure (with imitative openings for new lines of text) found in chansons.

Sweeping scale passages are present in superius (mm. 43 ff.), tenor (mm. 47 ff.), and contra (mm. 52 ff.). One voice is at times static while the other two show an interplay of rhythmic figures (mm. 21 ff., mm. 54 ff.), thus momentarily upsetting the balance of melodic activity. In measures 37–40, essentially the same figure is treated in all voices both sequentially and in imitation. A similar treatment appears in the two lower voices (mm. 54 ff.), while the superius serves as anchor with its long held tones. From measure 60:2 a combination of sequence and imitation is used to build up to a climax, producing much the same effect as does a stretto in a fugue. This effect is further enhanced by the conflict in rhythms resulting from the recurrent use of a three-beat figure in duple meter (superius, mm. 60:2 ff.; tenor, mm. 60:4 ff.).

The title of the work is provocative. Although not directly parallel with titles of other instrumental *tricinia* such as *La Morra* (*Odhecaton* 44) or *La Alfonsina* (*Odhecaton* 80), which were perhaps honoring some prominent person of the day, *Adieu, fillette de regnon* may have been composed for some gay occasion, for *fillette* meant not only "a girle, young maid, little wench," but also "a smalle wine vessell," and *fillette de Bourgogne* was a measure of wine.[117]

45. *CHANTER NE PUIS*[118]   Compere   3 v.
f. 49'-50

CONCORDANCES:
Heilbronn X. 2, no. 20, Compere. Contra only, with incipit.
Egenolff [c. 1535][14] *Lieder*, Vol. III, no. 19, Anon. Superius only, with incipit.

TEXT:

> At the fair one's house I may not (c)haunt
> Where in love's joy I'd gladly stay.
> Why not? Because the fair one runs away.
> This answer logic does not want.
>
> I see to me she'd say "Avaunt!"
> And that my love brings her dismay.
>   At the fair one's house, etc.
>
> Oft among folks her I do taunt:
> "She's all noise and empty clay."
> But Fortune wrongs me all the way,
> And so her coolness me does daunt.
>   At the fair one's house, etc.

The only known source of this *rondeau quatrain*, Paris 1719 (f. 117), as edited by Schwob (*Parnasse satyrique*, no. 52, p. 108), begins "Hanter ne puis. . . ." No text beginning with "chanter" has been found, although one may conjecture that an illuminated *C* might have been overlooked in copying. Either word may be used, however, without changing appreciably the sense of the *rondeau*.

1. chieux = chez
2. deduyt = divertissement
6. duyt = attire, charme
8. blasonne = critique
10. mes = mais

MUSIC:
The first nine measures of this composition are of unusual interest. The composer writes a motive that descends stepwise through the interval of a fifth and then, after a measure's rest, is reproduced sequentially a step lower. Tenor and contra imitate after one and two measures, the tenor at the fifth below and the

contra a fifth below the tenor. One hears in succession, then, scale segments (dominant down to tonic) in D minor, G minor, C major (contra), C major (superius), F major, and B-flat major. These motives dovetail perfectly, and the only accidental required is an E-flat in the last of the statements. One is reminded of Josquin's arrangement of *Fortuna d'un gran tempo* (*Odhecaton* 74), in which a motive with much the same characteristics is treated similarly at the start of the work, but leads to more interesting developments.[119]

46. *JE VOUS EMPRIE*   Agricola   3 v.   f. 50'-51

CONCORDANCES:
Florence 178, f. 23'-24, Alexander. Incipit "Ie uous uous eri" in S only.
Florence 229, f. 275'-277, Anon. Incipit "je vous" (or "ie vous") in each voice.
Florence 2794, f. 30'-31, Agricola. Text "Se vous voulez" in S; incipit, T, C.
London 20 A XVI, f. 5'-7, Anon. Text "Se vous voulez" in S; incipit, T, C.
Paris 1597, f. 17'-19, Anon. Text "Se vous voulez" in S, T; incipit, C.
Egenolff [c. 1535][14] *Lieder*, Vol. III, no. 20, Anon. Superius only, with incipit "Je vous empire."

MODERN EDITION:
Shipp, "Paris MS f. fr. 1597," no. 18, pp. 306-9, Anon.

TEXT:

> If you will good and faithful stay,
> Never pardon me, to God I pray,
> You for whom my love is whole,
> Lady, if ever I love, body and soul,
> Save you who o'er my heart hold sway.
>
> Am I not right? For she in whom all virtues grow,
> In whom there's not the slightest flaw to show,
> Of all the wishes to be wished on earth,
> Will be, now and ever, high and low,
> Rich in blessings. Thus do I know
> I must be hers alone, steadfast in worth.

No text beginning with "Je vous emprie" has been found. However, a *virelai* with five-line refrain beginning "Se vous voulez . . ." was also sung to Agricola's setting of *Je vous emprie*. No extant text gives the complete *virelai*, so this version, after Florence 2794, is really a *bergerette*. Even this text is incomplete since

---

[117] Randle Cotgrave, *A Dictionarie of the French and English Tongues*, s.v. "fillette."
[118] The edition of 1502 (Bologna copy) shows "Chanter," that of 1503 (Paris copy) "Chauter," an obvious typographical error.

[119] See Lowinsky, "The Goddess Fortuna in Music," pp. 45-53.

it consists of the five-line refrain plus an *ouvert* and a *clos* of three lines each, but lacks the *tierce*.

1. Paris 1597: omits "m'"; se = si
2. ja ne = jamais
3. Paris 1597: ma maistresse et . . .
4. ou = au; ne = ni
5. Paris 1597: sa donne = s'adonne
7. Paris 1597: En qui n'a point tant soit peu de deffault
11. "Tout" substituted from Paris 1597 as preferable to Florence 2794 "ton."

Lines nine to eleven are written beneath lines six to eight in the manuscript, since the musical phrases for the *ouvert* are merely repeated for the *clos*. The final syllables of line eight and of line eleven are written but once although serving both words.

MUSIC:

A comparison of the music of *Canti B* with the readings in the manuscripts shows consistent rhythmical disagreement; nearly every note of the Petrucci print that is a *brevis* or dotted *brevis* (excepting long notes found at or near cadential points) is replaced in the manuscripts by two or three semibreves, as may be needed. This is a unique example (in respect to the *A* and *B* collections) of a serious conflict with the sources.

One example will suffice. The tenor of *Canti B* starts with three half notes on G in agreement with the manuscript sources. In measure 7 the contra imitates exactly; in measure 3, however, the superius begins with a dotted whole note. This voice would normally be expected to imitate the tenor motive with three half notes, and the manuscripts agree in fulfilling this expectation.

These changes in rhythm may have been called for by the different text. Since the text *Je vous emprie* of *Canti B* has not been found, the text offered in the manuscripts, *Se vous voulez*, is used in the present edition, together with the half-note readings.

47. *A QUI DIRAGE MES PENSÉES* Anon. 3 v.
f. 51'–52

CONCORDANCES:
Bologna Q 16, f. 15'–16', Anon. Incipit in all voices.
Heilbronn X. 2, no. 24, Anon. Contra only, with incipit.
Rome 2856, f. 104'–106, Compere. Incipit in all voices.
Egenolff [c. 1535][14] *Lieder*, Vol. III, no. 21, Anon.
Superius only, with incipit.

TEXT:

A text beginning "A qui diray je ma doulleur" is found in the purely literary sources, Löpelmann, *Liederhandschrift des Cardinals de Rohan*, no. 353 (after Berlin 78. B. 17, f. 132), and Vérard, *Le Jardin de plaisance*, f. 91–91'. Although it has an incipit similar to that of *Canti B*, this is probably not the required text since Bologna Q 16, a source containing the *Canti B* music, supplies an *ouvert* incipit, "Or sus donc," not that of Löpelmann and Vérard. Furthermore, the setting by Compère calls for a five-line refrain whereas these texts give a refrain of but four lines.

MUSIC:

The music exhibits the style characterized as "late Burgundian." There is no sign as yet of that systematic use of initial imitation which was to become the hallmark of the Franco-Flemish style. Only three of the eight settings of the eight lines of text show any attempt at initial imitation; in the other five all voices move forward together. Usually each line of words is set to longer notes at the start, these notes giving way to quicker ones as the music nears the cadence, a stylistic feature retained until the newer, syllabic style of writing was adopted. The tenor approaches the final through the supertonic, the soprano through the leading tone, and several cadences throughout the work are virtually identical (mm. 5, 16, 37,[120] 43, 60, and 63). The contra is at times less melodic than the upper voices as it provides harmonic support. In this work one notices a great abundance of chords in root position.

The close of the refrain is marked by a strong cadence, a double bar, and repetition of the metric signature. Something akin to first and second endings (for *ouvert* and *clos*) seems to be supplied by the composer in measures 59 and 64. Although the Petrucci print gives no mark for a return after the first ending, MS Bologna Q 16 shows a *signum* in each voice at measure 59. The manuscripts of the period leave us uncertain as to what should be done with this music the second time through (the *clos*). It would seem that, in contrast to the modern practice of omitting certain measures on the repeat, the music following the *signum* was merely added to the preceding music as an intensification of the cadence.

One other feature of this work should be mentioned. At measure 22 there is an unusually strong point of

---

[120] See footnote 5 to the transcription of this piece for the actual readings of this cadence in the two editions of 1502 and 1503.

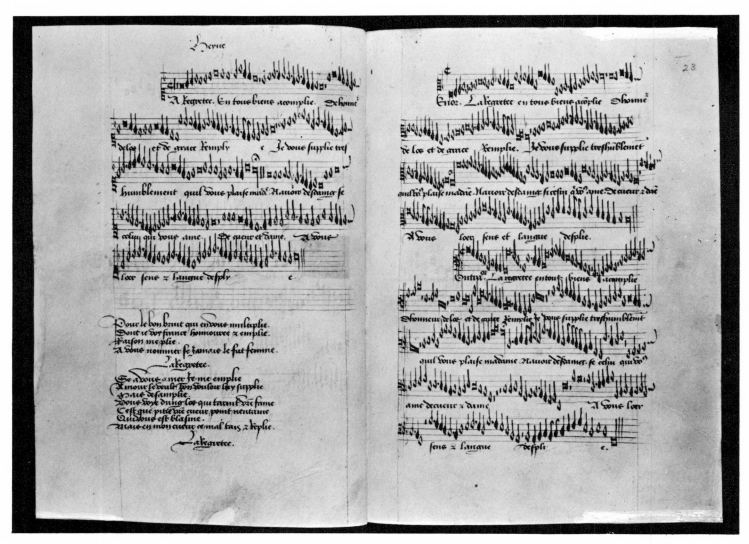

PLATE XV. London, British Museum, MS Royal 20 A XVI, f. 22'–23, Heyne, "La Regretée."

rest: each voice is marked with a *signum*, and all parts have rests for the first part of measure 23. This is a treatment one would expect at the midpoint of a *rondeau*, although no stop would be made at this point in a *virelai*. Occasional works of this period exhibit this peculiarity, and it is possible that in these pieces we have *rondeaux* which have been converted into *virelais* merely by the addition of more music and the substitution of a *virelai* text.

48. *LA REGRETÉE* Hayne 3 v. f. 52'–53

CONCORDANCES:

London 20 A XVI, f. 22'–23, Heyne. Text in all voices.
Paris 1597, f. 34'–35, Anon. Text, S, T; incipit, C.
Egenolff [c. 1535][14] *Lieder*, Vol. III, no. 22, Anon. Superius only, with incipit.

MODERN EDITIONS:

Marix, *Musiciens de Bourgogne*, no. 74, pp. 115–18 (after London 20 A XVI).
Shipp, "Paris MS f. fr. 1597," no. 35, pp. 376–81.

TEXT:

Perfect in virtues, source of my lament,
Whom honor, praise, and grace frequent,
Your gentle consent
Most humbly, Lady, I do pray.
Scorn not, nor heart and soul gainsay
Of him who, loving you, would say
With mind and tongue your praises eloquent.

Since your repute most excellent
All France's honor does augment,
Reason, this no accident,
Bids me name you, if e'er good name in woman
    lay.
    Perfect in virtues, etc.

If on loving you I'm so intent,
It is Love's will, I beg his assent.
Yet from you still absent
Is one grace, to your fame dismay.
No pity is there in your heart this day.
This one flaw only does you betray.
But I still this plaint in my heart's torment.
    Perfect in virtues, etc.

The text of this *rondeau cinquain layé* appears in London 20 A XVI, Paris 1597, and Paris 1722 (f. 73'). Marix (*Musiciens de Bourgogne*) and Wallis (*Anonymous French Verse*, no. 238) have published London 20 A XVI. Paris 1597 gives but the refrain; Paris 1722 gives the refrain and the second stanza only. This version follows London 20 A XVI.

1. Paris 1597: en tous lieux
   Paris 1722: de tous biens
2. Paris 1722: L'honneur
   London 20 A XVI: De honneur (in one voice)
4. Paris 1597 omits "très humblement," making a six-line stanza with line three reading, "Je vous supplye très humblement, Madame."
5. London 20 A XVI: se = si (T); cf. lines 11 and 13
6. Paris 1597: De arceur et de âme
   Paris 1722: De corps et d'âme
7. Paris 1597: A vous servir . . .
13. Paris 1722 gives a reading better fitted to the rhythm: S'à vous aymer de bon cueur je m'emplye. Marix added brackets to show need of another syllable.
16. Paris 1722: "termist," from "termer" = borner, limiter
    Marix: tarnit
19. Paris 1722: à mon cueur

MUSIC:

La Regretée, as a *rondeau layé*, shows shorter lines (here of four syllables) inserted between the lines of full length (here decasyllables) that echo the rhyme of the preceding long lines. Although the poetry links the short line with the line of verse preceding it, the music links it with the following line. An example occurs in measure 30. The same procedure is followed with the second "short line" (mm. 64:3 ff.). Hayne thus achieves a fine integration of poetry and music, at the same time preserving the very long phrase treasured in this style. Although a cadence does appear in measure 70 (marking the close of the second "short line"), the music continues without real pause, and this final "phrase" seems to be lengthened to some seventeen measures (mm. 64:3—80)!

49. *EN AMOURS QUE COGNOIST* Brumel 3 v. f. 53'-54

CONCORDANCES:

Heilbronn X. 2, no. 25, Brumel. Contra only, with incipit.
Egenolff [c. 1535][14] *Lieder*, Vol. III, no. 23, Anon. Superius only, with incipit.

MUSIC:

This work seems to have been written for instruments. The phrase structure of *rondeau* or *virelai* (marked by initial imitation and strong cadences) is lacking, and such bits of imitation as do occur (as, for example, mm. 44 ff.) are too casually treated to be considered the openings of new lines of text.

The work begins with a strong, impressive head-motive.[121] The long scale passsages usually found in this type of composition are kept within moderate limits. One sequential passage slips quite inconspicuously into the contra: a pattern three measures in length is reproduced at first a third and then a fifth higher (mm. 15:4 ff.). Another interesting touch is the short "hocket-like" passage beginning in the superius (m. 36:2). The passage is accompanied in the contra by an ostinato figure that might be described as a written-out turn. On its second appearance this figure is lifted to the octave above, a practice not likely to be followed in a vocal setting.

50. *JE DESPITE TOUS* Brumel 3 v. f. 54'-55

CONCORDANCES:

Heilbronn X. 2, no. 26, Anon. Contra only, with incipit.
Egenolff [c. 1535][14] *Lieder*, Vol. III, no. 24, Anon. Superius only, with incipit.

MUSIC:

Again Brumel shows originality. A feeling of unity and coherence rare in this period is manifested in techniques later periods would term "thematic development" or "transformation of themes."

The opening motive starts with repeated notes in the "*canzona* rhythm" that recur in the tenor and are used thematically in measures 45–48. The ascending minor third (a favorite interval of Brumel) reappears a degree higher, "filled in" and introduced by a "mordent." This filled-in third expanded to a fourth is now detached from the preceding passage and treated sequentially. A variation of this opening gambit begins in the superius (mm. 35 ff.) where the "filled-in" third is similarly treated.

After the cadence in measure 25, the theme of a new point of imitation again covers the interval of a fourth, this time syncopated and not scalar. The new motive is also related to an accompanimental motive

---

[121] Brumel seems to have liked this type of opening. Note its similarity to the opening motives of *Ave, Ancilla Trinitatis* (*Canti B* 39) and *Mater patris* (*Odhecaton* 62).

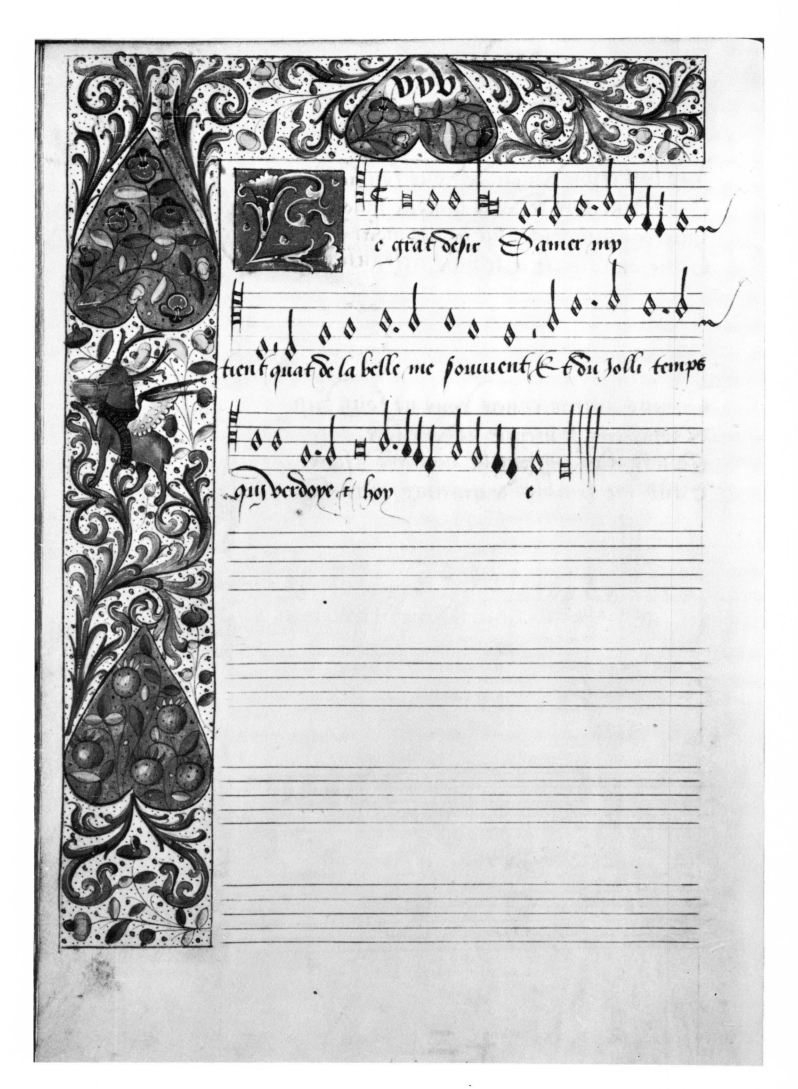

PLATE XVI. Paris, Bibliothèque Nationale, Fonds fr. 9346

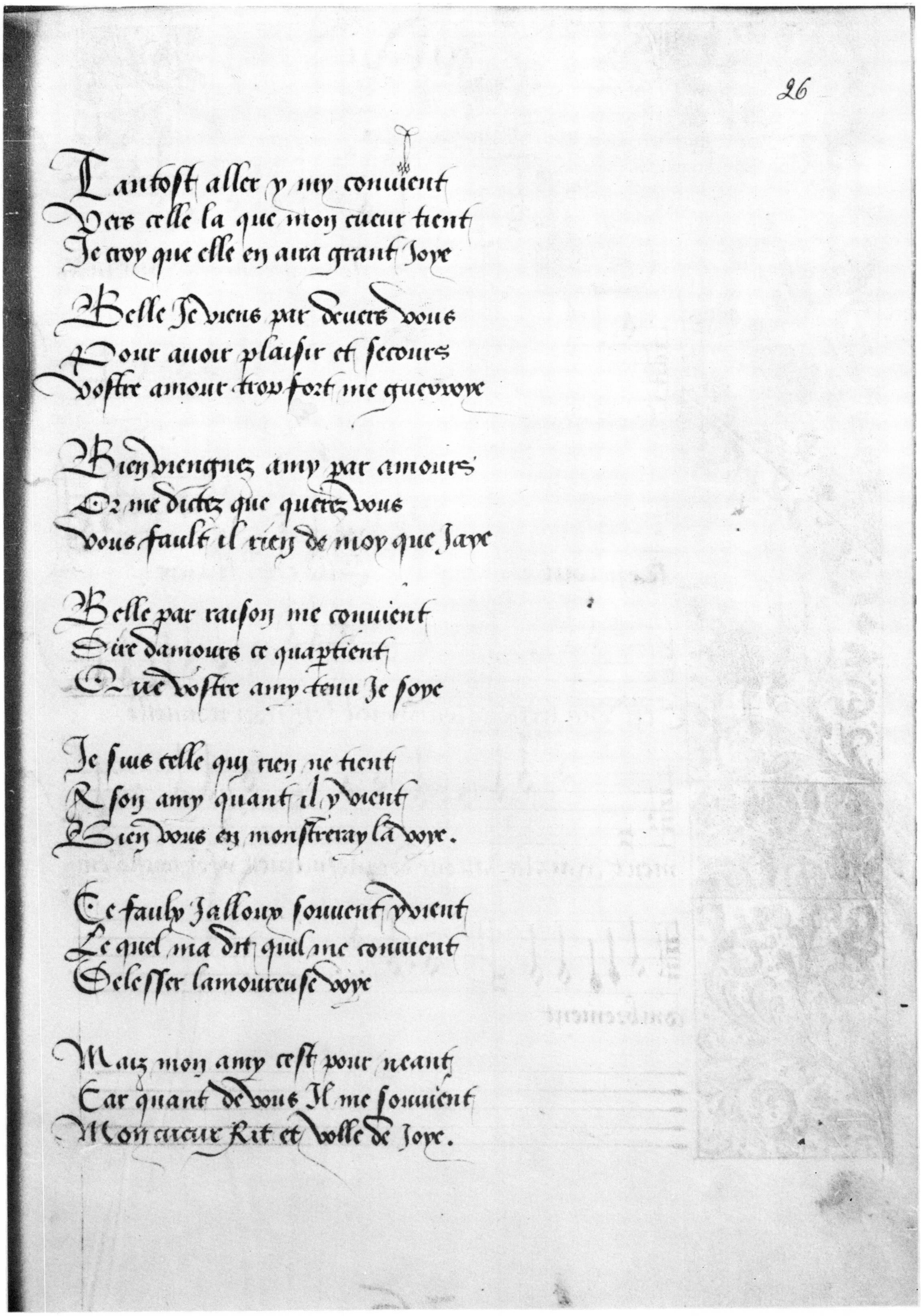

Tantost aller y my conuient
Vers celle la que mon cueur tient
Ie croy que elle en aura grant Ioye

Belle Ie viens par deuers vous
Pour auoir plaisir et secours
Vostre amour trop fort me queuroye

Bien vienguiez amy par amours
Or me dictez que querez vous
Vous fault il riens de moy que Iaye

Belle par raison me conuient
Dire damours ce quapptient
Or ne vostre amy tenu Ie soye

Ie suis celle quy riens ne tient
Aisoy amy quant il y vient
Bien vous en monstreray la voye.

Ce fauly Iallouy souuent y vient
Le quel ma dit quil me conuient
Delesser lamoureuse voye

Maiz mon amy cest pour neant
Car quant de vous Il me souuient
Mon cueur Rit et volle de Ioye.

(Le Manuscrit de Bayeux), no. 25, "Le grant désir."

in contra (mm. 31 ff.) and tenor (mm. 38 ff.). This figure, with its leap of a third, is added to the opening filled-in third to produce the figure starting in the superius (m. 54, after a rather weak cadence in the middle of m. 53). The combined motive is treated sequentially and in imitation by all voices. Since it is in diminution in relation to the previous motives, it creates the effect of a stretto and leads to the final cadence.

So tentative is the attempt here to unify and yet vary the thematic motives that one hesitates to decide whether it was made consciously or unconsciously. But that few composers of the day worked in this fashion is certain.

51. *LE GRANT DÉSIR* Compere 3 v. f. 55′

CONCORDANCES:
  Copenhagen 1848, p. 203, Anon. Text in contra only.
  Egenolff [c. 1535][14] *Lieder*, Vol. III, no. 25, Anon. Superius only, with incipit.

MONOPHONIC VERSIONS:
  Paris 9346, no. 25. Published in Gérold, *Manuscrit de Bayeux*, no. 25.
  Paris 12744, f. 93′. Published in Paris-Gevaert, *Chansons*, no. 135.

MODERN EDITION:
  Bordes, *Trois chansons*, no. III (doubtless after *Canti B*, though source is not told).

FACSIMILE:
  Kinsky, *Geschichte der Musik*, p. 72.

RELATED COMPOSITIONS:
  1. Antico 1536[1] *La Courone et fleur*, f. 5, Jo. Mouton. Text in each of three voices.
  2a. Antico 1520[6] *Chansons à troys*, no. 32, Anon. Superius and contra only, with text.
  2b. Rhaw 1542[8] *Tricinia*, no. 77, Iohan. Mouton. *Ad pares*; text in each of three voices.
      This is a second arrangement of the song attributed to Mouton.
  3. Phalèse 1569[11] *Recueil des fleurs*, f. 14, Adrianus Willaert. Text in each of three voices.

TEXT:

> Desire for love holds me in thrall
> When this fair maid I do recall
> And pretty spring in green array,
> Hey! Hey!
>
> Straight unto her I now must go,
> The one for whom my heart longs so.
> Joyous she'll be, I think, and gay,
> Hey! Hey!

> "To you I come, my lovely maid,
> For sweet delight and comfort, aid.
> Love's fierce attack does me dismay,
> Hey! Hey!"
>
> "For love's sake, welcome, dearest heart.
> Your wish to me you must impart.
> Have you cares I can allay?
> Hey! Hey!"
>
> "Fair maid, now reason me constrains
> To ask for what to love pertains,
> That I may be your love, I pray,
> Hey! Hey!"
>
> "Now I can naught refuse at all
> Whene'er my love on me does call.
> Indeed I will show you the way,
> Hey! Hey!
>
> That jealous wretch does often squall
> And urge on me complete withdrawal
> From love's gay, delightful way,
> Hey! Hey!
>
> But he succeeds, love, not at all.
> For when I, love, do you recall,
> My heart in joy soars all the day,
> Hey! Hey!"

This chanson *à refrain* is found in Paris 12744, Paris 9346, Antico 1520[6] *Chansons à troys*, Lotrian 1543 *Sensuyt plusieurs belles chansons* (f. 79), and elsewhere. The Paris-Gevaert edition (after Paris 12744) consists of seven three-line stanzas without refrain and with the final stanza in brackets. Gérold, *Manuscrit de Bayeux*, has eight stanzas. The refrain "Et hoye" appears after the first stanza and is evidently to be sung after each succeeding stanza. The two texts are generally alike in content, but Paris-Gevaert, *Chansons*, gives a different reading after the first stanza, and lacks the last two stanzas as found in Gérold. This edition follows Gérold.

  25. Gasté, in his edition of the Bayeux Manuscript, no. 25, reads "se" (si) for "ce," regarding the three lines as a question.

The Paris-Gevaert reading follows:

> Le grant désir d'aymer me tient
> Quant de la belle me souvient
> Et du joly temps qui verdoye;
>
> Tantoust partir il me convient
> Pour veoir celle qui mon cueur tient,
> Car de la veoir j'ay tresgrant joye.

"Ma dame, Dieu vous doint bon jour!
Je suis venu par devers vous:
Vostre amour sy fort me guerroye!"

"Amy, bien venu soiez-vous!
Vous fault-il rien? Que voulez-vous?
Vous fault-il la chose que j'aye?"

"Ouy, ma dame, en vérité:
De vostre amour suis tant navré
Que j'en meurs sy on n'y pourvoye."

"Et je suis celle à qui ne tient
Sy son amy pas ne parvient
A prendre l'amoureuse proye."

[Dieu garde de mal mon bel amy,
Et tous ceulx qui l'ayment aussy,
Et tous ceulx de sa compaignye!]

(Desire for love holds me in thrall
When this fair maid I do recall
And pretty spring in green array.

And now I must straightway depart
To see the one who holds my heart,
For seeing her does make me gay.

"God keep you this day, Milady fair!
To come to you I needs must dare,
Love's fierce attack does me dismay!"

"Sweet friend, welcome ever be!
Is there aught you want of me
That I may have? Tell me, pray."

"Lady, yes, in truth I know
My love of you does wound me so,
I'll die if none my pain allay."

"And I'm the one herself will blame
If her lover miss his aim
And fail to take this sweetest game.

[God keep from harm my own dear love,
And all who love him and approve,
And all his friends who 'round him move!])

MUSIC:

Compère gives us here a memorable piece of music: a simple setting of a popular song, which lies in the tenor. The two variants of this melody, found in Paris 9346 and 12744, are in general more elaborate than this tenor; if Compère "simplified" the melody as he knew it, he did it no disservice. His arrangement is so transparent that any comment may seem superfluous, yet a few touches may be mentioned. At the start, the two lower voices are at the unison, the superius at the octave above, for three beats forming an anacrusis; they then fan out to sound the complete chord of D minor on the strong beat. The first phrase, which seems to start in the Dorian mode, closes in the Lydian; the second phrase starts as if in the Lydian, but closes in the Dorian. This delightful wavering between major and minor, with its inevitable change of mood, continues throughout the song.

For the second line of words (phrase three), Compère introduces imitation: he anticipates the tenor motive (mm. 7:4 ff.) in the contra (mm. 7:2 ff.) and then imitates this motive in the superius (mm. 8:4 ff.). He repeats this procedure at the opening of the last line of the stanza. This phrase is now united with the refrain phrase by the descending sequences Compère wrote for the accompanying parts; in this passage the tenor notes act as foils for the syncopated outer parts. This third phrase and refrain are now repeated, note for note, with the single exception that, on the repeat, the contra rises from the dominant, where it rested before, to take the tonic tone in the last measure.

Although the outer parts could receive words without much difficulty, I believe they were written for instruments. A performance for solo voice and two accompanying instruments would seem to do justice to the lyrical character of the composition. Even with the repetition of the last long phrase the work runs to only twenty-seven measures, but, like many miniatures, makes up for its small size by its delicacy and simple charm.

CANTI B

1. L'omme armé

2. Virgo celesti

Compere

3. J'ay pris amours

f. 3'—4

Obreht

Superius

J'ay pris a - mours

Altus

J'ay pris a - mours

Tenor

Bassus

94

98

4. Vray Dieu, qui m'y confortera

f. 7'—8

(A. Bruhier) [1]

[1] Brussels 11239 attributes this work to "A. Bruhier."
[2] Original text incipit: "Vray dieu qui me confortera." The text is after Paris-Gevaert, *Chansons*.
[3] Orig.: G; emendation follows Brussels 11239.
[4] Brussels 11239 has a signature of one flat in alto and bass.

⁵) Orig.: these two notes appear as one (𝅗𝅥.); emendation follows Brussels 11239.
⁶) Brussels 11239 gives ₵ 3 as metric signature.

Roussignolet du boys plaisant,
Pourquoy me vas ainsy chantant,
Puisqu'au veillart suis mariée?

Amy, tu sois le bienvenu:
Long temps a que t'ay attendu
Au joly boys soubz la ramée.

⁷) The parallel fifths between soprano and alto are original.

5. Lourdault, lourdault

1) Original text incipit: "Lourdault lourdault." The text is after Paris-Gevaert, *Chansons*.
2) Basel F. X. 1—4 shows a signature of two flats in the alto.

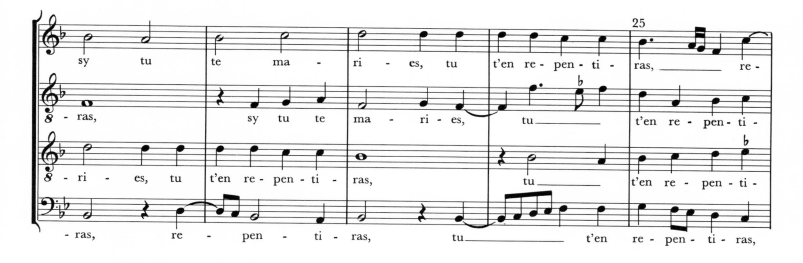

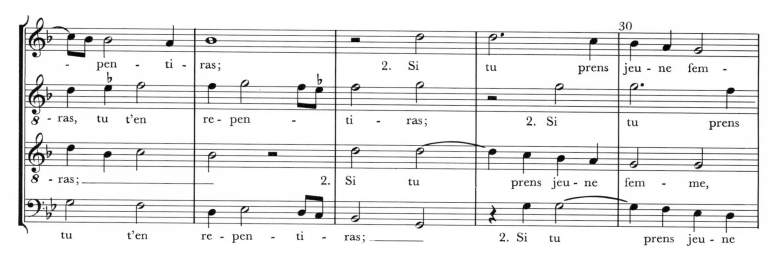

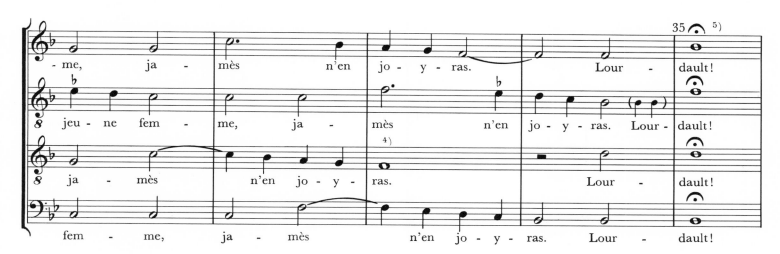

3) Orig.: these two notes appear as one (♩); emendation follows Paris 1597.
4) Orig.: ♩ ♩; emended version found in Paris 1597, Paris 1817, and Regensburg C 120.
5) Returns to the beginning for later pairs of stanzas are made at this point. The final refrain, mm. 36—55, is sung only after the last stanza.

Lourdault, etc.

3. Elle yra à l'église, le presbtre la verra;
4. La merra en sa chambre et la confecera;

Lourdault, etc.

5. Luy fera les enffanz et ren tu n'en sçauras.
6. Et quant el sera grosse, il la te renvoira;

Lourdault, etc.

7. Et nourriras l'enffant qui riens ne te sera.
8. Encor seras bien aise quant huchera papa.

Lourdault, etc.

6) Cortona 96 and Regensburg C 120 show a quarter rest on the third beat.
7) Orig.: these two notes appear as one (o); emendation follows Regensburg C 120.

6. Je suis trop jeunette

(Raulin) [1]

1) Florence 176 attributes this work to an unknown composer, "Raulin."
2) Original text incipit: "Se suis trop ionnette." The text is after Paris-Gevaert, *Chansons*.
3) Florence 176 gives E-flat; Florence 176 shows a signature of two flats in the bass.

4) Florence 176 gives two dotted *maximae* and a *longa;* that is, no rests from m. 28 to m. 41.

112

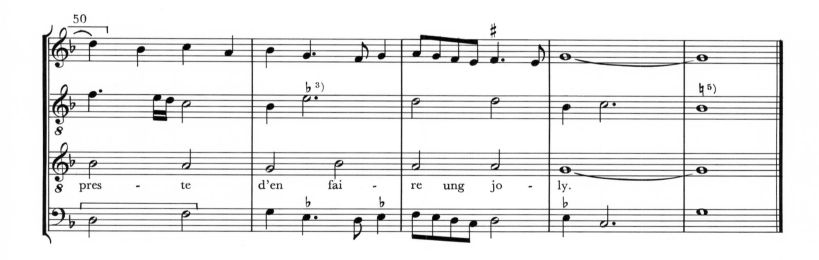

S'il me veut promettre et me tenir seur
D'estre seulle amée, prisée, et de tout son cueur,
Jamais n'auray autre seullement que luy,
Pour roy, duc ne conte qui vive au jour d'uy.
    Je suis trop jeunette, etc.

⁵) Florence 176 gives D, *longa*.

7. Ce n'est pas jeu

Pe. de la rue

f. 10′—11

1) Original text incipit: "Ce nest pas jeu." The text is after Brussels 228.

114

²) Orig.: ♩ ♩; emendation follows Brussels 228 and Brussels 11239, also alto, m. 18:4 f.

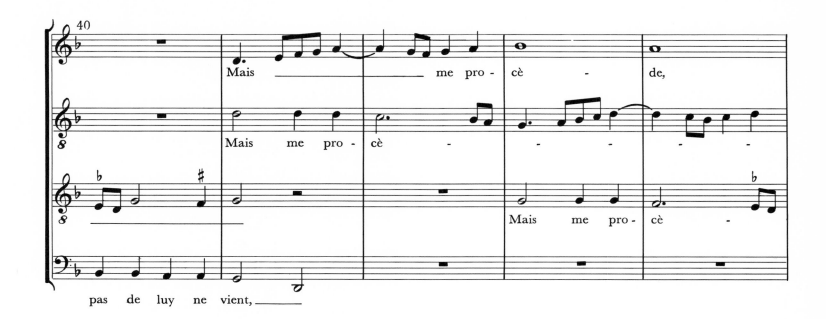

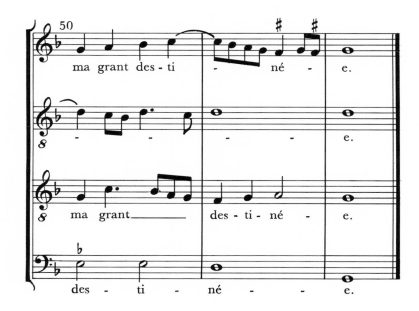

Dictes-vous donc que je suis esgarée
Quant je me voy séparée de mon bien:
  Ce n'est pas jeu, etc.

J'ay le rebours de toute ma pensée,
Et sy n'ay nul qui me conforte en rien;
De tout cecy je le porteray bien,
Mais que de luy je ne soye oublyée.
  Ce n'est pas jeu, etc.

8. L'autrier que passa

9. Réveillez-vous

f. 12′—13

Anon.

Superius

Altus

[1) Ré - veil - lez - vous,   Pic - cars   et Bour - - - gui -

Tenor

Bassus

Ré - veil - lez - vous,   Pic - cars et Bour - gui-

Ré - veil - lez - vous,   Pic - cars   et Bour - - - gui -

- gnons, _____   2)

- gnons, _____   et Bour - - gui - gnons,

et Bour - - - gui - gnons,

Ré - veil - lez - vous,   Pic - cars et Bour - gui -

- gnons,   Pic - cars _____   et _____ Bour - gui -

1) Original text incipit: "Reuelies vous." The text is after Paris-Gevaert, *Chansons.*
2) The parallel fifths between soprano and alto are original.

120

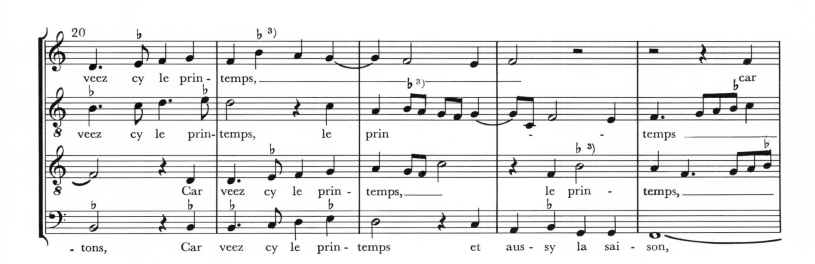

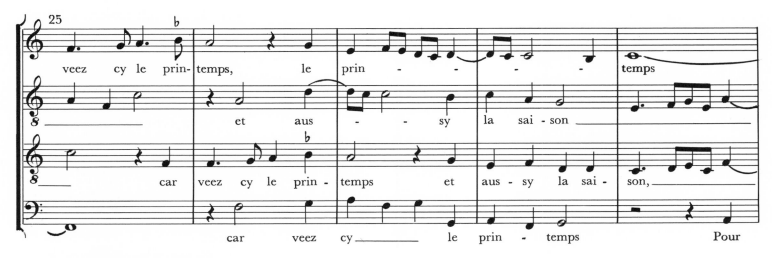

3) Regensburg C 120 gives B-flat.

Tel parle de la guerre qui ne scet pas que c'est;
Je vous jure mon âme que c'est ung piteux fait,
Et que maint homme d'armes et gentil compaignon
Y ont perdu la vie et robbe et chaperon.

Où est ce duc d'Aultriche? Il est ou Pais Bas;
Il est en basse Flandre avecques ses Piccars,
Qui nuyt et jour le prient qu'il les vueille mener
En la haulte Bourgoingne pour la luy conquester.

Adieu, adieu Salins, Salins et Bezançon,
Et la ville de Beaulne là où les bons vins sont;
Les Piccarz les ont beuz, les Flamans les payeront
Quatre pastars la pinte, ou bien bastuz seront.

10. En chambre polie

1) The parallel fifths are original.

11. Je suiz amie du fourrier

f. 14'—15

(Loyset Compere)[1]

Superius
[2] Je   suiz   a - mie   du   four - rier,   Or   a-

Altus
Je   suiz   a - mie

Tenor

Bassus

[2] Orig.: F.

[1] Rome C. G. XIII, 27 ascribes this composition to "Loyset Compere."

[2] Original text incipit: "Je suis amie du forier." The text is after Gröber, "Liederbücher von Cortona."

3) Cortona 95—96, Florence 107bis, and Florence 164—167: ♩♩ ♩ ♩♩
4) Orig.: ♩ ♩; emendation follows Cortona 95—96, Florence 107bis, and Florence 164—167.
5) Cortona 95—96, Florence 107bis, and Florence 164—167: G.
6) Orig.: E; Cortona 95—96, Florence 107bis, and Florence 164—167: F.

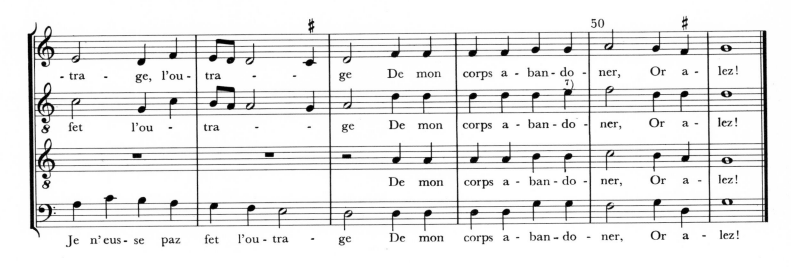

12. Mon mary m'a diffamée

De Orto

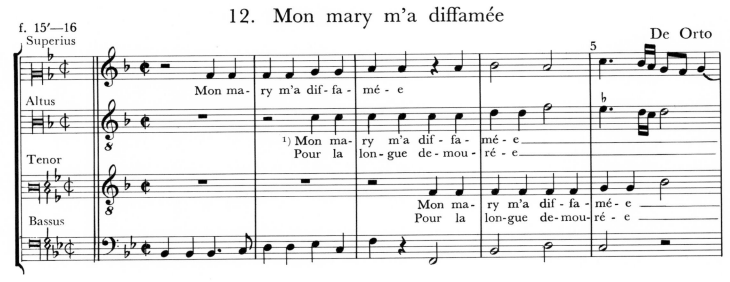

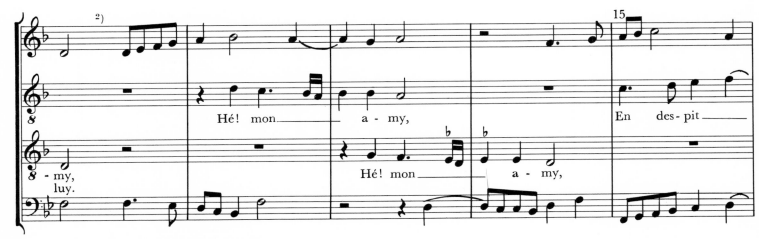

7) Cortona 95—96, Florence 107bis and Florence 164—167: D.

1) Original text incipit: "Mon mari ma deffamee." The text is after Paris-Gevaert, *Chansons*.

2) If the words are sung, a repeat (not indicated in *Canti B)* may be made at this point to accommodate the third and fourth lines of the stanza.

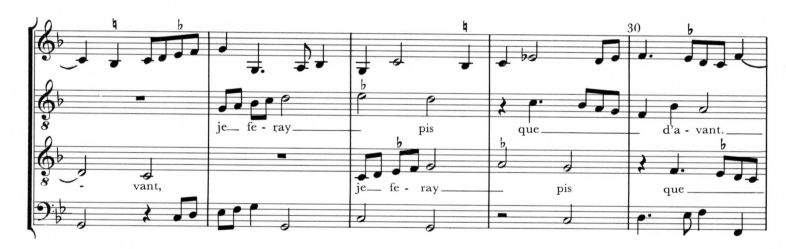

Aucunes gens m'ont blasmée
Disant que j'ay fait amy:
La chose trèsfort m'agrée,
Mon trèsgracieulx soucy.
  Hé! mon amy,
En despit de mon mary
Qui ne vault pas ung grant blanc,
Je feray pis que d'avant.

Quant je suis la nuyt couchée
Entre les braz mon amy,
Je deviens presque pasmée
Du plaisir que prens en luy.
  Hé! mon amy,
Pleust à Dieu que mon mary
Je ne veisse de trente ans!
Nous nous donrrions du bon temps.

Sy m'amye est courroucée,
Pensez que j'en suis marry;
Car elle est sy mal traictée
Pour l'amour de son amy.
  Hé! mon amy,
En despit de mon mary
Qui ne m'ayme tant ne quant,
Je feray pis que d'avant.

Si je pers ma renommée
Pour l'amour de mon amy,
Point n'en doy estre blasmée,
Car il est coincte et joly.
  Hé! mon amy,
Je n'ay bon jour ne demy
Avec ce mary meschant:
Je feray pis que d'avant.

13. Cela sans plus

f. 16'--17

Obreht In missa [1]

[1] The Index of *Canti B* gives only "Obreht"; the inscription with the music, however, reads "Obreht In missa," which may mean that this music once formed a movement of a Mass based on *Cela sans plus*. Today we have no proof that such a Mass ever existed.

[2] Original text incipit: "Cela sans plus." The text is after Florence 176.

14. Bon temps

f. 17'—18

Superius

Altus

Tenor

Bassus

Anon.

f. 17'—18

1) Original text incipit: ".Bon temps." The text is after Gustave Cohen (ed.), *Recueil de farces françaises inédites du XVe siècle* (Cambridge, Mass., 1949), Farce No. XLVII p. 379.

132

-vien - dras - tu ja - - mais

A ta no -

-ble puis - san - - - ce, Que nous

15. A qui dir'elle sa pencée

f. 18'—19

Anon.

Superius

Altus

Tenor

Bassus

puis - sions tous vi - vre en paix

Au roy - - aul - me de Fran - ce?

A qui di - r'el - le sa pen - cé - e, La

A qui di - r'el - le sa pen - cé - e, La

[1] A qui di - r'el - le sa pen - cé - e, La fil - le

A qui di - r'el - le sa pen - cé - e,

- cé - e, La fil - le qui n'a point d'a -

fil - le qui n'a point d'a - my?

qui n'a point d'a - my?

La fil - le qui n'a point d'a -

[1] Original text incipit: "A qui direlle sa pense" ("pensee" in alto). The popular melody and text are found in Paris-Gevaert, *Chansons*.

2) Orig.: ♩ ♩ ; emendation follows Regensburg C 120 and tenor, mm. 41—42.
3) Regensburg C 120.
4) Orig.: D; Regensburg C 120 shows E-flat.

La fil - le qui n'a _____ point d'a- my?

La fil - le qui n'a point _____ d'a - my?

La fil - le qui n'a point _____ d'a - - my?

La fil - le qui _____ n'a _____ point ____ d'a - my?

Il en a bien qui en ont deux,
  Deux, troys, ou quatre;
Mais je n'en ay pas ung tout seul
  Pour moy esbatre;
Héllas! mon jolly temps se passe;
Mon tétin commence à mollir.
  A qui dir'elle, etc.

J'ay le vouloir si treshumain
  Et tel couraige,
Que plus toust annuyt que demain,
  En mon jeune aage,
J'aymeroys mieulx mourir de rage
Que de vivre en un tel ennuy.
  A qui dir'elle, etc.

16. Cela sans plus

f. 19′—20
Superius   Lannoy [1]
Contra
Tenor
Contra
[Si placet Jo. Martini] [2]

Ce - la sans plus [3]
et puis _____ o - la.
- la sans plus et puis

[1]) The Index of *Canti B* ascribes this composition to Lannoy.
[2]) This piece has only three voices in all the sources except *Canti B* and Rome 2856, which give the added bass. Above the bass in Rome 2856 appears "Jo. Martinj"; below the bass, "Si placet."
[3]) Original text incipit: "Cela sans plus." The text is taken from Florence 176, where it appears in the superius only.
[4]) Rome 2856 has a signature of one flat in all voices; Washington, Wolffheim has B-flat here (m. 6) in the tenor.

5) Florence 176 shows E-flat.

6) Florence 176 and Florence 229 show B-flat.

7) Rome 2856 and Bologna Q 17 show ♩♩♩

8) Rome 2856 and Bologna Q 17 show ♩♩♩

9) Rome 2856 has a whole rest here, placing this phrase one-half measure later than in *Canti B;* values are then the same to m. 25, where Rome 2856 shows C, half; quarter rest; D, quarter note.

10) Orig.: ♩♩♩; emended version follows Rome 2856.

138

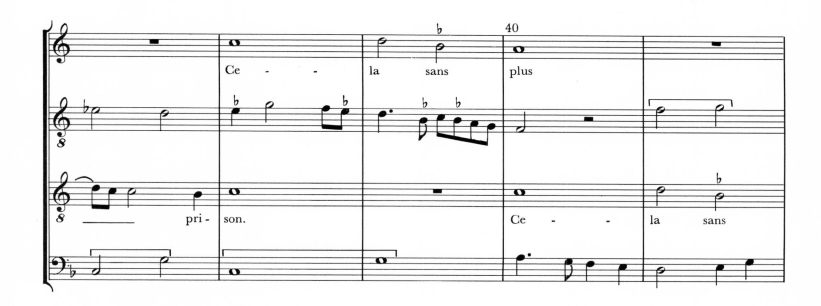

11) Orig.: ○♩♩ ; Rome 2856 and Bologna Q 17 have emended version.

12) Rome 2856 has a different reading, mm. 42—45:

17. Mon père m'a mariée

f. 20'—21   Anon.

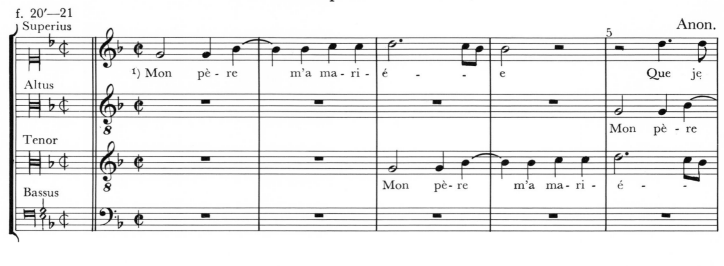

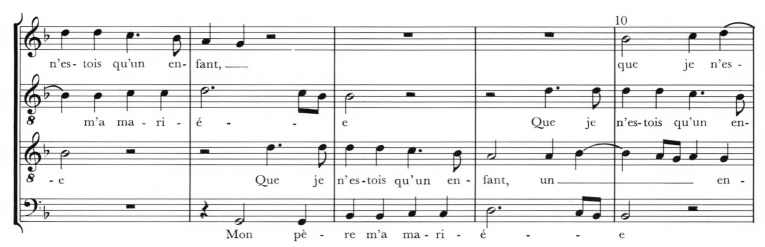

1) Original text incipit: "Mon pere ma mariee." The text is from "La Comédie de chansons" (*Ancien Théâtre François*, IX, 99—229), at the opening of Act III, Scene 1.

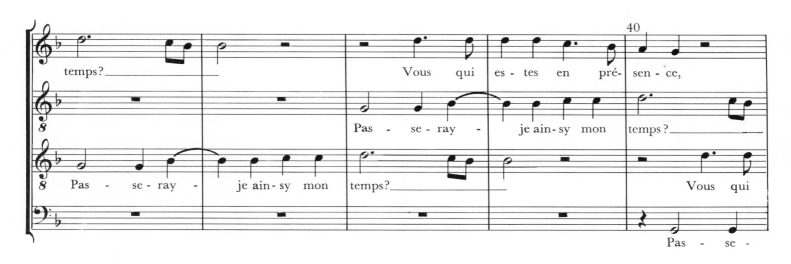

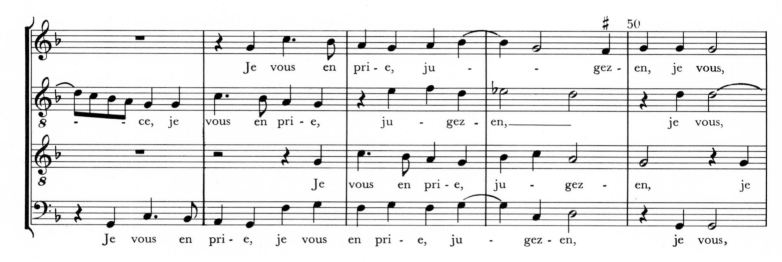

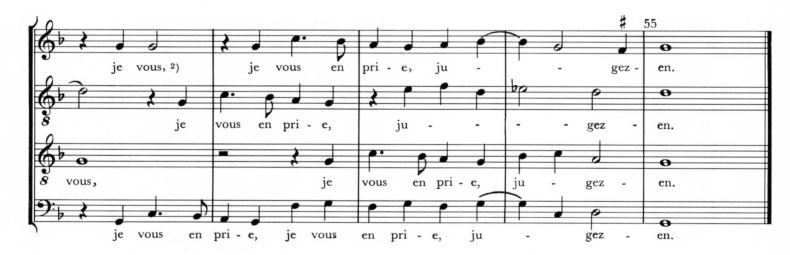

Miray-je rendre nonette
Dans quelque joly couvent,
Priant le dieu d'amourette
Qu'il me donne allègement,
Ou que j'aye en mariage
Celuy-là que j'aime tant.
Tant et tant il m'ennuye,
Tant et tant il m'ennuye tant.

2) See Introduction, pp. vii—viii.

142

18. Mijn morken gaf

veryhighf. 21'—22

Anon.

1) Original text incipit: "Myn morghen ghaf." The text follows Wolf, *Oud-Nederlandsche Liederen*.

lief had _____ zij ver - lo - - ren.

Haer lief had zij ver - lo - - - ren.

- lo - - - - - - ren.

had zij ver - lo - - - - ren.

19. Comment peult avoir joye

f. 22'—23

Josquin

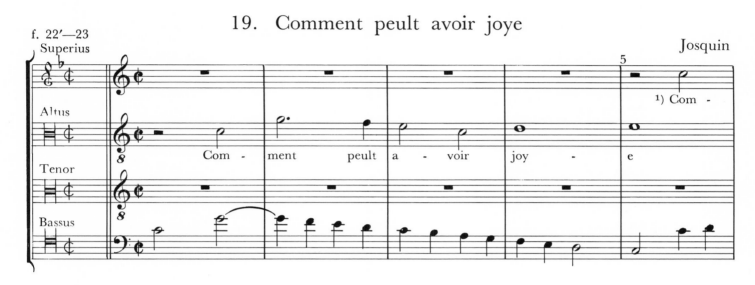

Superius

Altus

Com - ment peult a - voir joy - e

Tenor

Bassus

[1]) Com -

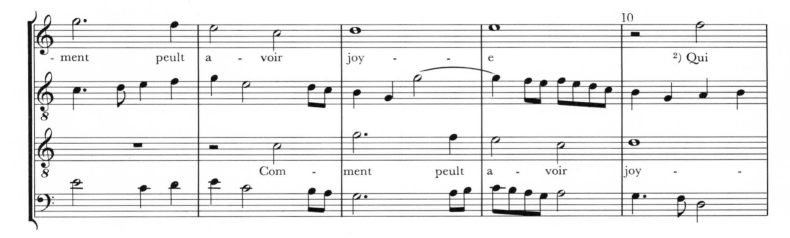

- ment peult a - voir joy - - e

[2]) Qui

Com - ment peult a - voir joy - -

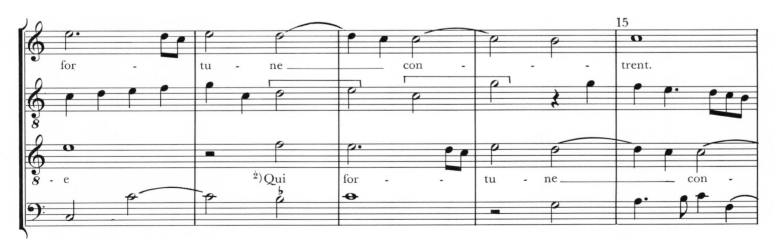

for - tu - ne _____ con - - trent.

[2])Qui for - - tu - ne _____ con -

- e

[1]) Original text incipit: "Coment peult hauer ioye." With the exception of line 2, this text follows London Add. 35087.
[2]) Florence 164—167; London Add. 35087 lacks line 2 of the stanza.

3) Rome C. G. XIII, 27 has a signature of one flat in the alto on each of its five staves.
4) Bologna Q 17 shows B-flat.

146

5) Florence 178 shows B-flat.
6) Florence 178 and Rome C. G. XIII, 27 show B-flat.

20. Comment peult

¹) *Canti B,* the only source for this work, gives G incorrectly.

148

21. Hélas, hélas, hélas

Ninot

f. 24'—25

Superius

Hé - las, hé - las, hé - las

Altus

Tenor

Hé - las, hé - las, hé - las

Bassus

1) Orig.: 𝆺; emendation follows Regensburg C 120.

3) Orig.: ♩ ♮; Regensburg C 120 has emended version.
4) A blackened *semibrevis* appears incorrectly in both editions of *Canti B.*

22. Tous les regretz

1) Original text incipit: "Tous les regres." The text is after Quicherat, *Vers d'Henri Baude*.

153

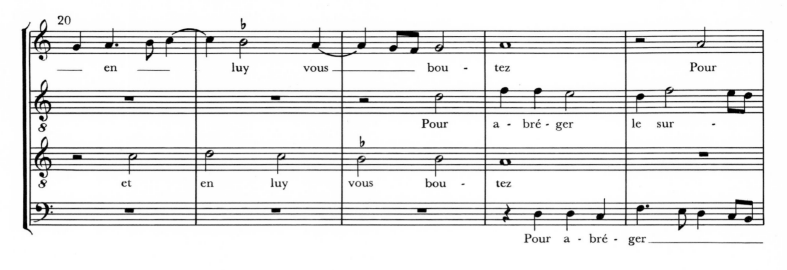

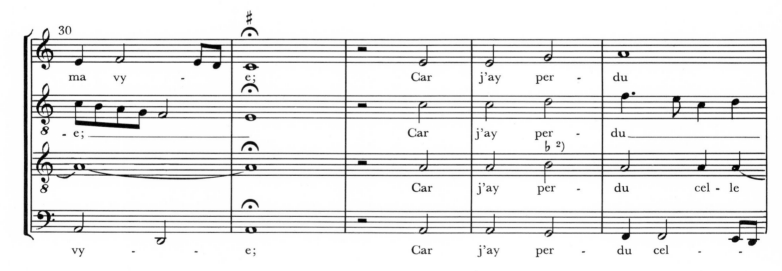

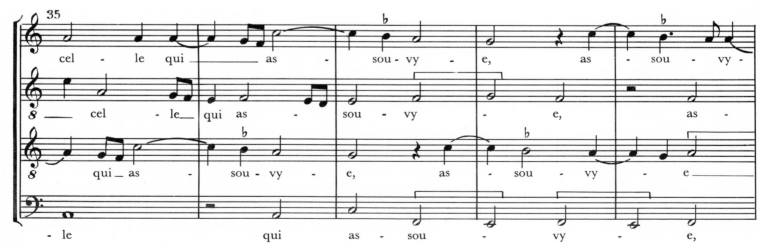

2) Vienna 18810.

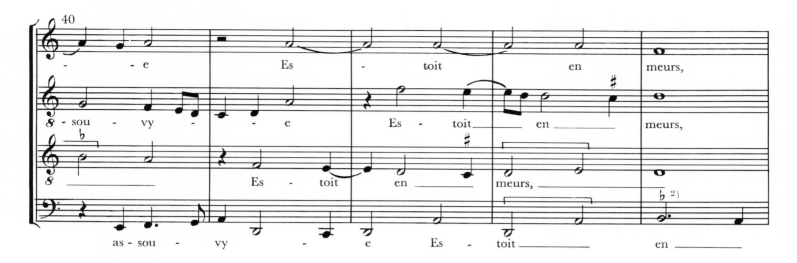

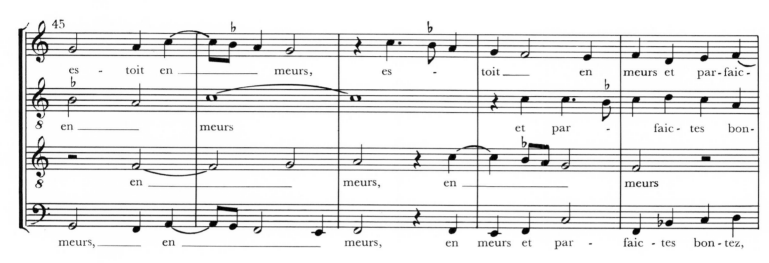

Venez doncques et plus rien ne doubtez,
Car mes cinq sens sont du tout aprestez
Vous recueillir. Pour tant, je vous convye,
   Tous les regretz, etc.

Si vous supply que de moy vous ostez
Joye et plaisir, lesquelz m'avoit prestez
Pour aucun temps Fortune sans envye.
J'ay triste soing qui veult que je desvye:
Pour ce venez et vous dilligentez,
   Tous les regretz, etc.

3) Vienna 18810.

23. Veci la danse barbari

f. 26'—27

Vaqueras

1) Original text incipit: "Veci la danse barbarj." The text is taken from Cortona 95—96, Paris 1817, where it occurs with the popular melody in a different composition.
2) Florence 107bis and Segovia both give B-flat.

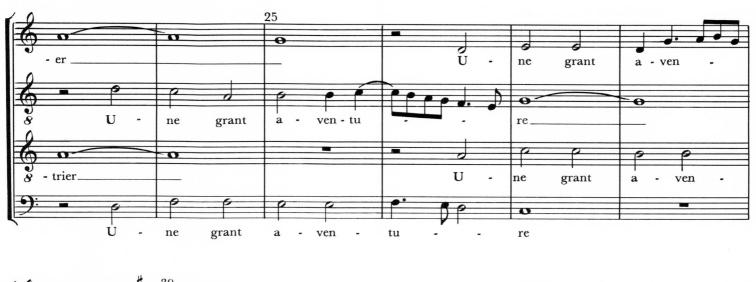

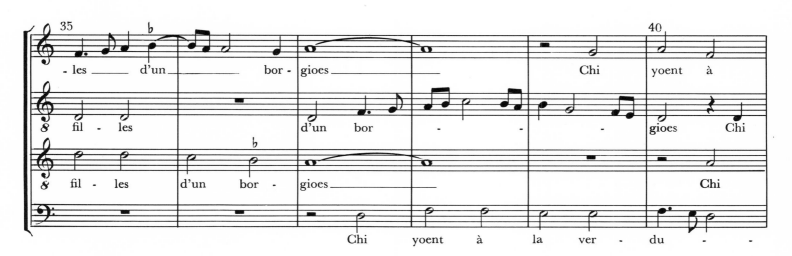

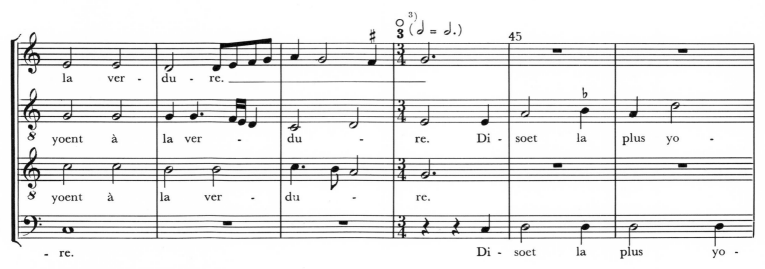

[3] Florence 107[bis] and Segovia both give merely "3."

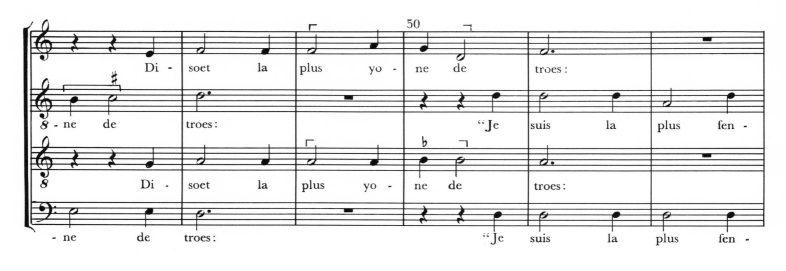

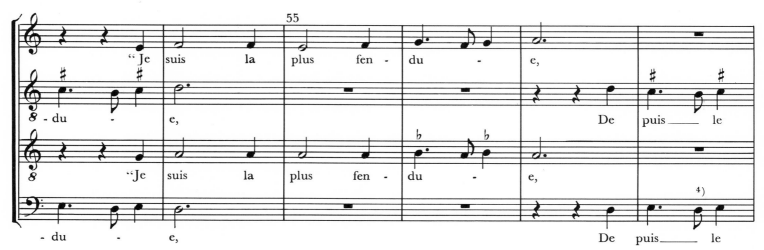

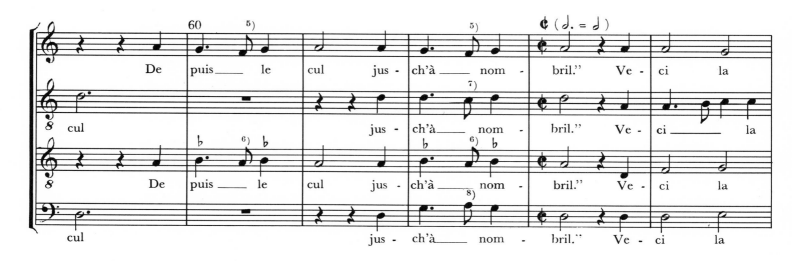

4) Orig.: E; emendation follows m. 53.
5) Orig.: G; emendation follows m. 56.
6) Orig.: B; emendation follows m. 56.
7) Orig.: D.
8) Orig.: G.

24. D'ung aultre amer

De orto [1]

f. 27'—28

Superius: [2] D'ung aul - tre a - mer _____ mon cueur s'a -

Contra: Obelus quinis sedibus ip(s)e volat

Tenor: Quartus confortatinus

Bassus: Obelus quinis sedibus ip(s)e volat

D'ung aultre amer (Contra)

D'ung aultre amer (Tenor)

- - bes - se - roit, Il ne fault

pas pen - - ser que je _____

_____ l'es - tran - - - ge,

---

[1]) With the music, *Canti B* ascribes this piece to "De orto"; the Index gives merely "Orto."

[2]) Original text incipit: "Dung aultre amer." The edition of the text follows Smijers, *Van Ockeghem tot Sweelinck,* Vol. I, No. 3, p. 12 (from Florence 2794).

[3]) If the words are sung, returns to the beginning may be made from this point. Alto and bass are so constructed that no confusion should result from this procedure.

4) The parallel fifths between alto and bass are original.
5) Orig.: A (m. 41 : 2, therefore, E).

Je l'aime tant que jamais ne seroit
Possible à moy d'en consentir l'échange.
    D'ung aultre amer, etc.

La mort, par Dieu, avant me defferoit,
Qu'en mon vivant j'acointasse ung estrange.
Ne cuide nul qu'à cela je me renge,
Ma loyaulté trop fort se mesferoit.
    D'ung aultre amer, etc.

25. Noé, noé, noé

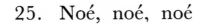

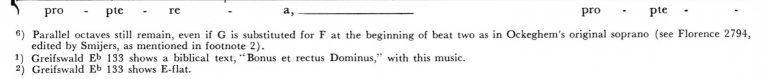

---

6) Parallel octaves still remain, even if G is substituted for F at the beginning of beat two as in Ockeghem's original soprano (see Florence 2794, edited by Smijers, as mentioned in footnote 2).

1) Greifswald Eb 133 shows a biblical text, "Bonus et rectus Dominus," with this music.

2) Greifswald Eb 133 shows E-flat.

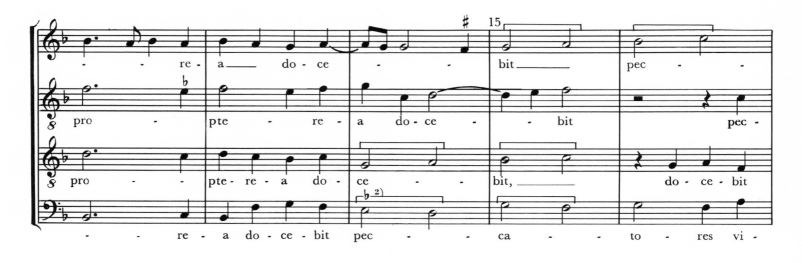

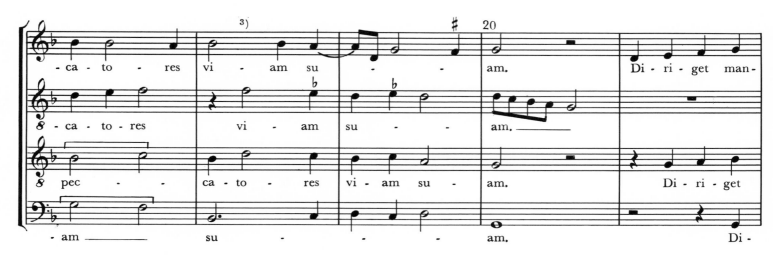

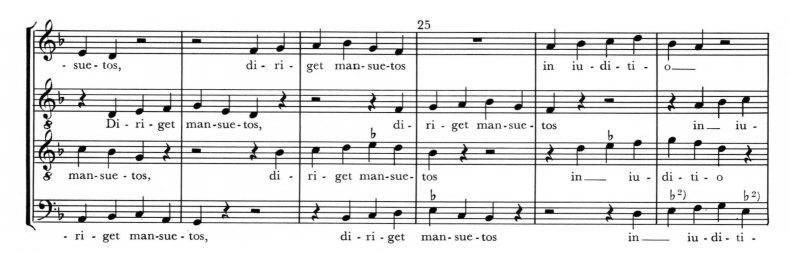

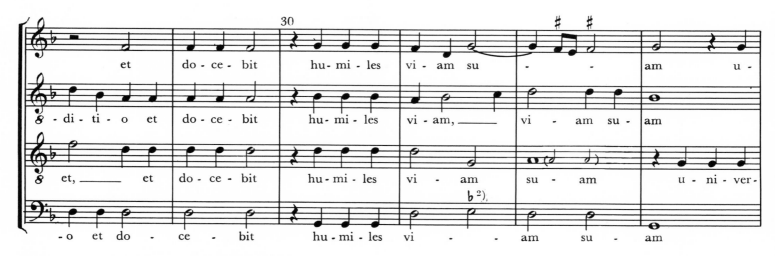

3) Greifswald E♭ 133: these two notes appear as one.

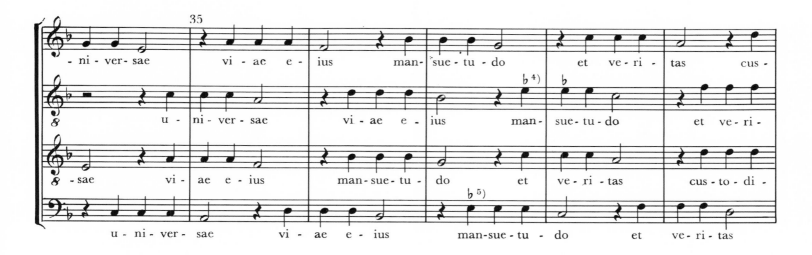

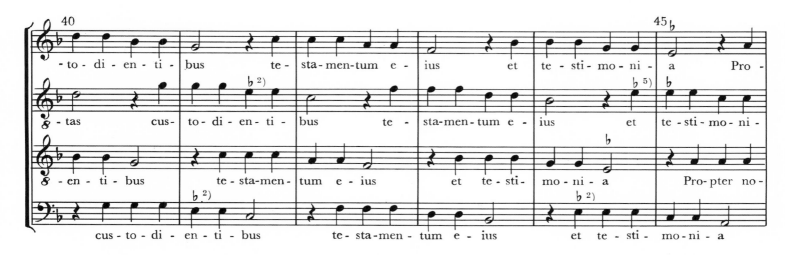

4) Greifswald Eb 133 and Bologna Q 18 have E-flat.
5) Bologna Q 18 has E-flat.

26. Una moza falle yo

f. 29'—30

Anon.

27. Et la la la

f. 30'—31

(Ninot le petit) [1]

Superius

Et la la la la la la la, Faic-tez-luy bon-ne chie - re.

Altus

Et la la la la la, Faic-

Tenor

Faic-tez-luy bon-ne chie - re.

Bassus

[2] Et la la la la la la la, Faic-

-tez-luy bon-ne chie - re.

Mi le-vay par ung ma-tin, par

Mi le-

-tez-luy bon-ne chie - re.

Mi le-vay par ung ma-tin,

Mi le-vay par ung ma-

ung ma-tin, La fres-che ma-ti-né - e, M'en en-tray en

-vay par ung ma-tin, La fres-che ma-ti-né - e, M'en en-tray en

La fres - che ma-ti-né - - - e, M'en en-

- tin, La fres-che ma-ti-né - e, M'en en-tray en

no jar-din Pour coeul-lier gi-rouf-flé - e. La la la la la la la la, Faic-

no jar-din Pour coeul-lier gi-rouf-flé - e. La la la la la la la, Faic-

-tray en no jar - din Pour coeul-lier gi-rouf-flé - e. La la la la la la la, Faic-

no jar-din Pour coeul-lier gi-rouf-flé - e. La la la la la la la, Faic-

1) This work is attributed to Ninot Le Petit in Florence 2442.
2) Original text incipit: "E la la la " (in soprano and alto); "Fates lui bona chiera " (in tenor and bass). The text is after Florence 2442.
3) Orig.: E; emendation follows Florence 164—167 and Florence 2442.
4) Florence 164—167 and Florence 2442: o
5) Florence 164—167 and Florence 2442: ♩

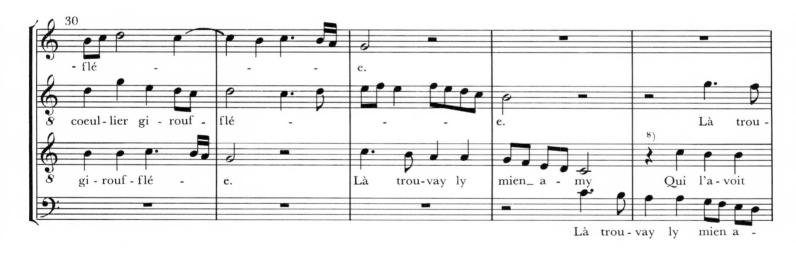

6) Orig.: ♩·; both Florence 164—167 and Florence 2442 have emended version.
7) Orig.: ○; emendation follows Florence 164—167 and Florence 2442.
8) Orig.: C quarter note; Florence 164—167 and Florence 2442 have quarter rest.
9) Florence 164—167: ○

28. Fors seullement

f. 31'—32

Pe. de la rue [1]

la la la, Faic - tez - luy bon - ne chie - re A la bel - le ber - gè - re.

la la la, Faic - tez - luy bon - ne chie - re A la bel - le ber - gè - re.

la la, la, Faic - tez - luy bon - ne chie - re A la bel - le ber - gè - re.

la la la, Faic - tez - luy bon - ne chie - re A la bel - le ber - gè - re.

Fors seul - le -

[4] Fors seul - le - ment, fors [8]

Fors seul - le - ment, fors

Fors seul - le -

[1] Mattheus Pipelare is given as composer in Basel F. X. 1—4, Bologna Q 19, Regensburg C 120, Segovia, and St. Gall 461.
[2] Florence 164—167.
[3] Orig.: o ; emendation follows Paris 1597.
[4] Original text incipit: "Fors seule ment." The text is after Löpelman *Liederhandschrift des Cardinals de Rohan.*
[5] Orig.: o ; Florence 164—167 and Segovia have emended version.
[6] Orig.: ♩♩ ; emendation follows Florence 164—167.
[7] The Bologna edition of *Canti B* has
[8] All sources except *Canti B,* which has B.

168

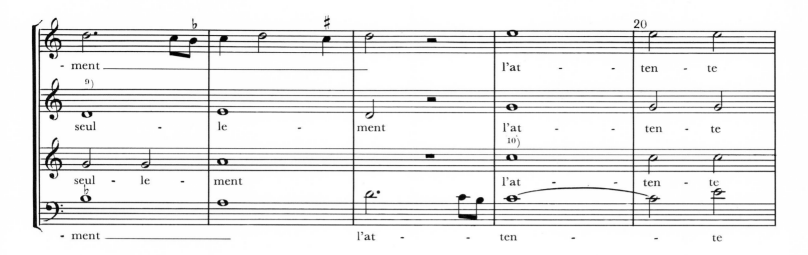

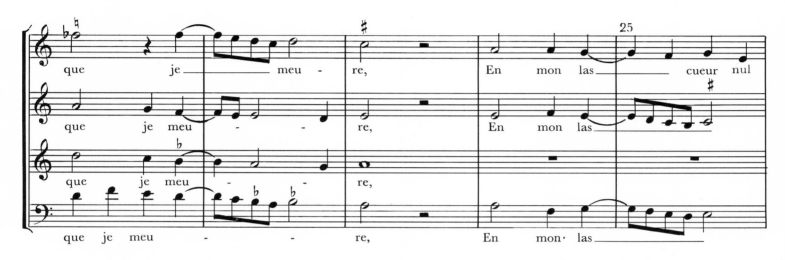

9) Orig.: two half notes in this and the following measure; emendation follows Florence 164—167.
10) Orig.: 𝅘𝅥𝅭 𝅗𝅥; Florence 164—167 has emended version.
11) Florence 164—167; in *Canti B,* A lasts for three measures.
12) Bologna Q 19 and Tournai 94.
13) Tournai 94.

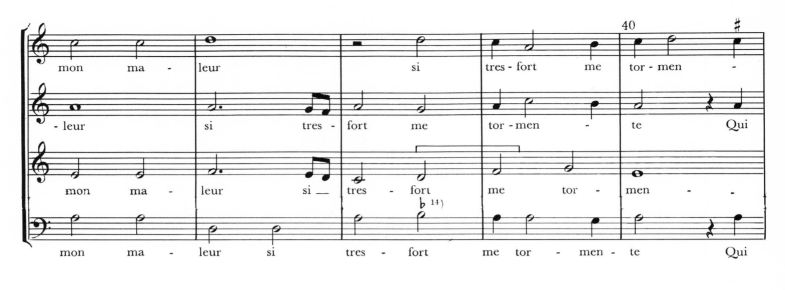

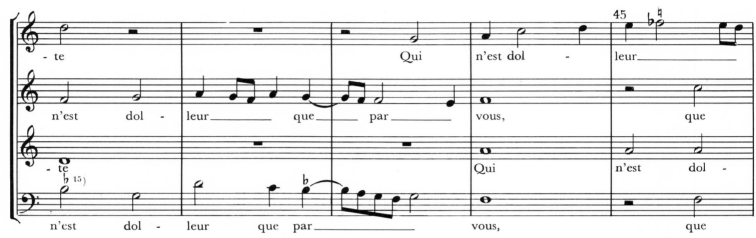

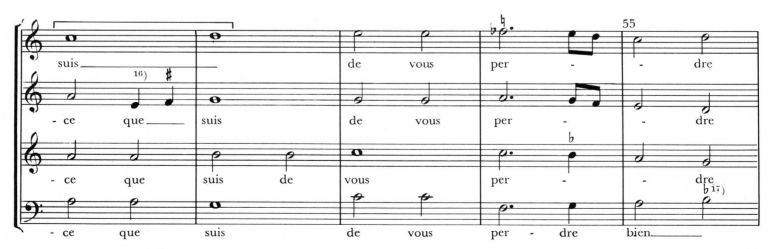

14) Florence 164—167 and Bologna Q 19.
15) Bologna Q 19.
16) Florence 164—167 and Paris 1597 have E half note.
17) Florence 164—167 and Segovia.

Vostre rigueur si tresfort me court seure
Qu'en ce party n'ay chose qui m'asseure,
Ne bien aucun qui en riens me contente
Fors seullement, etc.

Mon desconfort toute seulle je pleure,
En maudissant, sur ma foy, à toute heure
Ma loiaulté qui tant me fait dolente.
Las! que je suis de vivre mal contente,
Quant de par vous n'ay riens qui me sequeure
Fors seullement, etc.

29. Et dunt revenis vous

1) *Canti B,* edition of 1502, has A; edition of 1503, B.

²) There is an error here in the tenor in both editions of *Canti B*. The first edition (1502) has the right number of beats, but seems incorrect since it produces six-four chords, m. 48 : 4 and 49 : 2 (see Ex. 1), and also fails to produce the effect of hocket suggested by the other parts. It appears that this reading was retained in the second edition (1503); subsequently the error was discovered, and an effort made to correct it. It was noticed that the quarter rest and D, quarter note, of m. 49 (Ex. 1) were repeated. Omission of the second D would have corrected this end of the passage; instead, the first rest and D were deleted, leaving a vacant space. At the beginning of the passage a "correction" by hand is so untidy that the intended reading is uncertain. One can detect three C's, all with stems (the first, probably unintentionally, filled in). The first two of them are drawn by hand, and traces may be detected of an original (printed) C between them. An original rest seems to have been used for part of the head of the second hand-written note. As the passage now stands, it lacks two beats (rests). An editorial rest has been placed in m. 47, beat 3, and m. 49, beat 4. The readings of the two editions follow:

30. J'ay pris amours

f. 33'—34

Japart

1) In the Petrucci print, this canon appears above this voice which, however, occupies the position normally taken by the superius; that is, at the top of the folio verso.

174

²) Florence 229 shows B-flat.

31. Je cuide/De tous biens

Japart

32. Franc coeur qu'as tu/Fortuna d'un gran tempo

f. 35'—36

De Vigne [1]

[1] With the music, *Canti B* attributes this piece to "De Vigne"; the Index gives "Deuigna."
[2] Original text incipit: "Franch cor quastu." The text is taken from the farce, *Le Médecin et le badin* (see Commentary).
[3] Original text incipit: "Fortuna." See Hewitt, *Odhecaton*, "Notes on the Literary Texts," no. 74, for the continuation of this text, which is taken from Florence 229, f. 156'—158.
[4] Original text incipit: "Fortuna dun gran tempo."

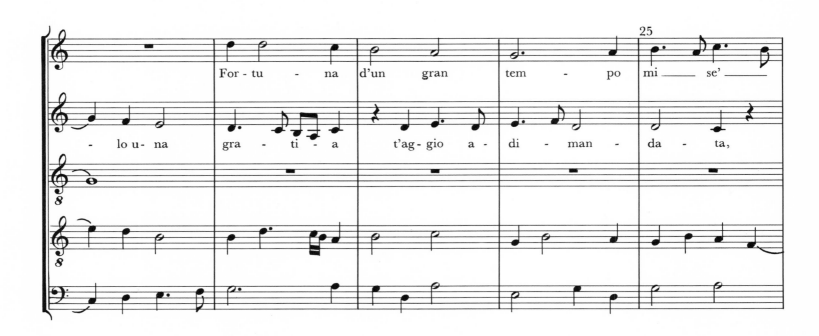

33. Amours me trocte par la pance

f. 36'—37

Superius

Lourdoys[1]

Altus

[2] A - mours me troc - te par la

Tenor

A - mours me troc - te par la

Bassus

[3] A - mours me troc - te par la

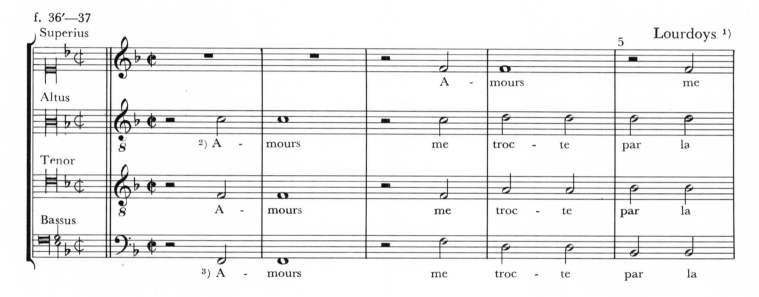

troc - te par la pan - ce Com - me re - gnart

pan - - ce, par la pan - - ce Com - me re -

pan - ce Com - me re - gnart a -

pan - - - ce Com - me re - gnart a -

[1] "Lourdoys" (given as composer of this work in *Canti B*) or, more frequently, "Lourdault" was the nickname of Jean Braconnier. The nick-name was derived from the popular song arranged in *Canti B* 5.
[2] Original text incipit: "Amours me trotent sur la pance." The text is taken from Florence 2442.
[3] The text of the bass follows that of the other voices, for the bass part-book of Florence 2442 is missing.

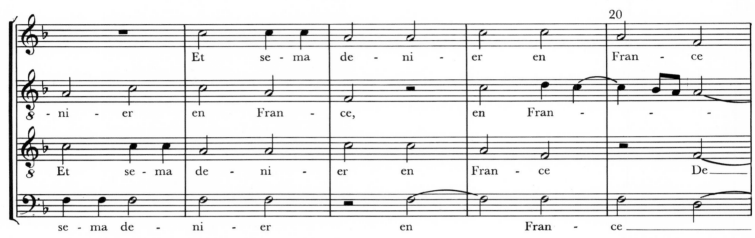

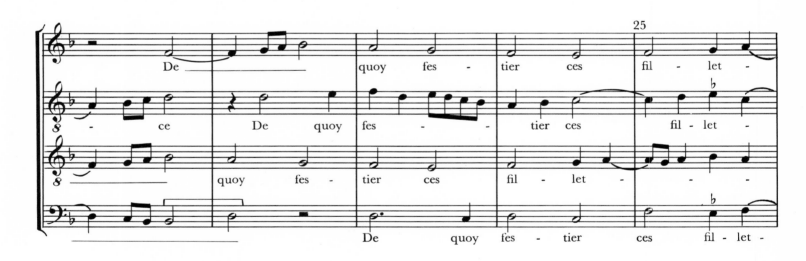

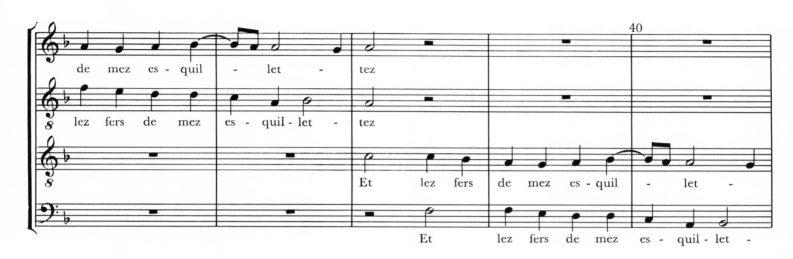

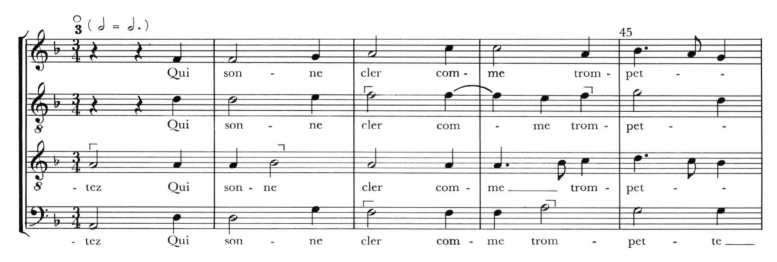

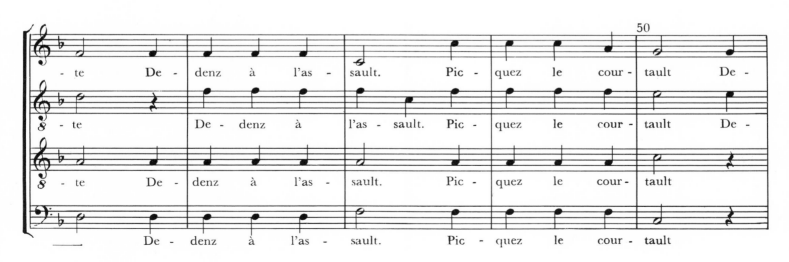

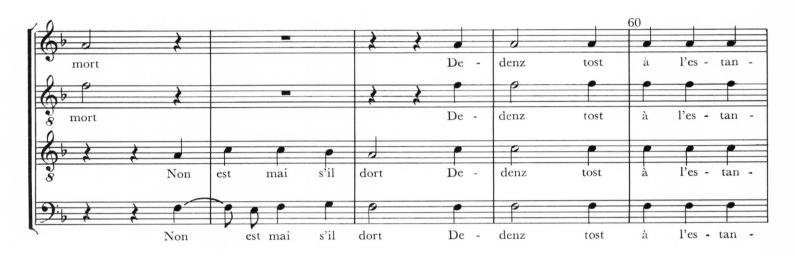

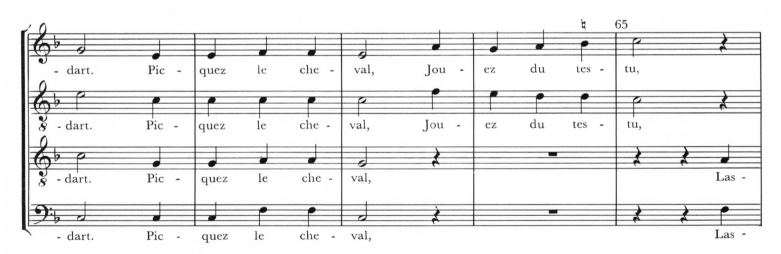

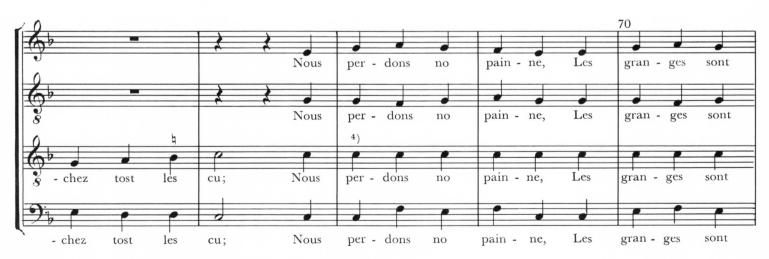

[4]) Measures 68—71 are from Florence 2442; *Canti B* has a *maxima*.

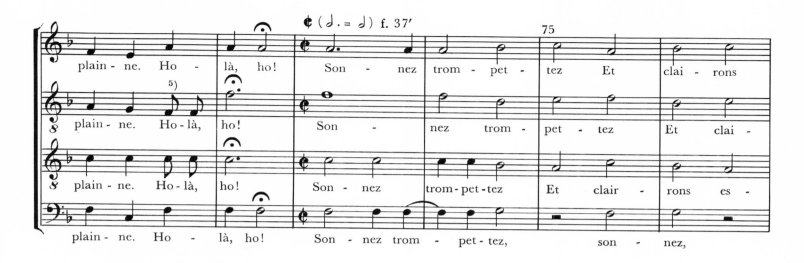

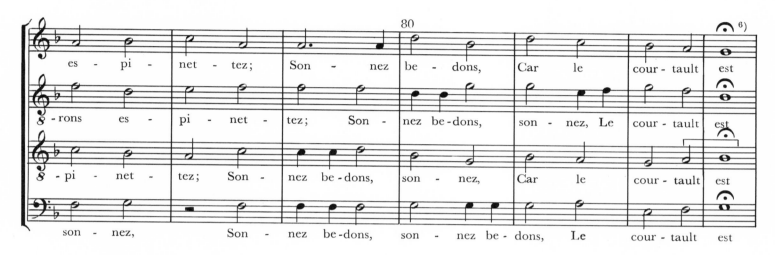

⁵) Orig.: ♩ ; emendation follows Florence 2442.
⁶) Orig.: ♩ ; Florence 2442 has emended version.

34. Baisés moy

1) The Index of *Canti B* ascribes this work to Josquin.
2) Original text incipit: "Basies moy." The edition of the text is after Gérold, *Manuscrit de Bayeux*.

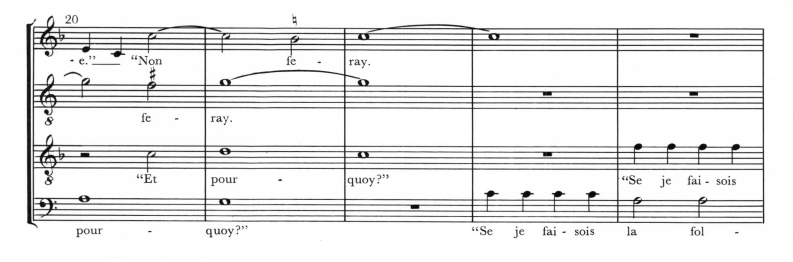

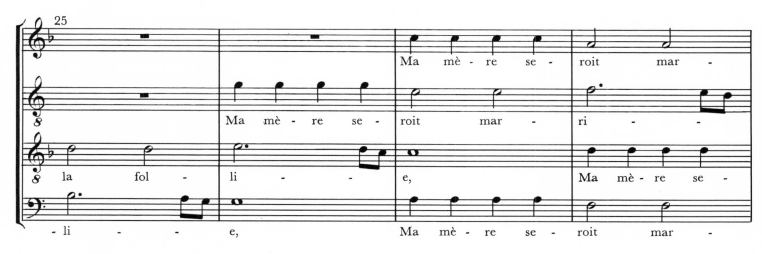

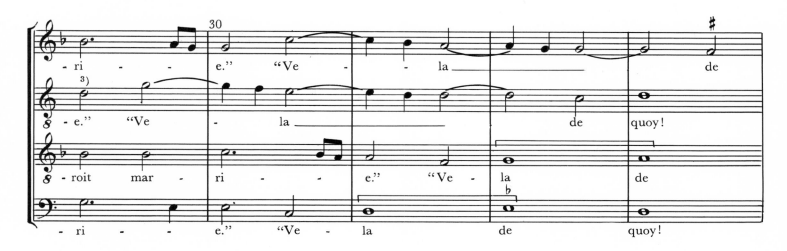

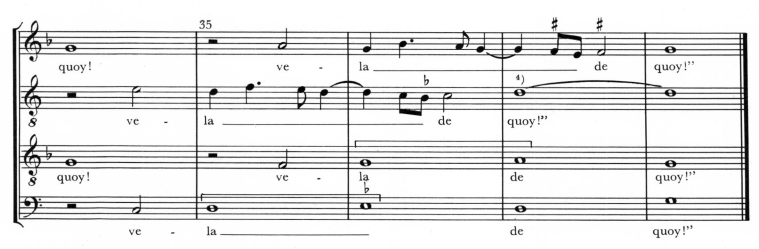

3) Antico 1520³ *Motetti novi e chanzoni,* alone, gives **D** whole, C half (soprano, m. 30: G whole, F half).
4) Antico 1520³ *Motetti novi e chanzoni; Canti B* and Cortona 95 – 96, Paris 1817 give **D** *brevis, longa* (in transcription: two whole notes).

35. Va uilment (= Wat willen) [1]

f. 38'—39

Obreht

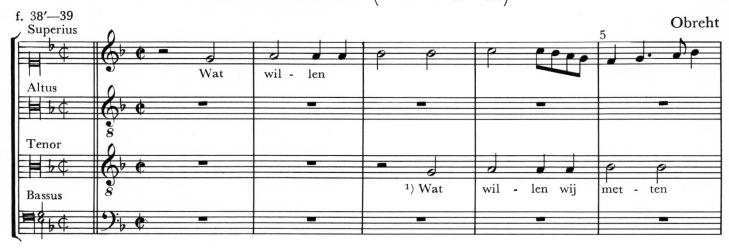

Superius

Wat wil - len

Altus

Tenor

Bassus

[1]) Wat wil - len wij met - ten

bu - del spe - len ons ghelt es uut

Wat wil - len

[1]) *Canti B* gives "Va uilment," a corruption of the opening words of the Flemish text "Wat willen." One line of this text appears in Segovia in each voice, the last four words in the alto only.

[2]) Orig.: ◖ ; emendation follows Segovia.

3) Segovia.
4) Rome C. G. XIII, 27.

5) Orig.: o ; emendation follows Segovia in mm. 51—53, 55—58, 60—62, 64, 68, and 70 (tenor); and 91 (alto).
6) These parallel fifths also occur in Segovia and in Rome C. G. XIII, 27.

7) Segovia: ♩ ♪
8) Rome C. G. XIII, 27.

36. Or sus, or sus, bovier

Bulkyn

37. Baisés moy

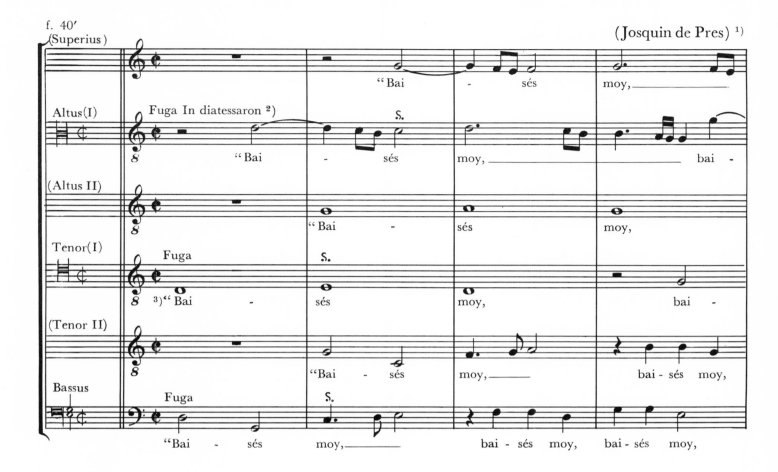

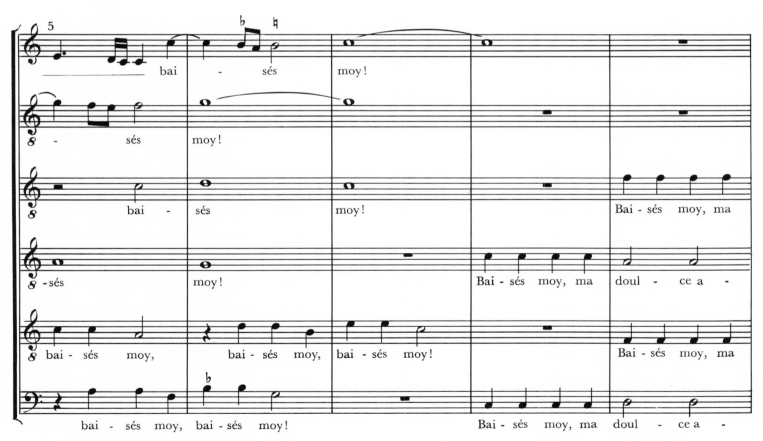

1) The four-part version of this work *(Canti B* 34) is assigned to "Josquin" in *Canti B.* The six-part form, published by both Susato and Attaingnant, is also attributed to Josquin des Prez by these printers.
2) Only the antecedents of the three canons are given in *Canti B.* A *signum congruentiae* in each part marks the point of entry of the consequent, and the accompanying instruction directs that the canon be sung at the fourth.
3) Original text incipit: "Basies moy." The text is after Gérold, *Manuscrit de Bayeux.*

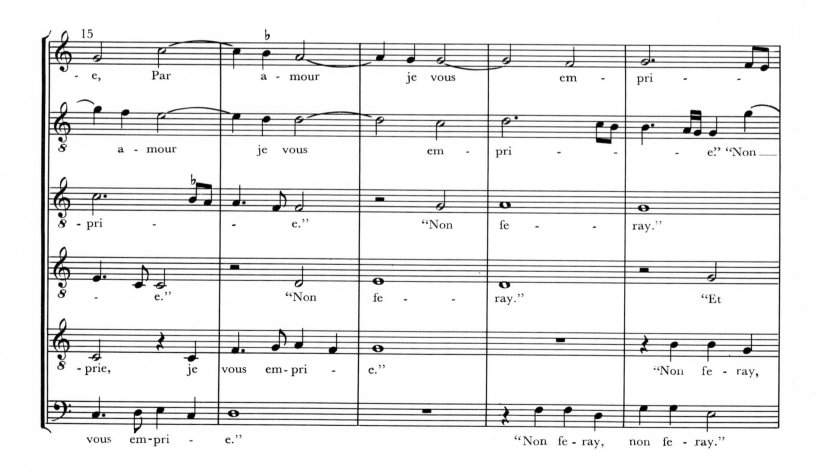

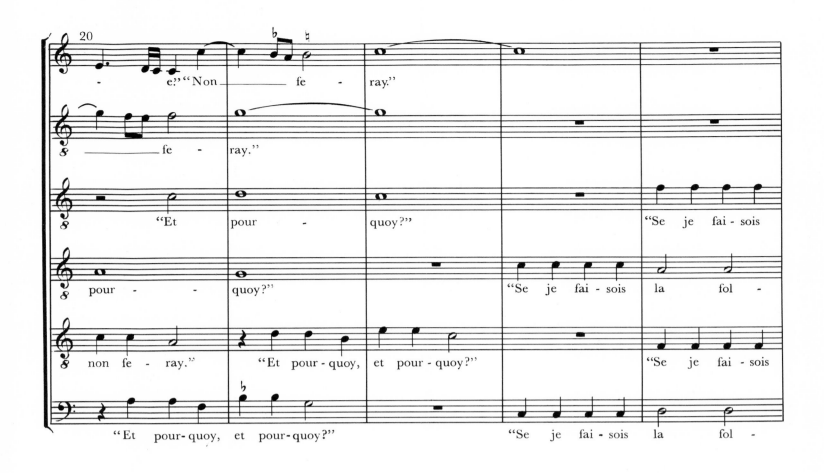

197

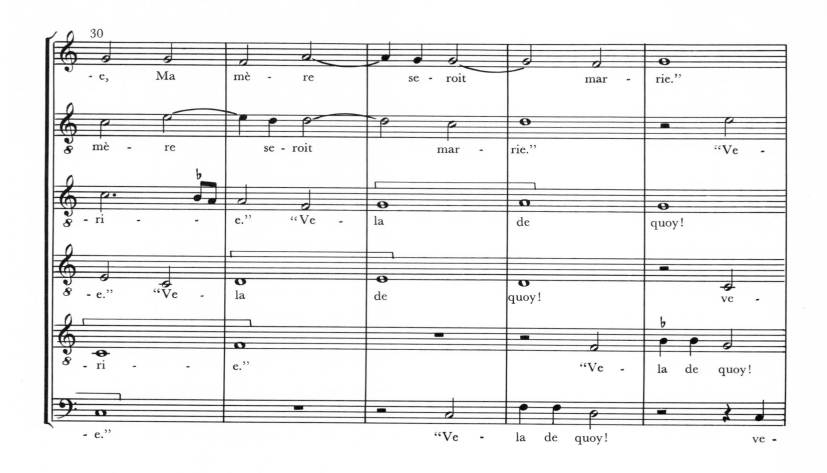

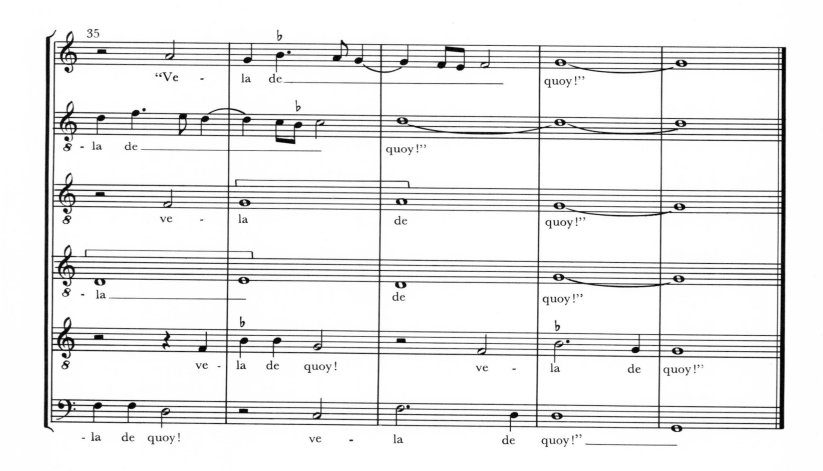

38. Avant, avant

f. 41

Superius

In subdiatessaron

Anon.

(Altus)

Avant, avant

Tenor

Bassus

39. Ave, Ancilla Trinitatis

1) Original text incipit: "Aue ancilla trinitatis." The text is after Munich 322—325 and Segovia.
2) Orig.: these two notes are contracted into one, and the two following notes appear as a whole note; emendation follows Segovia.

201

³⁾ Munich 322—325, Petreius 1541² *Trium vocum cantiones*,
and Segovia give a different reading for the contra, mm. 76—84:

Note that the **contra** of *Canti B* runs in parallel thirds with the tenor, mm. 75:2—79:1, while the **contra** of the other sources runs in
parallel tenths with the superius, mm 76:2—83:3.

203

la - ti - o - ni - bus ___ me - is, tri - bu - la ___ ti -
- o - ni - bus ___ me - is, tri - bu - la ___ ti - o - ni -
- o - ni - bus ___ me - is, tri - bu - la ti -

- o - ni - bus me - is. A - men, ___ a - men.
- bus me - is. A - men, a - men, ___ a - men. ___
- o - ni - bus me - is. A - men, ___ a - men, a - men.

40. Si sumpsero

f. 42'—43

Superius

Obreht

Si sump - se - ro

Tenor

Contra

Si

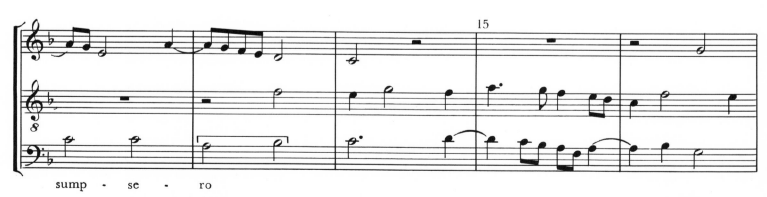

sump - se - ro

---

⁴) The contra of Munich 322—325, Petreius 1541² *Trium vocum cantiones,* and Segovia also differs from that of
Canti B in m. 87:

87

1) Orig.: double whole note; Brussels 11239 and Paris 1597 have emended version.
2) Here, and in the imitations in tenor and superius, Brussels 11239 and Paris 1597 have two half notes.
3) Orig.: ♩♩𝅝 emendation follows Formschneider 1538⁹ *Trium vocum carmina*.

4) Orig.: C; Brussels 11239 and Formschneider 1538⁹ *Trium vocum carmina* both have D.
5) Formschneider 1538⁹ *Trium vocum carmina* gives C.

41. Mon père m'a donné mari

¹) Original text incipit: "Mon pere ma dona mari."

42. De tous biens

f. 45'—46

Ghiselin

De tous biens

De tous biens

212

43. Pour quoy fu fait ceste emprise

f. 46'—47

Superius

Tenor

Contra

Anon.

Pour quoy   fu fait ceste emprise

Pour quoy fu fait   ceste emprise

215

44. Adieu, fillette de regnon

1) This work is attributed to "Isaac" in Zwickau 78, 3.
2) Formschneider 1538⁹ *Trium vocum carmina.*

45. Chanter ne puis

f. 49'—50

Compere

Superius

Tenor

[1] (C)han - ter_____ ne puis, (c)han -

- ter_____ ne puis chieux la my - non - - -

Contra

(C)han - ter_____ ne puis,

(C)han - ter_____ ne puis,

(c)han - ter_____ ne puis chieux la my - - -

(c)han - ter_____ ne puis chieux la my - -

[3] Formschneider 1538[9] *Trium vocum carmina* has E-flat here, yet lacks a flat before E in the superius of m. 62.
[1] Original text incipit: "Chanter ne puis" (Bologna. 1502 edition); Paris (1503) copy has "Chauter ne puis." The text is after Paris 1719.

Car j'apparçoy qu'on m'abandonne
Et que mon amour ne luy duyt.
    (C)hanter ne puis, etc.

Souvent entre gens la blasonne
Et dis d'elle que c'est tout bruyt.
Mes veslà: Fortune me nuyt;
Aussi son frès maintien m'estonne.
    (C)hanter ne puis, etc.

46. Je vous emprie

Agricola

1) The Bologna (1502) copy gives "impire" with the music, "empire" in the Index; the Paris (1503) copy gives "Je vous emprie" throughout. The text, "Se vous voulez," used here (and required by all the sources except *Canti B*) is taken from Florence 2794.
2) Orig.: ᴏ. in superius (mm. 3, 24–25, 37, 86), tenor (m. 48), and **contra** (mm. 39–40); emendation follows Paris 1597 and Florence 2794. The emendation in superius (mm. 39–40) is after Paris 1597.
3) Orig.: ᴏ in superius (mm. 7, 10, 11, 17, 18, 19, 21, 22, 36, 41, 58, 59, 60, 66, 85) and tenor (mm. 5, 19, 20, 21, 23, 27, 35, 36, 46, 56, 68, 70); emendation after Paris 1597 and Florence 2794.

4) Orig.: in tenor (mm. 11—12, 58—59); emendation follows Paris 1597 and Florence 2794.

5) Orig.: o ◻ in tenor, beginning in m. 40; emendation after Paris 1597 and Florence 2794.
6) Orig.: o ♩ in superius, mm. 46—47; emendation after Paris 1597 and Florence 2794.

224

qui tant vault, _____ Et
bas et hault, _____ Heu -

tant vault, _____ et _____ hault, _____

qui _____ tant vault, _____
bas _____ et hault, _____

en qui n'a _____ tant soit _____ pour
-reu - se en bien: _____ ve - la _____ tant

Et en qui n'a tant
Heu - reu - se en bien: _____ ve -

Et _____ en _____
Heu - - reu - - se

peu de def - fault, tant soit peu de def - fault, _____
quoy il _____ fault, ve - la pour ____ quoy il fault _____

soit peu de def - fault, _____ tant soit peu de def -
-la pour _____ quoy il ___ fault, _____ pour _____ quoy il fault

qui n'a _____ tant soit peu de def - fault,
en bien _____ ve - la pour quoy il fault

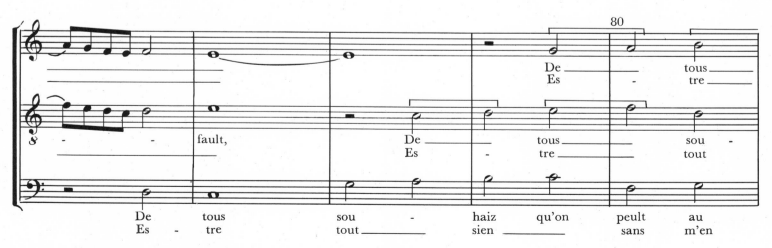

fault, De _____ tous _____ sou -
Es - tre _____ tout

De _____ tous _____
Es - tre _____

De tous sou - haiz qu'on peult au
Es - tre tout _____ sien _____ sans m'en

7) Orig.: 𝅗𝅥 𝅝 in tenor, mm. 62—63; emendation after Paris 1597 and Florence 2794.

47. A qui dirage mes pensées

(Compere) [1]

1) Rome 2856 attributes this work to Compere.
2) Orig.: ♩. ; emendation follows Bologna Q 16.

3) Rome 2856 has a different reading for the contra, mm. 25—28:

4) Rome 2856 has a different reading for the contra, mm. 32—38:

5) *Canti B* (1502)   *Canti B* (1503)

6) Orig.: ♩. ♪♩ ; emended version is found in Bologna Q 16.
7) This F is correctly a minim in the Bologna copy, incorrectly a semiminim in the Paris copy.
8) A *signum* appears here in Bologna Q 16.

48. La Regretée

f. 52'—53

Hayne

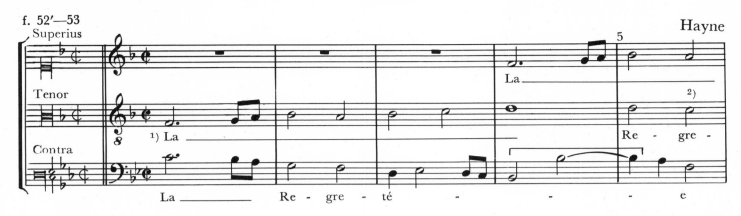

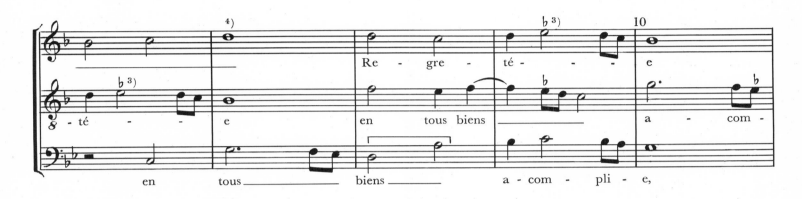

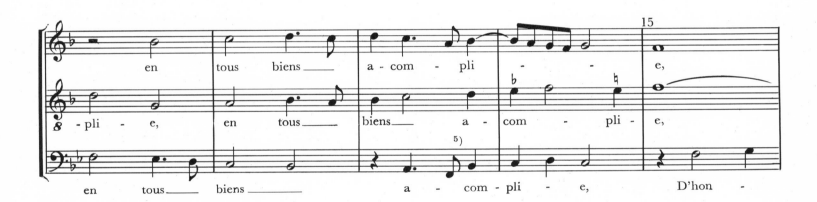

1) Original text incipit: "La regretee." The text is after Marix, *Musiciens de Bourgogne*.

2) Orig.: ; emendation follows London 20 A XVI and Paris 1597.

3) London 20 A XVI.
4) Orig.: ○ ♩ ; both concordances have emended version.
5) Orig.: G; London 20 A XVI has F.

6) Orig.: ♩ ♩ ; both concordances have emended version.

7) Orig.: o ; emended version found in both concordances.

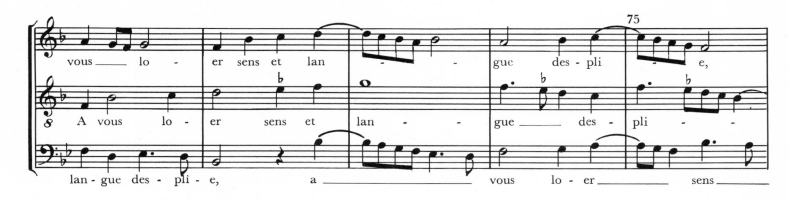

Pour le bon bruit qui en vous multiplie,
Dont je voy France honnourée et emplie,
Raison me plie
A vous nommer, se jamais le fut femme,
　La Regretée, etc.

Se à vous amer je me emplie,
Amour le veult, bon vouloir luy supplie.
Mais desamplie
Vous voye d'ung los qui tarnit votre fame:
C'est que pitié votre cueur point n'entame
Qui vous est blasme;
Mais en mon cueur ce mal tais et replie.
　La Regretée, etc.

49. En amours que cognoist

Brumel

233

50. Je despite tous

f. 54'—55

Brumel

235

51. Le grant désir

Compere

Superius

Tenor

Le grant dé - sir

Contra

1) Le grant dé - sir   d'ay- mer___ m'y tient, d'ay- mer,   d'ay-

8- mer___ m'y   tient   Quant de la   bel - le   me___ sou-

8- vient,   Et du   jo - ly   temps qui   ver- doy - e.

1) Original text incipit: "Le grant desir." The text is after Gérold, *Manuscrit de Bayeux*.

Et hoy - e, et hoy - - e! Et du jo - ly temps

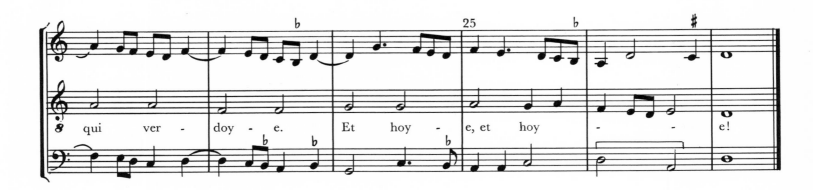

qui ver - doy - e. Et hoy - e, et hoy - - e!

Tantost aller y m'y convient
Vers celle-là qui mon cueur tient;
Je croy qu'el en aura grant joye.
  (Et hoye!)

"Belle, je viens par devers vous
Pour avoir plaisir et secours:
Vostre amour trop fort me guerroye."
  (Et hoye!)

"Bienviengnez, amy, par amours;
Or me dictes: que quérez-vous?
Vous fault-il rien que de moy j'aye?"
  (Et hoye!)

"Belle, par raison me convient
Dire d'amours ce qu'apartient,
Que vostre amy tenu je soye."
  (Et hoye!)

"Je suys celle qui rien ne tient
A son amy, quant il y vient,
Bien vous en monstreray la voye."
  (Et hoye!)

"Ce faulx jalloux souvent y vient,
Lequel m'a dict qu'il me convient
Délaisser l'amoureuse voye."
  (Et hoye!)

"Maiz, mon amy, c'est pour néant;
Car quant de vous il me souvient,
Mon cueur vit et volle de joye."
  (Et hoye!)

238

INDEX OF COMPOSERS

The use of italics for a textual incipit signifies that the attribution of the work to the composer under whose name it is listed is derived from a source other than *Canti B*.

The use of parentheses around an incipit indicates that the text derives from another source and is used because that required by *Canti B* could not be found.

The diagonal line (/) separates incipits of texts used in different voices of the same composition. Capital letters following these incipits show their location in soprano (S), alto (A), tenor (T), or bass (B). The first page number refers to text, the second to music.

[1] All sources containing words call for this text; "Je vous emprie" is wanting.

[2] Florence 2442 gives "Lourdault," *Canti B* the variant spelling "Lourdoys," the nickname of Jean Braconnier.

[3] Greifswald E♭ 133 gives this text in place of "Noé, noé, noé," which is wanting.

[4] Basel F. X. 1–4 gives "Josquin," Bologna Q 17, "Nino petit."

[5] Florence 178 gives "Josquin," probably incorrectly.

[6] Basel F. X. 1–4, Bologna Q 19, Regensburg C 120, Segovia, and St. Gall 461 attribute this work to Matthaeus Pipelare.

[7] Regensburg C 120 is the only source to assign this work to "Josquin."

[8] "Wat willen" is the Dutch incipit of which "Va uilment" is a corruption.

[9] Segovia gives "Loysette Compere."

INDEX OF COMPOSITIONS

The use of italics for a composer's name signifies that the attribution has been derived from a source other than *Canti B*.

The diagonal line (/) separates incipits of texts used in different voices of the same composition. Capital letters following these incipits show their location in soprano (S), alto (A), tenor (T), or bass (B).

All incipits found in lower voices (but not used in the soprano) are listed, but are indented. The first page number refers to text, the second to music.

[1] Florence 2442 gives "Lourdault," *Canti B* the variant spelling "Lourdoys," the nickname of Jean Braconnier.

[2] Greifswald E♭ 133 gives this text in place of "Noé, noé, noé," which is wanting.

[3] Florence 178 gives "Josquin," probably incorrectly.

[4] Basel F. X. 1–4, Bologna Q 19, Regensburg C 120, Segovia, and St. Gall 461 attribute this work to Matthaeus Pipelare.

[5] Basel F. X. 1–4 gives "Josquin," Bologna Q 17, "Nino petit."

[6] All sources containing words call for this text; "Je vous emprie" is wanting.

[7] Regensburg C 120 is the only source to assign this work to "Josquin."

[8] This incipit is a corruption of "Wat willen."

[9] Segovia gives "Loysette Compere."